Construction Purchasing & Supply Chain Management

W. C. Benton, Jr.
Linda F. McHenry

New York Chicago San Francisco
Lisbon London Madrid Mexico City
Milan New Delhi San Juan
Seoul Singapore Sydney Toronto

The **McGraw·Hill** Companies

Cataloging-in-Publication Data is on file with the Library of Congress.

McGraw-Hill books are available at special quantity discounts to use as premiums and sales promotions, or for use in corporate training programs. To contact a representative please e-mail us at bulksales@mcgraw-hill.com.

Construction Purchasing and Supply Chain Management

Copyright ©2010 by The McGraw-Hill Companies, Inc. All rights reserved. Printed in the United States of America. Except as permitted under the United States Copyright Act of 1976, no part of this publication may be reproduced or distributed in any form or by any means, or stored in a data base or retrieval system, without the prior written permission of the publisher.

1 2 3 4 5 6 7 8 9 0   DOC/DOC   0 1 4 3 2 1 0 9

ISBN 978-0-07-154885-4
MHID 0-07-154885-8

The pages within this book were printed on acid-free paper.

Sponsoring Editor
  Joy Bramble Oehlkers
Acquisitions Coordinator
  Michael Mulcahy
Editorial Supervisor
  David E. Fogarty
Project Manager
  Preeti Longia Sinha,
  International Typesetting and
  Composition
Copy Editor
  Shivani Arora

Proofreader
  Manish Tiwari, International
  Typesetting and Composition
Indexer
  WordCo Indexing Services, Inc.
Production Supervisor
  Richard C. Ruzycka
Composition
  International Typesetting and
  Composition
Art Director, Cover
  Jeff Weeks

Information contained in this work has been obtained by The McGraw-Hill Companies, Inc. ("McGraw-Hill") from sources believed to be reliable. However, neither McGraw-Hill nor its authors guarantee the accuracy or completeness of any information published herein, and neither McGraw-Hill nor its authors shall be responsible for any errors, omissions, or damages arising out of use of this information. This work is published with the understanding that McGraw-Hill and its authors are supplying information but are not attempting to render engineering or other professional services. If such services are required, the assistance of an appropriate professional should be sought.

Contents

Preface		ix
Acknowledgments		xiv

1 Introduction to Construction Purchasing and Supply Chain Management ... 1

Manufacturing Risks versus Construction Risks	2
Types of Construction Projects	7
Preconstruction Design and Contractor Selection	9
Construction	10
Information Management	10
Risk Management	10
Critical Elements for Best Practice Construction	10
Supply Chain Management and Competitive Construction Operations	13
Barriers to Supply Chain Management	14
Supply Chain Partnerships	16
Traditional Construction Supply Chain	16
Benefits of Supplier Partnerships	18
Risks of Supplier-Contractor Partnerships	20
Joint Venture Supply Chain Partnership	21
Conclusion	23
References	24

2 The Construction Supply Sourcing Process and Procedures ... 25

Objectives and Activities of Construction Supply Sourcing	28
The Supply Management Process	30
Supply Sourcing Dollar Responsibility	32
Competitive Pressures	32
Material Shortages	32
Inflation	32
Complex, High-Value Projects	33
Potential for Profit	33
Purchasing and Competitive Strategy Linkage	34
Competitive Strategy	34
Supply Chain Strategy	36
The Project Sourcing Plan	37
Purchase Order	39

	The Subcontract Document	41
	The Sourcing Cycle	42
	Construction Sourcing Documents	43
	Prime Contract	43
	Purchase Order	44
	Subcontract	44
	Leases and other Agreements	44
	Subcontracting versus Materials Purchasing	44
	The Subcontracting Sourcing Process	44
	Materials Purchasing	46
	Maintenance, Repair, and Operating Supplies	47
	Conclusion	48
3	**Construction Supply Chain Relationship Management**	**49**
	Construction Supply Chain Relationship Management	50
	Subcontractor and Supplier Reduction	51
	Four Dimensions of Supply Chain Relationships	52
	Supplier Relationship Management Segmentation	53
	Preferred Supplier Relationship Management	54
	Strategic Supplier Relationship Management	54
	Strategic Source Performance Review Process	56
	Strategic Supplier Relationship Scoring System	57
	Conclusion	59
	Tier 1 Supplier Profile Example	60
	References	62
4	**Construction Supplier Selection and Evaluation**	**63**
	Construction Purchasing Mistakes	64
	Construction Sourcing Success Factors	64
	Sources of Supplier Information	66
	Strategic Selection	66
	Criteria for Supplier Evaluation	67
	Three Common Supplier Evaluation Systems	67
	Categorical Method	67
	Cost-Ratio Method	68
	Linear Averaging	70
	Single versus Multiple Sources	72
	Advantages of Multiple Sourcing	72
	Advantages of Single Sourcing	72
	Advantages of Dual Sourcing	73

Contents v

	Long-Term Relationship Issues	73
	Cross-Sourcing	74
	Supplier Reduction	74
	Grade	74
	Hurdle	75
	Certification	75
	Conclusion	76
5	**Purchasing Subcontracting Services**	**77**
	Preliminary Subcontracting Planning	80
	Subcontracting Source Selection	80
	Preparation of the Bid Package or Request for Quotation	80
	Components of the Bid Package	83
	Pre-Bid Conference	85
	Purchasing/Supply Management (Large Construction Organizations)	86
	Evaluation of Bid Packages	86
	Submitting Bids by E-mail, Facsimile, and Telephone	86
	Contract Types	88
	Lump Sum Contracts	90
	Unit Price Contracts	90
	Cost-Plus Contracts	91
	Design-Build Contracts	93
	Negotiated Contracts	93
	Contract Negotiations	93
	Awarding Major Subcontractors	95
	Subcontractor and Supplier Quality Assurance and Quality Control Expectations	95
	Strategic Construction QA and QC	98
	Change Orders	99
	Conclusion	100
	References	102
6	**Construction Equipment Planning, Purchasing, and Leasing**	**103**
	Requisition	105
	Company Goals and Objectives	105
	New Market Niche Ideas	105
	Cash-Flow Analysis	108
	Economic Evaluation	109
	Example: Motor Grader	109
	Selection	112
	Financial Plan Analysis	112

Contents

	Implementation	118
	Expenditure Control	119
	Audits	119
	Disposal of Capital Equipment	119
	Purchasing New versus Used Construction Equipment	124
	Conclusion	125
7	**Construction Supply Chain Complexity, Profitability, and Information Sharing**	**127**
	Construction Supply Chain Management	128
	Information Sharing	129
	Project Execution	140
	Conclusion	142
	References	143
8	**Construction Supply Chain Management Business Models**	**145**
	Public and Private Sector Heavy Construction and Horizontal Supply Chain Models	145
	The Components of the Heavy Construction Supply Chain Model	147
	Public versus Private Construction Projects	154
	Supply Chain Document Flows	154
	Supply Chain Coordination and Information Flows	155
	Supply Chain Money Flows	155
	Private and Public Sector (Vertical) Construction Supply Chain Models	156
	Supply Chain Document Flows	160
	Supply Chain Coordination and Information Flows	160
	Supply Chain Money Flows	160
	Implementation of Construction Supply Chain Management	161
	Conclusion	162
	Reference	162
A	**Joint Venture Agreement**	**163**
B	**Subcontractor's Bid Package and Pre-Bid Invitation**	**173**

C	CD 300, Standard Form of Tri-Party Agreement for Collaborative Project Delivery	191
D	Standard Form of Agreement Between Owner and Contractor for Integrated Project Delivery	197
E	Construction Manager At Risk Contract	205
	Glossary	209
	Index	233

About the Authors

W.C. Benton, Jr. is the Edwin D. Dodd Professor of Management and Distinguished Research Professor of Operations and Supply Chain Management at the Max M. Fisher College of Business at the Ohio State University where he teaches courses in purchasing/supply management manufacturing planning and control, operations analysis, and facility design to undergraduates, MBAs, and doctoral students. Dr. Benton earned his B.S. in Business Administration at Texas Christian University, Ft. Worth, Texas, and received his doctorate in both operations and systems management and quantitative business analysis from Indiana University, Bloomington, Indiana. His research and writing accomplishments include more than 120 articles. He is the author of two books.

Dr. Benton's expert contribution to the business and governmental arena includes consultancy for Grant Hospital, Ashland, IBM, RCA, Frigidaire, the Ohio Department of Transportation, the Florida Department of Transportation, the Indiana Department of Transportation, the South Carolina Department of Transportation, the Alabama Department of Transportation, the Kentucky Department of Transportation Cabinet, the Federal Highway Administration, Battelle Institute, the United States Air Force, Gelzer Automated Assembly Systems, Bitronics, Inc., the Ohio Rehabilitation Services Commission, Bio-Ohio, the Carter Group Canada, and others.

He currently serves as a panel member for the engineering and manufacturing divisions at the *National Science Foundation*. He also serves on the board of directors for the Healthcare Accreditation Colloquium, Inc., the Sleep Medicine Foundation, the House of Hope, the Supply Chain Research Group, and others.

Linda F. McHenry is chief operating officer for Benton and Associates, a construction management and engineering training firm. Ms. McHenry received her BA in political philosophy from Wellesley College, Wellesley, Massachusetts. She earned her law degree at Indiana University, Bloomington, Indiana. She also studied accounting and business administration at the Ohio State University. Ms. McHenry is admitted to the practice of law in four jurisdictions—Ohio, Indiana, California, and Michigan (inactive). Ms. McHenry was formerly an attorney for the Dow Chemical Company, Midland, Michigan, where she was responsible for advising 10 product groups. Later she was assistant general counsel at ITT-O. M. Scott-Burpee, Marysville, Ohio. At ITT-Scott, Ms. McHenry also served as manager of corporate planning with overall responsibility for the annual business plan cycle and presentation to the president of ITT. Ms. McHenry is the project manager for training programs presented by Benton and Associates. She is responsible for program and creative design and also offers courses on entrepreneurship, how to purchase legal and other professional services and construction law. Ms. McHenry has authored more than 18 construction educational manuals developed specifically for state departments of transportation and the Federal Highway Administration in Indiana, Kentucky, South Carolina, North Carolina, Alabama, Mississippi, Tennessee, Georgia, Florida, and Ohio.

Preface

Construction Purchasing & Supply Chain Management is an authoritative guide that provides proven strategies for the construction supply chain management (CSCM) function. The material in this book explains how to achieve maximum integration with upstream and downstream supply chain members using the latest methodologies and technologies. It is also a comprehensive step-by-step guide to CSCM that is intended to help project owners, design engineers, architects, prime contractors, subcontractors, suppliers, and construction managers involved in construction projects throughout the world establish a strategic framework to meet the budgetary and scheduling goals of any project. This book can be used to teach the fundamentals of construction purchasing and supply management in a logical, simple, and concise format in construction management courses designed for undergraduate business and civil engineering students or for construction management graduate students. CSCM focuses on strategies for Lean construction including just-in-time purchasing, supplier evaluation, subcontractor selection, subcontractor relationship management, equipment acquisition, information sharing, and project quality management. The treatment of CSCM in this book is extensive and complete. There are more than 70 illustrations and ready-to-use forms.

The construction industry has changed in its complexity over time. However, the primary objective of the industry is basically the same as it was 100 years ago: to build communities, roads, schools, homes, businesses, and hospitals. In 2007 approximately $2 trillion was spent in the construction industry. A unique project-delivery system is the cornerstone of the construction industry. The industry is fragmented and distinguished by a collection of large and small firms, related bulk material suppliers, and many other support professionals. The typical supply chain for any given construction project could include architects and engineers, prime contractors, specialty subcontractors, and material suppliers that come together one time to build a single project for a specific owner. This complex supply chain is characterized by adversarial short-term relationships driven by the competitive bidding process. Except for the architect, support engineer, or other construction professional whose fees are negotiated, the low bid win is the pricing model that repeats itself in each link of the supply chain. The project owner selects a prime contractor who is the low bidder. In turn, the prime contractor uses price as the basis for selecting subcontractors and suppliers. This approach continues even if a subcontractor hires his or her own subcontractor; again, the low bid wins. In most private and some public markets it is an industry practice after the contract is awarded and the overall project price is known, for the prime contractor to "shop" the prices of subcontractors before deciding which to use. Likewise, prime contractors may receive unsolicited quotes from subcontractors who aggressively pedal their low prices after the contract award. This adversarial behavior causes dissatisfaction throughout the supply chain and results in arms-length, one-time, project-focused relationships.

Time is one of the most critical factors in construction operations and has significant legal consequences. The project owner sets rigid beginning and ending dates for the construction process. Delays are costly and are specifically addressed in contract documents in anticipation of liquidated and other damages. Pricing in construction can be lump sum, cost plus, negotiated, or unit price. All pricing in construction depends on the time that the contractor determines it will take to complete a job. Barring any circumstances caused by the project owner and outside of the control of the contractor, the contractor must meet the time set by the project owner or lose money. Time factors are even more complicated in construction because the working environment may be outside for part or all of a project, which means that progress is influenced by weather conditions.

The labor-intensive construction operation is characterized by decentralization. A prime contractor may self-perform a portion of the work as other specialty subcontractors move in and out of the project as their sections of work are ready. Over time, the jobsite is transformed from a temporary production facility with materials and heavy equipment to the actual completed project, a school or a hospital. Projects are typically located near the project owner who is either hands-on or represented by an architect or construction manager. There is limited coordination and collaboration between the design professionals, prime contractors, subcontractors, and suppliers involved during the life-cycle aspects of the project. Information generated by various sources, at many levels of abstraction and detail, contributes to the fragmentation. Traditionally, the project information exchanged between architects/engineers and a prime contractor is compliant and has been mainly based on paper documents. These documents come in the form of architectural and engineering drawings, specifications, bills of quantities, and materials and change orders. This lack of communication and implementation leads to significant negative impacts—low productivity, cost and time overruns, change orders, inadequate design specifications, liability claims, and generally, conflicts and disputes—which directly impact the customer by increasing project-completion time and cost.

As flawed as the individual entities of a construction supply chain may be, they are even more troublesome because a new supply chain or operations component must be developed each time a new project begins. The reality is that the learning that takes place in manufacturing is circumvented in construction by the changes from one project to the next. Construction supply chain management poses an excellent opportunity to at least mitigate some risks by partially integrating some of the lessons learned from the manufacturing sector. A systematic step-by-step approach to operating a value-driven construction company must be adopted.

The topical coverage includes an introduction to construction purchasing and supply chain management; construction supply sourcing process and procedures; construction supply chain relationship management; construction supplier selection and evaluation; purchasing subcontracting services; equipment purchasing, planning, and leasing; supply chain complexity, profitability, and information sharing; and construction supply chain management business models.

Chapter 1 establishes construction supply chain management's potential for contributing to profitability. The fragmentation and adversarial relationships between owners, prime contractors, subcontractors, and suppliers in public and private, and vertical and horizontal sectors of the construction industry are a harsh reality. Construction sourcing risks involve not only the project owner, but all entities in the supply chain. At the same time, the construction industry faces new levels of complexity as it moves forward and tries to keep pace with increasing energy, materials, and labor costs. Construction supply chain management poses an excellent opportunity to mitigate risks by partially integrating the lessons of continuous improvement learned from the manufacturing sector.

In **Chap. 2**, the construction supply sourcing process and procedures have historically been among the most arbitrary elements in the construction process. Only when the cost of materials and subcontracting services increased did management attempt to solve sourcing problems. The focus on labor was logical simply because the construction process is labor intensive. Recently, some construction market segments have investigated new technologies and invested in a technology-driven construction purchasing systems. Although these new systems are up and running, too frequently they are being operated just like the old construction business models, thus defeating the very purpose the system was designed to achieve. The reality is that technology and advanced management systems are rapidly displacing labor.

Construction supply chain relationship management is addressed in **Chap. 3**. Construction organizations cannot afford to ignore subcontractor/supplier relationship management. Competitive advantages can be gained through superior subcontractor/supplier management. Given the competitive nature of the current business environment, a firm could potentially go out of business if it neglects proper management of strategic subcontractor/supplier relationships. The supply chain management approach encourages a prime contractor to compete by adding supply chain value and eliminating waste. Establishing long-term relationships with strategic subcontractors and suppliers is one of the most important principles of the supply chain paradigm. True information sharing can only be accomplished with both upstream and downstream information technology. Finally, the theme of continuous improvement must permeate all relationships and activities throughout the supply chain.

Construction supplier selection and evaluation is the focus of **Chap. 4**. Construction organizations are not proficient at identifying the capabilities of their suppliers and sometimes rationalize decisions for the selection of materials suppliers based on convenience. This integral function—materials supplier selection process—should be integrated into the supply chain management environment so that the availability of bulk materials is ensured. The mistakes made by many organizations in supplier selection can be avoided with three factors for success. Prime contractors should assess the core competencies and capabilities of each supplier and then ask if that supplier could be replaced. Since firms exit the market for various reasons, prime contractors should be prepared to establish alternative partnerships. Lastly, the prime contractor should share information with all team members and request their input.

In **Chap. 5** purchasing subcontracting services is presented. Planning the use of subcontractor services can account for improved supply chain performance, thereby substantially increasing the probability of a successful project. Prime contractors should not wait until they receive bid proposals to evaluate subcontracting expertise. The dollar magnitude of subcontracting is motivation for the supply chain management-oriented construction organization to ensure that the appropriate subcontractor is selected. The subcontractor selection process involves many important factors including the evaluation of a subcontractor's capacity and performing a SWOT (strengths, weaknesses, opportunities, and threats) analysis. An equitable bid submission and evaluation process, along with mutually satisfactory negotiations set the tone for sound relationships with subcontractors once the project begins.

Equipment purchasing, planning, and leasing are presented in **Chap. 6**. The capital equipment acquisition is a specialized function for the purchasing department. A step-by-step capital acquisition process includes (1) requisition, (2) company objectives, (3) new product ideas, (4) cash-flow analysis, (5) economic evaluation, (6) financial plan analysis, and (7) expenditure control. The decision to lease or buy capital equipment requires both analytical analysis and normative judgments.

When does it make more sense to invest in construction capital equipment instead of leasing it? Another element of the capital acquisition process is whether to purchase new or used equipment. But, whatever the reason for the purchase or lease, technology-driven equipment acquisitions can be a formidable competitive weapon.

Construction supply chain complexity, profitability, and information sharing are presented in **Chap. 7**. The concept of construction supply chain has gained significance because of the increasing number of potential complex private and public sector construction projects. In the short run, contractors may be able to survive with losses; however, in the long run, *every* construction business *must* generate a profit. Niche marketing, decreasing total costs, and decreasing overhead are traditional means of increasing profits. In the construction process costly delays in materials, equipments, and services erode profits. Construction supply chain management through the integration and coordination of materials, information, and money flows between the various project partners resolves delays and offers a new means of increasing profitability. CSCM's emphasis on information sharing and communications fosters cooperation and collaboration among supply chain members. Contract arrangements that promote core values across all levels of the supply chain depart from traditional practices by advancing successful project outcomes instead of individual firm successes. Project management and execution are the final tests of how well the supply chain is working. Tracking progress in the field ensures that a project will be on-time and under-budget and within specifications. Sharing field measurements with all members in accordance with supply chain values is the final predictor of a profitable project.

The book concludes with a focus on construction supply chain management business models in **Chap. 8**. Two construction supply chain models encompass the variety of specific project types discussed in Chap. 1. Horizontal projects are usually publicly funded and characterized by government agencies in the role of the project owner. In addition to the project owner's own in-house technical capabilities, the supply chain members have substantial engineering expertise. Vertical projects may have public or private funding. Construction managers are a key supply chain entity in the vertical model. Because of private ownership issues there can be vulnerability to bankruptcy in some variations of the vertical model. The CSCM models and methods described in this chapter and throughout this book can be customized to meet specific project requirements. A systematic CSCM approach will lead to increased integration and profitability.

W. C. Benton, Jr.
Linda F. McHenry

Acknowledgments

Our ideas have been greatly shaped by the many contractors, engineers and our colleagues at Benton and Associates who we have worked with over the years. We have learned as much from them as they learned from us. We are fortunate to have worked with some of the most progressive project owners in the construction industry: the Federal Highway Administration, the Ohio Department of Transportation, the Florida Department of Transportation, the Indiana Department of Transportation, the South Carolina Department of Transportation, the North Carolina Department of Transportation, the South Carolina Department of Transportation, the Georgia Department of Transportation, the Alabama Department of Transportation, the Kentucky Transportation Cabinet, and the Mississippi Department of Transportation. We are especially grateful to the Indiana Department of Transportation's Division of Economic Opportunity and the Federal Highway Administration Indiana Division who have made significant contributions to the construction knowledge base throughout the industry. Our greatest appreciation goes to the hundreds of contractors and engineers whom we have taught in our Entrepreneurial Development Institute programs.

In terms of actually creating this book, we would like to thank our executive editor, Joy Bramble. We sincerely thank Joy and her team of professionals at McGraw-Hill for their contributions toword completing this publishing project.

W. C. Benton Jr.
Linda F. McHenry
Semper Fidelis
www.constructionsupplychain.com

CHAPTER 1
Introduction to Construction Purchasing and Supply Chain Management

> The Future Is Now

The essential ingredients in any business are mental, not physical. The methodologies and processes used to organize the labor, materials, equipment, and financial resources needed to produce a product are at the core of a successful business model, more so than the physical tasks required to make the individual product itself. The reason for acquiring knowledge of methodologies is to prevent mistakes from being repeated. To this end, the primary purpose of business schools and business education is to teach the minimization of risks and improve the probability of success.

Knowledge, whether gained through experience or education, is both conceptual and analytical. *Conceptual knowledge* comes from years of experience: "We know how to build a sports arena because we have done it time and time again." On the other hand, *analytical knowledge* encompasses technology: "We use the Critical Path Method to track actual to budgeted production performance." Even with an increased knowledge base and cumulative learning, however, there will still be risks. The challenge for business owners is to be willing to take *reasonable* risks.

Manufacturing Risks versus Construction Risks

Knight[2] defined the difference between risk and uncertainty: Risk is measurable, but uncertainty cannot be measured. Therefore, supplier and contractor risks can be defined as SCR = PA × NC, where SCR = supplier and contractor risks, PA = the probability that an adverse event will occur, and NC = negative consequences if the adverse event occurs, assuming that each of the adverse events is independent.

The notion of risk versus reward in the construction industry is counterintuitive because the expected risk reward curve in the manufacturing industry is positively correlated, meaning that for each unit of risk an approximate reward follows (Ceteris paribus). See Fig. 1.1. On the other hand, the risk reward curve for the construction industry is negatively correlated. See Fig. 1.2.

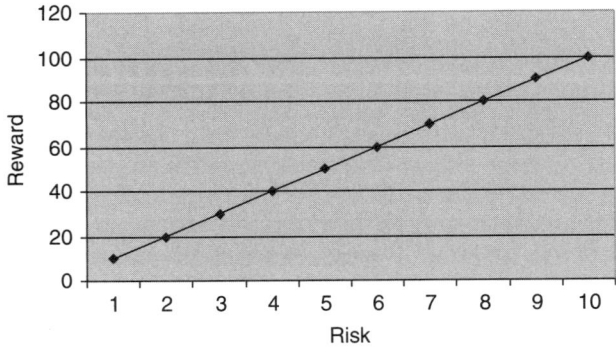

FIGURE 1.1 Risk versus reward for the manufacturing sector.

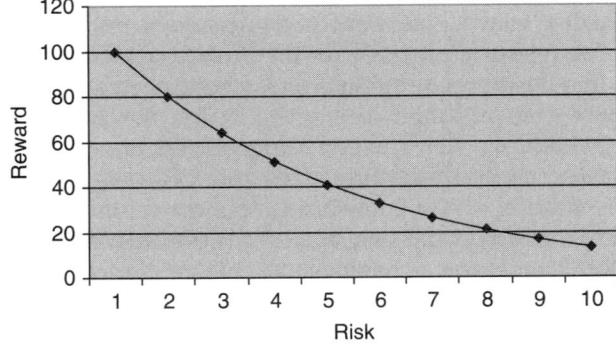

FIGURE 1.2 Risk versus reward for the construction sector.

Introduction to Construction Purchasing and Supply Chain Management

Construction sourcing risks involve all of the entities in the supply chain: the project owner, architect, prime contractor, subcontractors, and suppliers. The potential for mistakes and problems is magnified by the interrelationships between these entities. Some of the risks include:

- Internal financial problems
- Working capital problems
- Slow payment from project owner
- Inferior plans and specifications
- Inadequate technical capabilities
- Insufficient information technology
- Lack of communication between supply chain partners
- Productivity inefficiencies
- Work quality problems
- Work method problems
- Delivery reliability problems
- Bulk materials quality problems

Any of these adverse events independently or together could cause the entire supply chain to go bankrupt. Supply risk management involves identifying and assessing alternative strategies for eliminating and reducing supply chain sourcing risks. Perhaps the most important component of risk management is the certification, prequalification, and monitoring of all supply chain participants.

Operations, how to generate a product or service and get it to market, is a critical business function. The contrasts between the risks in manufacturing and construction are significant when one compares the operations component (project delivery system, product/service, employees, response time, and location) in both industries. The differences suggest the need for knowledge-based solutions like supply chain management that can achieve process improvements in the construction business model. A classic manufacturing process is predictable, stable, capital-intensive, and technocratic. The typical supply chain network is simple and centralized, and includes multiple suppliers, the manufacturer, and the ultimate customer. See Fig. 1.3.

The customer is isolated from the process and for the most part, is only affected indirectly, if at all, by any malfunction. The product in manufacturing is typically mass produced, standardized and durable, and can be transported. In addition, the product can usually be produced ahead of time, which makes it easier to balance resources with demand. Products can even be backordered. Employees in manufacturing sometimes have wages that are based on output. In the

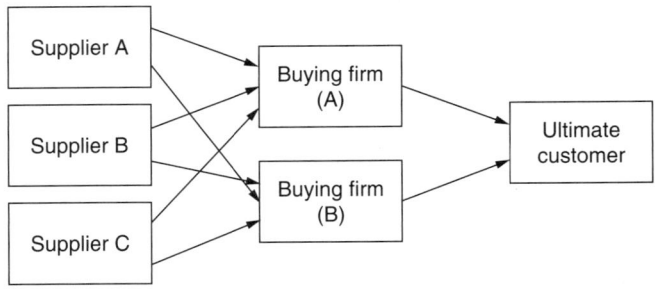

Figure 1.3 Typical supply chain network[1].

manufacturing sector, workers have technical skills, are closely supervised, in most instances exercise no or low personal judgment, and have little or no contact with the actual customer. A single plant or multiple facilities permanently house the equipment and production processes. The manufacturing sector is characterized by long response times for making a product. While labor, supply, and transportation are nearby for manufacturing entities, the market for the sale of a product can be both national and international.

Improvement curve techniques are well suited for manufacturing because of its repetitive production of individual durable units by a single business. The improvement curve is exponential and depicts a constant-percentage reduction of labor as a function of cumulative units produced. Put another way, as workers learn how to do their jobs better, they produce more and more units at a lower cost. The efficiencies that are achieved over time are a factor in a firm's competitive advantage and are the impact of cumulative learning in manufacturing. See Fig. 1.4.

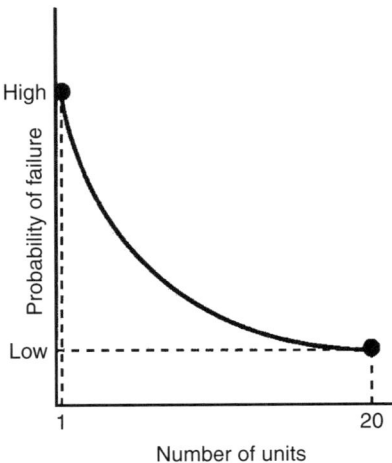

Figure 1.4 Probability of failure for the manufacturing industry.

Introduction to Construction Purchasing and Supply Chain Management

While construction has changed in complexity over time, the primary objective of the industry is basically the same as it was 100 years ago: to build infrastructure, roads, schools, homes, hospitals, factories, and other businesses. In 2007, approximately $3 trillion was spent in the United States in the construction industry. Unlike the widgets produced in manufacturing, the finished product in construction is customized and cannot be mass-produced. The operations function that shows improvement in the manufacturing sector has quite a different profile in the construction industry. The probability of failure remains constant for traditional construction organizations. See Fig. 1.5.

A unique project delivery system is the cornerstone of the construction industry. The industry is fragmented and distinguished by a collection of large and small firms, related bulk material suppliers, and many other support professionals. The typical supply chain for any given construction project could include architects and engineers, prime contractors, specialty subcontractors, and material suppliers that come together one time to build a single project for a specific owner. This complex supply chain is characterized by adversarial short-term relationships driven by the competitive bidding process. Except for the architect, support engineer, or other construction professional whose fees are negotiated, the "low bid wins" is the pricing model that repeats itself in each link of the supply chain. The project owner selects a prime contractor who is the low bidder. In turn, the prime contractor uses price as the basis for selecting subcontractors and suppliers. This approach continues even if a subcontractor hires his or her own subcontractor; again, the low bid wins. In most private and some public markets, it is an industry practice after the contract is awarded and the overall project price is known, for the prime contractor to

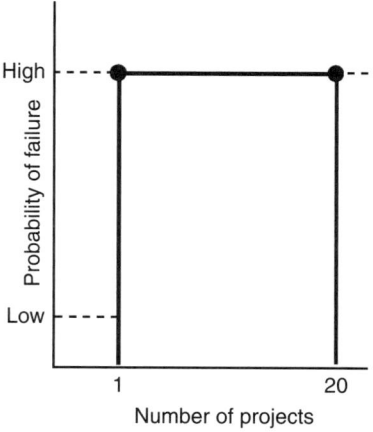

FIGURE 1.5 Probability of failure for the construction industry.

"shop" the prices of subcontractors before deciding which to use. Likewise, prime contractors may receive unsolicited quotes from subcontractors who aggressively pedele their low prices after the contract award. This adversarial behavior causes dissatisfaction throughout the supply chain and results in arms-length, one-time, project-focused relationships.

Time is one of the most critical factors in construction operations and has significant legal consequences. The project owner sets rigid beginning and ending dates for the construction process. Delays are costly and are specifically addressed in contract documents in anticipation of liquidated and other damages. Pricing in construction can be lump sum, cost plus, negotiated, or unit price. All pricing in construction depends on the time that the contractor determines it will take to complete a job. Barring any circumstances caused by the project owner and outside of the control of the contractor, the contractor must meet the time set by the project owner or lose money. Time factors are even more complicated in construction because the working environment may be outside for part or all of a project, which means that progress is influenced by weather conditions.

The labor-intensive construction operation is characterized by decentralization. A prime contractor may self-perform a portion of the work as other specialty subcontractors move in and out of the project as their sections of work are ready. Over time, the jobsite is transformed from a temporary production facility with materials and heavy equipment to the actual completed project, a school or a hospital. Projects are typically located near the project owner who is either hands-on or represented by an architect or construction manager. There is little or no coordination and collaboration between the design professionals, prime contractors, subcontractors, and suppliers involved during the life-cycle aspects of the project. Information generated by various sources, at many levels of abstraction and detail, contributes to the fragmentation. Traditionally, the project information exchanged between architects/engineers and a prime contractor is compliant and has been mainly based on paper documents. These documents come in the form of architectural and engineering drawings, specifications, bills of quantities and materials, and change orders. This lack of communication and implementation leads to significant negative impacts—low productivity, cost and time overruns, change orders, inadequate design specifications, liability claims, and, generally, conflicts and disputes—which directly impact the customer by increasing project completion time and cost.

As flawed as the individual entities of a construction supply chain may be, they are even more troublesome because a new supply chain or operations component must be developed each time a new project begins. The reality is that the learning that takes place in manufacturing is circumvented in construction by the changes from one project to the next. Construction supply chain management poses an excellent

Introduction to Construction Purchasing and Supply Chain Management

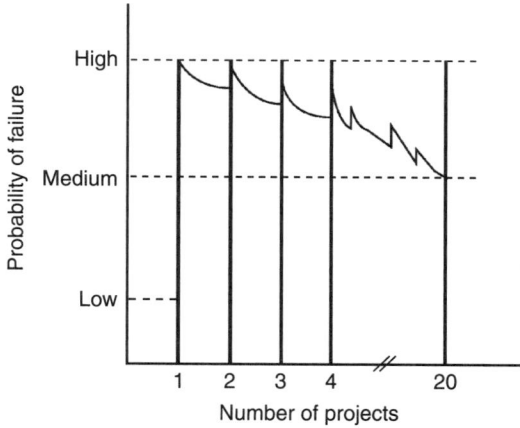

FIGURE 1.6 Probability of failure of the construction industry with supply chain management.

Project Category	Net Income (%)	Firms with Income (%)
Private sector project (residential)	5.2	65.2
Private sector project (commercial)	3.3	59.9
Public sector (building/vertical)	4.8	72.6
Public and private sector (heavy/horizontal)	4.6	67.7

TABLE 1.1 Average U.S. Construction Industry Profitability (2007)

opportunity to at least mitigate some risks by partially integrating some of the lessons learned from the manufacturing sector. See Fig. 1.6.

The translation of the operations function in the construction industry into financial measures can be demonstrated with average profit performance in the U.S. construction industry broken down by project type. See Table 1.1.

Types of Construction Projects

- Private sector housing (e.g., residential, apartment, and subdivision development projects)
- Private sector commercial (e.g., retail stores, manufacturing plants, businesses, restaurants, and warehouses)

- Public sector building/vertical (e.g., schools, universities, airports, hospitals, and state buildings)
- Public and private sector heavy/horizontal (e.g., highways, bridges, and dams)

The percentage of firms that broke even or showed a positive net income underscores just how risky the construction industry can be. For example, 40 percent of firms in the commercial construction market showed either no profit or lost money. The public sector building market was slightly better with only 28 percent of firms either losing money or breaking even. However, the stark reality is that across all categories, construction firms that are profitable show only modest returns from 3 to 5 percent. When one considers the risk, these gains cannot compete with investment earnings in a normal financial market. It is not surprising then that in the United States, construction firms have a one-in-five chance of being successful after 5 years. In other words, the risk of bankruptcy is 80 percent after 5 years. Moreover, with the fragmented project delivery system, with each new project there is an equal probability that any one or all of the firms could fail. The risk of failure for any individual construction business enterprise can be decreased by as much as 60 percent with increased knowledge.

Supply chain management (SCM) that is driven by information technology (IT) is recommended for the construction industry. The construction supply chain management (CSCM) concept has the potential, through information, and communication technologies, to overcome some of the fragmentation problems. When the manufacturing definition of SCM is extrapolated to construction, CSCM is defined as the strategic management of information flows, activities, tasks, and processes, involving various networks of independent organizations and linkages (upstream and downstream) which produce value that is delivered to the owner in the form of a finished project.

The upstream activities within CSCM from the perspective of a prime contractor involve the project owner and engineering/design teams as they engage in preparing for the construction process. The downstream activities, which include material suppliers and subcontractors who interact with the prime contractor to carry out the task of building the project, require substantial coordination among project partners. To marry and then manage the downstream and upstream elements of the supply chain, the prime contractor must develop an enabling structure and an efficient communication system for effective relationship management as part of the overall project management. CSCM can easily lead to a natural evolution toward productive relationships throughout the construction process. The considerable documentation, contracts, change orders, purchase orders, specifications, and so on generated both upstream and downstream during the life cycle of a construction project is another reason why the need for CSCM is significant.

Introduction to Construction Purchasing and Supply Chain Management

When integrated with continuous improvement, CSCM can successfully address major problems of the construction industry and its project owners.

CSCM can systematically reduce sources of uncertainty through the active cooperation of all entities in the supply chain in four functional areas: preconstruction design and contractor selection, construction, information management, and risk management.

Preconstruction Design and Contractor Selection

After the owner makes its own internal determination to proceed with a new project, a qualified architect or engineering firm is selected to develop a design. A request for proposal (RFP) is initiated to solicit architectural services. The architect's compensation is established by negotiations. The next step is to develop an appropriate design that meets the owner's requirements in terms of constructability and functionality. The architect then communicates the final project design, specifications, and bid to documents to a pool of qualified contractors. The prime contractor may be selected through a competitive bid process where the award is made to the most responsive low bidder or through negotiations. Whether prime contractor or subcontractor, there are four prevalent kinds of pricing methods that are widely used in the construction industry:

1. Single fixed price (lump sum)
2. Negotiated, cost plus a fee
3. Unit price
4. Design build

After the award, contract documents are signed between the owner and the prime contractor or construction manager. Those agreements are typically either customized or standardized industry forms, such as the family of construction documents available through the American Institute of Architects (AIA), the series of contract documents developed by the Engineers Joint Contract Documents Committee (EJCDC) in 1975 and revised in 2007, or a new set of agreements, ConsensusDOCS, which have been endorsed by 22 contractor and other industry groups led by the Associated General Contractors of America (AGC).[3] With a signed contract between the owner and the prime contractor or construction manager, the material suppliers and subcontractors are selected and similar documents are then signed by all entities downstream in the supply chain. Depending on the nature of the project, the selection of subcontractors can be ongoing as various segments of a project are "packaged" for bidding by trade. See Chap. 7 for more about CSCM and contract documents in the principal market segments discussed in this book.

Construction

This phase is the core of production, and it includes critical activities such as scheduling; site coordination; and resource, material, and logistics management. This phase might also include the selection of additional contractors if the project is presented to the industry in trade "packages."

Information Management

This area includes project information demand and supply (information transparency, flow, acquisition, availability, and sharing). The key elements in information management uncertainty are analyzed in terms of how they contribute to inefficiencies in information upstream and downstream of the construction process. At the same time, subcontractors, materials, equipment, and even funds move in response to signals from the information flow. However, in construction projects these flows take place in the context of linkages between independent organizations. In a pre-CSCM environment, there is an informal reliance on information management to coordinate the chain. The strength of CSCM is that it crosses organizational boundaries, organizing information and process flows, sending signals to operations, and evaluating results. As a result, information management is the life blood of *construction* SCM.

Risk Management

The potential for liability in any business has a direct correlation to the relationships in that business, that is, dealings with other businesses, employees, and the general public. Disputes between customers, subcontractors, and suppliers almost always occur because of poor initial communications and attempts to shift risk unfairly through egregious contractual provisions. Disgruntled employees negatively affect productivity. As ambassadors for the employer, dissatisfied workers can be detrimental to customer relationships. In construction, employees on the jobsite have substantial interactions with the project owner and other entities in the supply chain. Liability that stems from accidents is unfortunate and hard to predict; however, it can be reduced and managed through safety programs that foster a safe work environment. The paradigm of CSCM can play a significant role in developing relationships within the supply chain that reduce the exposure to contractual claims disputes. This development of relationships works to minimize accidents and create an overall environment of productive employees.

Critical Elements for Best Practice Construction

The construction industry has seen fierce price competition in the past decade, making survival a more arduous task. The competitive strategies of low-cost, high-quality, on-time project completion, and

Introduction to Construction Purchasing and Supply Chain Management

flexible leadership allow firms the ability to compete by positioning *operational efficiency* as a competitive weapon. In today's business environment, this competitive edge is not only a must for a market leader in the construction industry, but a necessity for all construction industry firms just to survive. The creation and maintenance of operational leadership, however, is a difficult and complex process, and construction firms must foster a set of new, critical elements in order to develop best practice construction operations. There are several established best practices for forecasting the benefits of CSCM. See Fig. 1.7.

First, the construction industry must develop a sincere *attitude adjustment* toward a strong dedication to operational efficiency. The belief and commitment toward developing operational efficiency as a profit driver requires a high level of organizational support that must be communicated throughout the firm. Operational analysis must play a prominent role in business strategy for successful construction operations. This leads to a second necessary operational element of *continuous improvement*. An established competitive advantage means little if the construction firm is not able to sustain it from project to project, and, thus, construction industry leaders must retain a fundamental spirit of anticipation (instead of reaction) to changes and problems. Realizing that most major advances result from small changes over time, the construction industry must create an environment of continuous project and process (work method) improvement. This requires employee training and empowerment as these small changes will more effectively come from the quality of the work force.

The third component required to position operations efficiency as a source of advantage is the *elimination of waste*. To be able to reduce costs

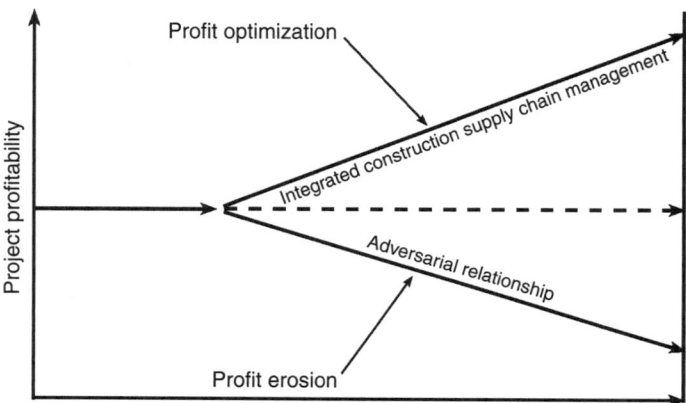

FIGURE 1.7 Best practices for forecasting the economic benefits of investing in construction supply chain management.

and react to change, construction firms must be lean and flexible. This necessitates a general attitude toward elimination of excess in materials, personnel, and processes. "Lean" construction has helped propel many responsive construction companies to success. A fourth element that fosters the environment for best practice operations is *technology*. Knowledge of company capabilities, competitors, and the business cycle is critical to success. Modern technology can also be utilized to enhance information flows both inside and outside the firm. Technology may be exploited to facilitate improved project selection, planning, scheduling, work methods, and materials flows. This "Lean" construction approach enhances the responsiveness and allows the construction firm to be on the cutting edge of competition. See Fig. 1.8.

The critical elements of attitude, process improvement, waste elimination, and technology are necessary in allowing operational efficiency to serve as a competitive advantage within a construction firm. An operations-oriented strategy, however, must extend beyond an individual construction firm. The project is delivered to the project owner via supply networks of firms consisting of architects, engineers, contractors, material suppliers, and related supply chain members. Most firms are simply a link in the supply chain, and a chain can only be as strong as its weakest link. Therefore, construction firms cannot be responsive without responsive subcontractors or material suppliers and technology implementation. As another example, a prime contractor cannot produce high-quality projects without quality materials and well-informed subcontractors, pushing quality responsibility down to its subcontractors and material suppliers.

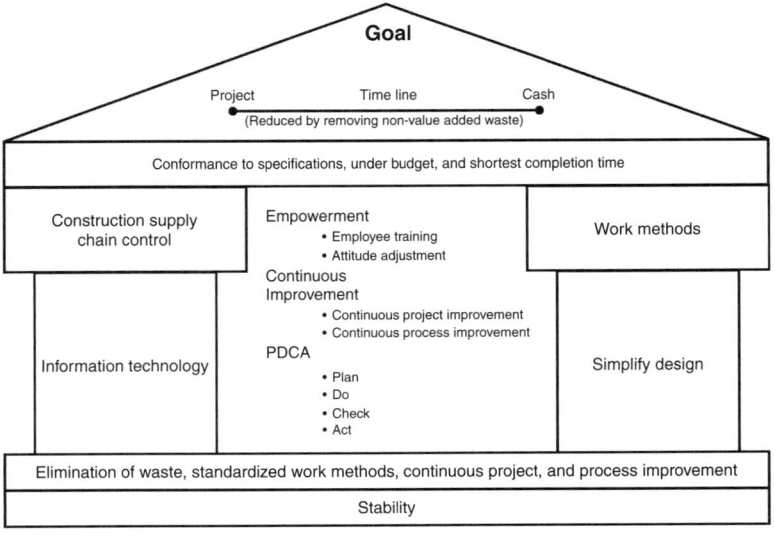

Figure 1.8 The Construction House of Lean.

Supply Chain Management and Competitive Construction Operations

This discussion leads to the conclusion that a single construction firm cannot necessarily position itself as an *operations efficiency* leader without the help of other firms in the chain. A fifth element necessary for a competitive construction operation is *supply chain control*. Specifically, the supply chain consists of all firms and organizations which contribute delivery of a high-quality project or service to the project owner. Japanese manufacturers achieved tight control over their supply chains with the *keiretsu*, which is described as a business cohort which relies on cooperation, coordination, and control to competitively position businesses and industry norms. While *keiretsu* activities are driven by the unique legal and cultural environment in Japan, transferring the keiretsu-like philosophy to the United States has yielded the concept of *supply chain management*.

Supply chain management involves the strategic and process coordination of subcontractors, material suppliers, and information within the supply chain to deliver satisfaction to the ultimate project owner. While each business entity in the supply chain has been traditionally driven by self-profitability, the notion of supply chain management involves optimization of synergistic relationships between supply chain members to ultimately satisfy the project owner. The concept evolves from controlling the supply chain as a single process rather than as a sum of independent transactional relationships. The expected end result is a mutually beneficial, win-win partnership that creates a synergistic supply chain in which the entire chain is more effective than the sum of its individual parts.

Ideally, supply chain management represents a win-win, utopian goal of circular benefits. See Fig. 1.9. Each company in the supply chain obtains its own profitability and success by creating customer value in terms of a functional, high-quality project at an acceptable price. Each organization within the supply chain can reduce its own costs and increase its project performance through supply chain management, thereby enabling the supply chain to deliver value to the project owner. The satisfied project owner in turn rewards the supply chain with loyal contracting power, allowing profitability to be transferred back down throughout the supply chain. This in turn fosters further supply chain integration and responsiveness, causing the cycle to repeat.

As mentioned above, a prime contractor may be able to position a firm as a market leader through exploitation of best practice operations, but the nature of the linked firms in the supply chain necessitates that subcontractors and material suppliers must be part of this strategy. The prime contractor cannot become an industry leader without supply chain support, and, thus, supply chain

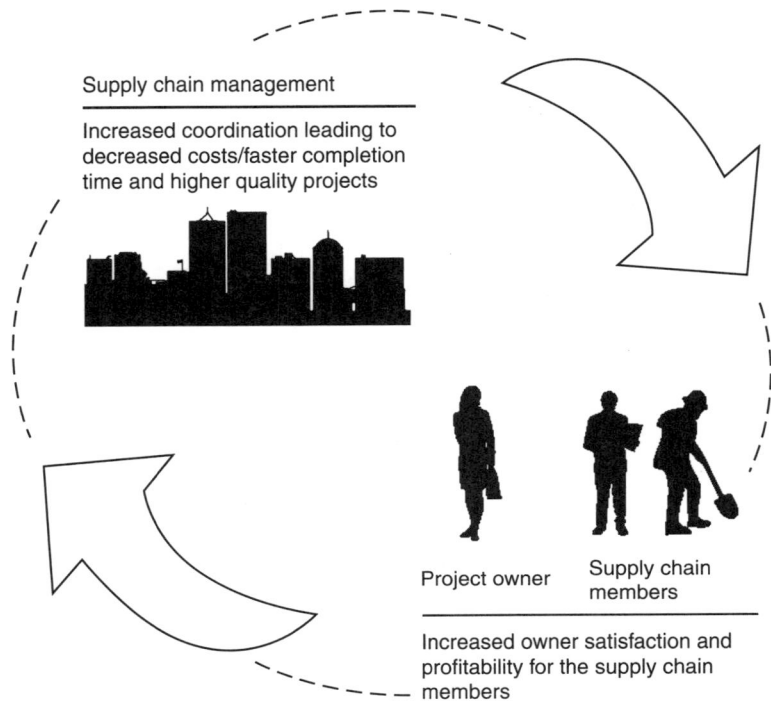

Figure 1.9 Circular benefits of construction supply chain management.

management is a prerequisite for developing a competitive advantage for successful construction operations. As an example, the Japanese auto manufacturers brought their cutting edge production and supply chain processes to the United States. The subsequent intense competition forced Chrysler and General Motors to bankruptcy. At a minimum, competitive auto manufacturers must focus on operations excellence throughout the supply chain. The next generation of auto manufacturers must therefore develop a new orientation to the supply chain, transferring design, cost reduction and quality issues to their suppliers.

Barriers to Supply Chain Management

Supply chain management offers promise for the construction industry. Intense implementation challenges, however, often prevent effective exploitation of supply chain management benefits and prove detrimental to any planned operational efficiency advantage. See Table 1.2. One barrier, the individualistic and adversarial history of the industry makes it difficult to create involved cooperative relationships with other construction-related entities. Specifically, supply

Introduction to Construction Purchasing and Supply Chain Management

- Failure to share project information
- Fear of loss of control
- Lack of self awareness
- Lack of partner awareness
- Enormity of the project complexity
- Inability to recognize project goals
- Lack of understanding project owner
- Lack of understanding of supply chain
- Myopic thinking
- Myopic strategies
- Deficiency of mutuality

TABLE 1.2 Barriers to Supply Chain Management

chain management necessitates sharing of traditionally proprietary information, strategy, planning and goals, and most construction firms do not feel comfortable exposing such elements to other firms, fearing loss of control. Furthermore, interfirm collaboration requires each participating firm to create a high level of awareness of both themselves and their partners, and such cognition is often difficult to accomplish effectively. Yet another problem involves the inability of chain members to focus on one mutual goal of the supply chain rather than individual performance. Other significant barriers to the execution of supply chain management include a lack of understanding of the project owner (who is the true customer and what do they really want?), communication gaps (in what ways is it difficult for separated members to communicate?), a lack of understanding of the true supply chain (what firms are in the chain?), the enormous size of many supply chains (is it difficult to coordinate many independent firms?), a lack of effective leadership (who is the best leader?), egocentrism (is pride creating a myopic strategy?), and finally, a deficiency of mutuality (are profits and rewards shared equally?).

On the basis of the above barriers to supply chain management, development of an integrated supply chain remains an extremely difficult task. It represents a new way of doing business, and most construction firms are not prepared or even necessarily willing to effectively integrate the chain. Though it is perhaps a distant goal, the concept of supply chain management remains a critical factor for the long-term success of construction firms. While complete supply chain management may be out of reach for most construction firms, application of its concepts will improve their competitive advantage. Furthermore, as the supply chain best practice firms are able to improve project quality, completion times, and work methods while decreasing costs, the demanding project owner will continue to demand more. As a result, the efficient construction supply chains will prosper, and the traditional, adversarial supply chains will not survive. For this reason, construction supply chain management remains a critical element for positioning operational efficiency as a source of competitive advantage, and serves as a desirable goal for leadership in the construction industry.

Supply Chain Partnerships

Critical to the implementation of construction supply chain management techniques is the construction supply chain partnership. Also termed a *strategic alliance*, a strategic supply chain partnership is a relationship formed between two independent entities in supply channels to achieve specific objectives and benefits. These partnerships form the essential building blocks of CSCM. The high levels of information flow and subsequent coordination of error-free planning and scheduling required by CSCM require prime contractors to build tighter bonds with a few strategic subcontractors and suppliers. Once traditionally driven by competition, the supplier *relationships* for many construction firms have thus matured from an adversarial relationship to one of a construction supply chain partnership.

Within the win-win construction partnership dyad, prime contractors and strategic (subcontractors and material) suppliers share goals as well as inherent risks through joint planning and control, seeking to create an effective supply chain with increased information flow and enhanced project owner loyalty. Like the overall goal of CSCM, such coordination allows for improved service, technological innovation, and project design with decreased cost. Ideally, the end result for all members of the construction supply chain should be a decreased uncertainty, yielding greater control of costs, activity times, materials, project quality, and, ultimately, project owner satisfaction.

Traditional Construction Supply Chain

Firms must take bold steps to break down intrafirm barriers to both smooth uncertainty and enhance control of the supply chain activities. See Fig. 1.10. The evolution of intrafirm functional integration has occurred for most progressive construction firms over the last few decades, and the current push is toward external integration with subcontractors, material suppliers, and project owners. Supply chain partnerships bridge the barrier between prime contractors, subcontractors, materials suppliers, and project owners.

Historically, contractors have formulated operations strategy around adversarial downstream relationships. This approach encourages competition which the prime contractors can exploit to shop for lower costs. Such a strategy enhances ultimate prime contactor bargaining power. This is clearly an unsustainable strategy. The most

Introduction to Construction Purchasing and Supply Chain Management

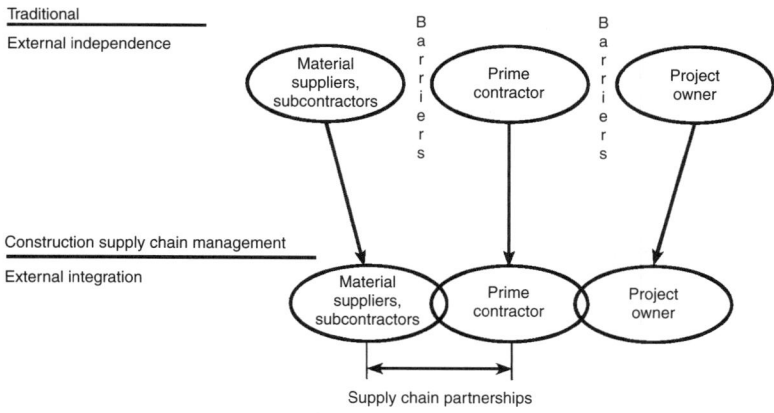

FIGURE 1.10 Evolution from traditional to construction supply chain management integration.

productive subcontractors and material suppliers will join progressive supply chain networks.

A Harvard Business School study concluded that a key driver in the decline of U.S. competitiveness in the international marketplace has originated from investing less in intangible benefits such as relationship building.[4] According to MacNeil, it is impossible to operate as a discrete entity. But, while virtually no firm has completely discrete engagements, conventional Western and American business practices have been more oriented toward discrete than relational strategies.[5] Traditionally, U.S. firms have based their drive for success on autonomy and have viewed competition as a Darwinistic keeper of American superiority. Long-run U.S. firm planning has been independent, and considerable efforts are taken to ensure privacy of company information.

Over recent decades, however, American firms within the supply chain have begun to realize the advantages enjoyed from sharing technology, information, and planning with other firms and even competitors. Many modernistic business thinkers will claim that a more open and relational attitude is not only advantageous, but is also actually essential and inevitable in maintaining a competitive advantage. The idea of relationalism between firms seeks to move away from the concept of discrete transactions, breaking down traditional intrafirm barriers. See Table 1.3. Firms unite to share information and planning efforts, thus reducing uncertainty as well as increasing control. In the end, supply chain partners reap the benefits of the joint effort.

Modern construction improvements such as Lean management methods require the tighter control generated by the construction supply chain partnership.

Contractual Element	Discrete Orientation	→	Relational Orientation
Duration	One payment only		Future payments
Attitude	Independent, suspicious		Open, trusting, cooperative
Communication	Very little		Complex
Information	Proprietary		Shared
Planning and goals	Individual, short-term		Joint, long term
Benefits and risks	Individual		Shared
Problem solving	Power driven		Mutual, judicious

TABLE 1.3 Discrete versus Relational Business Strategies

Strategic construction supply alliances, however, extend well beyond this notion to an even more relational level of exchange in which partners create an intensive, interdependent relationship from which both can mutually benefit. Strategic construction supply partnerships emphasize a direct, long-term association, encouraging mutual planning and problem-solving efforts. See Table 1.4.

Traditional Project Relationships	Supply Chain Project Partnerships
Short-term contracts for suppliers	Long-term alliances with suppliers
Bid evaluation	Intensive evaluation of supplier value-added
Many suppliers and subcontractors	Few suppliers and subcontractors
Proprietary information	Shared project information

• Power-driven problem solving
    Coercive relationships
	• Mutual problem solving
	    Improvement
	    Success sharing

TABLE 1.4 Traditional versus Partnership Supply Strategies

Benefits of Supplier Partnerships

Prime contractors, suppliers, and subcontractors can gain from quality improvements, and transaction costs may be reduced through economies of scale, decreased administrative and switching efforts, process integration, and coordination of processes. Furthermore, the strategic supply chain relationship will be enhanced by stability of market conditions and the benefits of construction strategic partnerships. See Table 1.5.

Reduced Uncertainty for Project Owners in	Cost Savings
• Material costs • Quality • Timing • Reduced supplier, subcontractor base easier to manage	• Economies of scale in • Scheduling • Purchasing • Logistics • Decreased administrative costs • Fewer switching costs • Enhanced project integration • Technical or physical integration • Improved equipment utilization
Reduced Uncertainty for Subcontractors and Suppliers in	**Time Management**
• Market • Understanding of project owner's needs • Project specifications	• Faster project completion • Improved cycle time for subcontractor
Reduced Uncertainty for Owners and Partners in	**Shared Risks and Rewards**
• Convergent expectation and goals • Reduced effects from externalities • Reduced opportunism • Increased communication and feedback	• Joint capability and development • Market shifts • Increased profitability • Project development • Accident reduction
Joint Work Method Development	**Stability**
• Increased shared technology • Greater joint involvement of project design	• Lead times • Priorities and attention
Greater Flexibility	

TABLE 1.5 Potential Benefits of Supplier Partnerships

Risks of Supplier-Contractor Partnerships

With its many benefits, construction supply chain partnerships retain several inherent risks that can be potentially damaging to participants. First and foremost, heavy reliance on one partner can be disastrous if the partner does not meet expectations.

The entire partnership implementation process holds many elements critical to the success of the relationship and several factors contribute to success (see Table 1.6). Table 1.7 provides general

1. Establish strategic need for partnership
2. Develop partner criteria, evaluate suppliers and subcontractors, and select partner
3. Formally establish partnership
4. Maintain and refine partnership

TABLE 1.6 Supplier Partnership Implementation Steps

Project Completion Time	
• Natural management support	
• Communication	
• Increased coordination	
Initial Strategic Analysis Phase	
• Social and attitudinal barriers	
• Procedural and structural barriers	
Subcontractor/Supplier Evaluation and Selection Phase	
• Total cost and profit benefit	• Partner capabilities
• Cultural compatibility	• Management compatibility
• Financial stability	• Location
Partnership Establishment Phase	
• Perception and needs analysis	
• Intense interaction	
• Documentation	
Maintenance Phase	
• Trust	• Social exchange
• Goodwill	• Boundary personnel
• Flexibility	• Performance measurement
• Conflict management skills	

TABLE 1.7 Supplier Partnership Critical Success Factors in the Phases of Implementation

Introduction to Construction Purchasing and Supply Chain Management

resources for success factors. In practice, overcoming the social and *attitudinal barriers* and managerial practices may prove to be extremely difficult if not impossible.

The most important attitudinal factors involve cooperation, trust, and goodwill, as well as the ability to be flexible and handle conflicts. Furthermore, attitude and shared goals are described as success factors. Other critical success factors will include effective performance measurement and proper establishment of boundary personnel and procedures. Ultimate dissolution of the partnership may be necessary if the firms are unable to successfully work through the critical steps of partnership formation or synergies cannot be recognized.

Joint Venture Supply Chain Partnership

A joint venture is a special type of a construction supply chain partnership. Specifically, a joint venture is a formal supply chain partnership formed to do a single project. Unless the joint venture functions as a team, it will not be successful. The ultimate goal of the joint venture is to deliver a high-quality project on time and under budget. If projects require one or more of the following conditions, a "joint venture approach" may be appropriate:

- A variety of skills, experiences, judgments, and abilities.
- Interdependence between partners
- Both entities all working toward the same goals
- Innovation and synergy
- Shared accountability among entities

The joint venture approach requires the joint venture partners to determine in advance the appropriate communication channels and problem-solving methods that will be followed to resolve conflicts. When a joint venture faces problems, the following questions must be asked:

- Are we stuck because of disagreement?
- What can we do to be more productive?
- How can we solve the problems of the team (joint venture)?

An overview of the steps to a successful joint venture is given here.

Phase I: Getting Organized
Step 1—Focus on team

- What is the reason for forming the joint venture?
- What is the goal or mission of the joint venture?
- What are the expected results of the joint venture?
- What is the expected completion date for the project?

There will always be resistance to the teamwork approach.

Step 2—Definition of roles for Contractors A and B

Contractor A

- Manage and coordinate the team toward completion of a specific project
- Provide project management (on-site)
- Members of Contactor B's staff should serve on Contractor A's staff

Contractor B

- Manage and coordinate the team toward completion of administrative functions
- Provide project management (fiscal control)
- Members of Contactor A's staff should serve on Contractor B's staff

Step 3—Establish ground rules within regulations

Joint venture meetings

- How frequent?
- Should they be regular?
- What are the attendance standards?
- How will the team handle differences of opinion?

Communication between meetings

- What method of communication will the team use?
- Who initiates communication among team members?

Behavior toward one another

- What behaviors are inappropriate?
- What behaviors will the team strive for?

Joint venture problems

- What problems does the team anticipate and how will the members work through them?
- How will the team handle rumors, confidentiality, and conflicts?

Phase II: Production

Step 4—Plan the specified work

- Lay out major steps or goals that will accomplish the mission
- Break down each major step or goal into manageable tasks
- Lay out time line for completion of goals and tasks
- Use scheduling tools as needed

Introduction to Construction Purchasing and Supply Chain Management

Step 5—Do the work

- Hold regular, productive team meetings
- Review and update schedule
- Re-plan when necessary
- Measure actual progress against budget using "S" curve
- Process progress reports and payments

Step 6—Review team performances

- Acknowledge the strengths and weaknesses of the joint venture's performance
- Assess all important areas of the project
- Design and implement a joint venture evaluation form

Step 7—Complete the work

Phase III: Wrap Up
Step 8—Acceptance and final payment

- Do punch list

See sample joint venture agreement in App. A.

Conclusion

The fragmentation and adversarial relationships between owners, prime contractors, subcontractors and suppliers in public and private, and, vertical and horizontal sectors of the construction industry is harsh reality. Project owners face internal financial problems, insufficient information technology, a lack of communication between supply chain partners, all coupled with the realization that in spite of these hurdles, they still must be willing to take reasonable risks. In fact, construction sourcing risks involve not only the project owner, but all entities in the supply chain. At the same time, the construction industry as a whole faces levels of complexity as it moves forward and tries to keep pace with increasing energy, materials, and labor costs.

Construction supply chain management poses an excellent opportunity to mitigate risks by partially integrating some of the lessons learned from the manufacturing sector. CSCM can replace fragmentation and inefficiencies with integration, value, and enhanced project quality. CSCM embraces the use of technology to enhance communication and information flows both in and outside of the firm. CSCM, driven by the "Lean" revolution will result in win-win benefits for the entire construction supply chain. Supply chain partnerships, such as joint ventures, are critical to the success of construction supply chain management. CSCM has enormous potential to make an important contribution to achieve continuous improvement and efficiencies in the design and execution of projects in all sectors of the industry.

References

1. Benton, W. C., *Purchasing and Supply Management*, McGraw-Hill, New York, 2007.
2. Knight, F., *Risk, Uncertainty and Profit*, Harper and Row, New York (first published in 1921), 1965.
3. Harris, L. D., and M. B. Perlberg, "The Advantage of the ConsensusDOCS," presented at Winds of Change, "The ConsensusDOCS," American Bar Association Forum on the Construction Industry, September 11–12, 2008, Chicago, IL.
4. MacBeth, D. K., and N. Ferguson, *Partnership Sourcing: An Integrated Supply Chain Management Approach*, Pitman Publishing, London, 1994.
5. MacNeil, Ian R., *The New Social Contract, An Inquiry into Modern Contractual Relations*, Yale University Press, New Haven, CT, 1980.

CHAPTER 2
The Construction Supply Sourcing Process and Procedures

> Reengineering Construction Organizations for the Twenty-First Century

The sourcing process for most construction firms is fragmented and not well documented. Since the beginning of the new millennium and even more so today, the construction marketplace has been in an economic and energy quandary. In addition to these industry wide challenges, individual construction firms have had to change radically in response to burgeoning technologies. Historically, the sourcing of subcontracting services was the most neglected element in the construction process. Only when the cost of materials and subcontracting services increased, did management attempt to investigate alternative methods to the planning and control of the acquisition and transformation functions in the organization. Instead, most firms emphasized minimizing the cost of labor. The focus on labor was logical because, by definition, the construction process is labor intensive. Some construction market segments have embraced new technologies and invested in technology-driven construction systems. Although these new systems are up and running, too frequently they are operated just like the old construction business models, thus defeating the very purpose the system was designed to achieve. The reality is that technology and advanced management systems are rapidly displacing labor.

As a functional area within a firm, purchasing and sourcing management grappled with the stigma of being labeled a clerical function. However, in the past 25 years, construction sourcing has made many strides toward shedding this label and has emerged as a viable professional career path. More importantly, during the next decade, sourcing, supply chain management, and continuous improvement are likely to contribute to profitability more than any other functions in the construction industry.

The life cycle of a typical construction project consists of the following stages. (Fig. 2.1):

1. Conceptualization
2. Engineering and design
3. Supply sourcing
4. Construction
5. Implementation
6. Utilization

In reality, the construction life cycle stages are not mutually exclusive or independent. Many of these stages occur concurrently. By definition, each construction project is unique and requires varying degrees of aggregation. Depending on the size of the construction

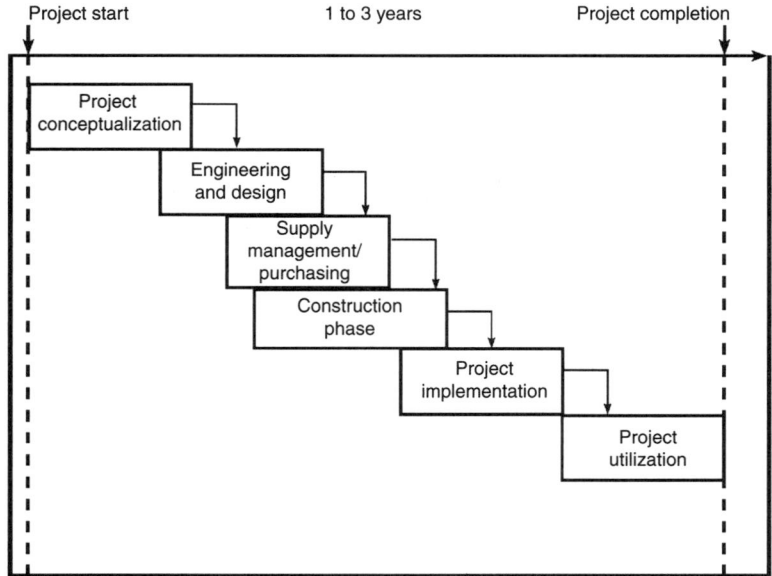

FIGURE 2.1 Typical industrial construction project life cycle.

organization, the supply sourcing function may be implemented with a single supply manager or a supply sourcing group. Regardless of the size of the organization, ownership in the supply sourcing function must be defined. In small construction organizations, the president of the company must exercise supply sourcing leadership. The supply sourcing function of the typical construction organization is the first stage of profit realization.

The primary responsibility of the supply function is to serve as the supply sourcing professional for the construction organization at both the project and home office levels. The supply sourcing activities must be carried out subject to specifications, budgetary, and scheduling constraints. Supply sourcing and purchasing activities are implemented at two levels of aggregation. The home office or owner usually purchases capital equipment and materials. Equipment renting and bulk materials are sourced from the field (i.e., the superintendent orders concrete the day before it is needed).

The focus of this book is on the supply sourcing and construction stages of the construction project life cycle. There is a high level of integration and interdependence between the sourcing and construction stages which increases the probability of project risks upstream and downstream. Project quality, budgets, and completion times can easily be compromised. Therefore, it is important to manage the communication and project integration in order to mitigate adverse project events. The supply sourcing function involves working with upstream and downstream relationships, inside and outside each Organization. The supply sourcing process involves assisting the project manager with subcontracting services, bulk materials, and equipment requirements. At a basic level, the construction organization transforms capital, engineering, labor, bulk materials, supplies, work methods, and technology into a completed, acceptable project. See Fig. 2.2. The percentage of the resource inputs sourced externally is constantly increasing compared to the in-house resources. There is a continuous trend toward specialization and integration. Subcontracting is basically specialized labor. In most cases, construction organizations can source specialized resources more efficiently than adding the needed capabilities in-house. Supply sourcing managers and the project manager have the responsibility and the authority to schedule and deliver the required resources to the project site. The supply sourcing manager must become an expert in sourcing for various project categories (i.e., bridge construction, office buildings, hospitals, etc.).

The supply sourcing manager, along with the prime contractor and project manager, usually prequalifies subcontractors and solicits competitive bids based on the engineering and design specifications. The key to construction sourcing coordination is effective project planning and scheduling. The construction stages shown in Fig. 2.1 involve converting labor, materials, and equipment into an acceptable completed project, as shown in Fig. 2.2. The construction manager or prime

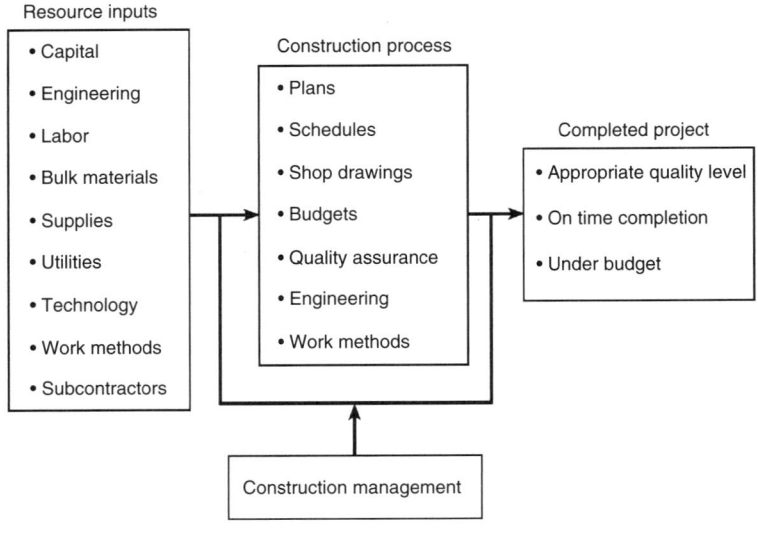

FIGURE 2.2 Construction transformation process.

contractor coordinates the transformation process based on three basic criteria—completing the project on time, coming in under budget, and delivering an acceptable high-quality project to the owner.

Objectives and Activities of Construction Supply Sourcing

The purpose of the supply sourcing function for construction organizations is to buy materials and services of the right quality, in the right quantity, and at the right price from the right source at the right time. The supply sourcing department assists the project team in performing their responsibilities within the project's budgetary and scheduling goals. Supply sourcing managers and purchasing agents seek to obtain the highest-quality subcontractors and materials at the lowest possible cost for their organizations. Sourcing managers determine which bulk materials, commodities, or services are best; choose the suppliers of the material or service; negotiate the lowest price and award contracts that ensure that the correct amount of the material or service is received at the appropriate time. In small construction firms, the owner is usually responsible for all of the sourcing and purchasing functions. In order to accomplish these tasks successfully, sourcing managers (owners) must identify the most qualified suppliers. Supply sourcing managers must also become experts on the materials and services that they purchase.

Managers in this critical sourcing function evaluate suppliers on the basis of quality, price, service support, availability, and reliability in order to purchase services competitively and wisely. To assist them in their search for the right subcontractors and suppliers, sourcing managers review catalogs, industry and company databases, government directories, and trade journals. Much of this information is now available on the Internet. Sourcing managers research the reputation and history of the subcontractors and suppliers, and advertise anticipated purchase actions in order to solicit bids. At meetings, trade shows, conferences, suppliers' plants, and field sites, they examine materials and services, assess a supplier's performance capabilities, and discuss other technical and business considerations that influence the sourcing decision. Once all of the necessary information on suppliers is gathered, purchase orders are placed and contracts are awarded to those suppliers who meet the contractor requirements.

To keep inventory investment to a minimum, the sourcing professional must implement just-in-time (lean) purchasing concepts. Just-in-time requires on-time, frequent deliveries of reliable small batches of high-quality materials. The supply manager is always developing reliable alternative suppliers and subcontractors. New sources for equipment and materials must be developed in order to eliminate single sourcing. The overall goal of the sourcing manager is to achieve maximum integration with upstream and downstream supply chain members. This integration involves communication and information sharing.

Several key objectives for construction supply sourcing applicable to both horizontal and vertical construction organizations are listed below. The guiding principle of these objectives is to obtain the maximum value for each dollar spent.

1. To assist the project team in performing their responsibilities within the project's budgetary and scheduling goals.
2. To purchase and source services competitively. (In order to source competitively and wisely, supply managers must be experts on the materials and subcontracting services that they purchase.)
3. To keep inventory investment (i.e., deterioration and theft) to a minimum by implementing just-in-time (lean) purchasing concepts for the jobsite.
4. To develop and maintain good relationships with supply chain members (suppliers and subcontractors).
5. To develop reliable alternative suppliers and subcontractors.
6. To achieve maximum integration with upstream and downstream supply chain members.
7. To continue to develop innovative systems for recruiting, training, and retaining purchasing and supply chain talent.

8. To prepare patterns of administration for sourcing materials, equipment, services, and subcontracts.
9. To prequalify, select, and evaluate suppliers and subcontractors.
10. To establish and update database of current and potential suppliers and subcontractors.
11. To conduct background checks on current and potential consultants, suppliers, and subcontractors.
12. To study scope of work for each active project.
13. To review and evaluate invitation to bid.
14. To conduct bid opening and/or participate in the proposal evaluation team.
15. To inform successful and unsuccessful bidders in timely manner.
16. To prepare contract and associated details.
17. To participate in the negotiations team.
18. To participate in change order variances from the initial contract.
19. To seek out bids from women- and minority-owned businesses and monitor compliance after selection and award.
20. To prepare purchase orders, contracts, and subcontracts for engineering and construction.
21. To coordinate submittal of shop drawings and other specification requirements.
22. To schedule shipping and transportation.
23. To prepare back charges with the assistance of the project manager.
24. To coordinate and track invoice approval process.
25. To participate in purchase order and subcontract closeout activities with the assistance of the project manager.
26. To develop a continuous improvement culture that permits the accomplishments of all of the preceding objectives.

The Supply Management Process

Changing economic and political environments, emerging technology versus labor, and the changing nature of construction as a discipline must influence the role of construction purchasing and supply chain management. To become more strategically competitive, construction firms must abandon fragmented purchasing and subcontracting approaches. The companies that invest in engineering-based construction methods ("hard" technology) must at the same time invest in result-oriented sourcing training programs ("soft technology"). The purchasing function must become an integral part of transforming materials and resources into an on time, under budget, and acceptable finished project.

In many construction firms, functional and project managers within each area make independent decisions using similar techniques. The approach introduced in this chapter proposes that the sourcing decision should be integrated. Integrative supply management consists of the planning, acquisition, and conversion of materials and subcontracted labor into a finished project. In this scenario, each field supervisor (foreman) reports to the same superior. Further, project managers should work for the overall purpose of delivering high-quality, efficient, on-time projects to the owner. An important objective of this approach is to provide high-quality customer service while minimizing the cost of producing the service or project. Integrative supply management is not related to the size of a firm. Realistically, the sourcing subfunctions must first be integrated before the supply function will be synergistic with other business functions.

The purpose of supply management is to support the construction function in the transformation of materials and labor into a completed project. The function of the supply chain is to integrate the entire transformation process. During the transformation process, materials are combined with labor, information, technology, and capital. The construction planning and scheduling system is central to the acquisition of subcontracting and materials in an effective construction environment. For complex projects, the critical path method (CPM) schedule is the most important input into a construction planning and control system. Many successful construction organizations have embraced just-in-time philosophies and use CPM concepts to enhance the effectiveness of the construction supply mission.

Perhaps the most significant change for construction firms in the past decade has been the acknowledgment of continuous improvement. Between 1960 and 1990, most construction firms performed 60 to 80 percent of the project through the combined efforts of a prime contractor and numerous subcontractors. Today, a large number of construction management and design engineering organizations serve as the owners' representative and subcontract 90 to 95 percent of the projects' values. Since this impressive shift in value percentages, the complexity of the construction process has been greatly reduced for the prime contractors. The complexity in the construction process has been shifted downstream to the supply chain (subcontractors and suppliers). Under the traditional construction model, the prime contractors transformed significantly more materials and labor for the project. Because prime construction firms are purchasing more and more subcontracting services, the construction focus is shifted downstream to operations efficiency. This significant shift has elevated the importance and profile of sourcing and supply sourcing professionals.

Supply Sourcing Dollar Responsibility

The dollar responsibility of supply management is very large in both relative and absolute terms in the construction industry. More importantly, if the supply sourcing management is responsible, it will contribute to the competitive stance and long-run survival of the construction organization.

The following are ratios of materials-related costs that are typically cited in the construction industry:

Total project cost of sales (labor, equipment, and materials)
= 75% of sales
Home office overhead (sales) = 15% of sales
Profit margin = 10% of sales

The labor, equipment, and materials ratios are increasing for various reasons: competitive pressures, material shortages, inflation, and thoroughly complex high-value projects.

Competitive Pressures

As the number of bidders increases for each project, the project prices decrease. Some competing construction organizations bid below the total project cost.

Material Shortages

As natural resources are consumed, more costly methods of exploration, extraction, and processing are necessary. Shortages also result from political events. Former colonies of Western nations, once a low-cost and ready source of supply, have gained their independence. As autonomous nations, these new nations manage their resources to achieve economic, social, and nationalistic objectives.

Inflation

Material prices usually adjust upward in response to the rising costs of energy and labor. Managing materials during inflationary periods result in decisions that would make little sense in stable environments.

Complex, High-Value Projects

Management in the construction industry frequently hears the complaint, "They don't build them like they used to." The industry's response is, "If we did, you wouldn't want them." Project owners demand ever more reliable and functional projects for lower prices. For these reasons, we should expect no reversal in the trends of increased dollar responsibility and the promise of effective construction supply chain management. Where else is the potential for cost reduction and competitive advantage so great?

Potential for Profit

All sourcing activities have the potential for increasing profit through cost reduction. The sourcing of materials is used to illustrate the "profit leverage" argument which emphasizes the importance of profit efficiency over market share. As an example, consider a construction firm's income statement is like the one given in Table 2.1. At the sales level of $1,000,000, the firm is expensing 50 percent of sales or $500,000 for the purchase of bulk materials while incurring a net profit of $50,000.

Suppose the firm sets a goal of increasing the net profit by $10,000 or 1 percent of current sales. One way to achieve this goal is to focus on market share and increase the firm's level of sales without changing the material costs. The required level of sales can be estimated using the following equation.

$$\text{Sales} = \text{variable cost} + \text{fixed cost} \pm \text{profit}$$

$$\chi = 0.5\chi + 0.4\chi + 50{,}000 + (10{,}000 + 50{,}000)$$

$$\chi = \$1{,}100{,}000$$

In order to increase the net profit by $10,000 or 1 percent of current sales, the required increase in sales is $100,000 or 10 percent of current sales. Also, the variable costs increase as the result of increased production.

Another way to achieve the same goal is to improve profit efficiency through the reduction of material costs by the supply manager's skillful negotiations while maintaining the current level of sales. In this case, the material cost is the only changing variable. As each $1 cost reduction is exactly reflected as an increase in profit, the required reduction in material cost is $10,000 or 2 percent of current material cost. The resulting income statement is like shown in Table 2.2.

When comparing the two methods, it can be seen that the required reduction in material costs which is 2 percent or $10,000 is far smaller in amount compared to the required 10 percent increase in sales. In addition, a sales increase of 10 percent could be considerable difficult

	(in 000s)
Sales	$1,000
Bulk material costs	(500)
Labor costs	(400)
Gross profit	$100
Project overhead	(50)
Net profit	$50

TABLE 2.1 Income Statement Example 1

	(in 000s)
Sales	$1,000
Bulk Material costs	(490)
Labor costs	(400)
Gross profit	$110
Project overhed	(50)
Net profit	$60

TABLE 2.2 Income Statement Example 2

depending on the firm's competitive position and market conditions. This is not to say that cost reductions in purchasing are achieved at no cost, but management must make sure that the operating costs are well in hand before trying to increase market share. Therefore, Profit efficiency, not market share, should the first concern. The same leverage analysis could also be applied to improving work methods in order to reduce labor costs.

Purchasing and Competitive Strategy Linkage

Supply sourcing managers need to devise sourcing actions so that they are consistent with each other and with the organization's competitive strategy. A framework for purchasing strategy can link a firm's competitive strategy with its purchasing policy. See Table 2.3 and Fig. 2.3. Competitive priorities are one means of articulating an organization's competitive strategy. The competitive priorities are a key determinant of the importance given to different criteria in the sourcing of materials and services. Performance measures or reward criteria are other factors that also influence the sourcing criteria. The competitive priorities define the intended or desired sourcing criteria, and the reward criteria determine how close the objectives are met. The decisions or actions that constitute project sourcing strategy are determined by the construction organization's competitive priorities, its resource capabilities, and the environment. Similarly, in the formulation of supply sourcing strategy, again the organization's competitive priorities, the organization's strengths and weaknesses, and the competitive environment must be considered.

Competitive Strategy

Construction organizations can compete in two broad alternate ways. They can either seek competitive advantages on *cost* or choose to *differentiate* themselves from their competitors based on some attributes of the final project or process efficiency. The notion of two generic competitive advantages—cost and differentiation—is important, but too broad to

Decision Area	Decision	Alternative
Supply management	Size of subcontracting firm	Small vs. large location, closed or geographically dispersed
	Managerial expertise	High or low
	Financial health	High or low
	Amount of purchase or subcontract	Restrict to a certain percentage of supplier's output or no constraint
	Engineering	Developmental vs. experienced
	Relationship	Strategic partner vs. transactional focused
	Extent of technology (computerization)	Manual vs. systems
	Communication (integration)	Share plans and information vs. not sharing plans and information
	Value engineering	Active program vs. no program
Sourcing	Criteria	Cost, quality, delivery, or lead time, perceived delivery reliability or reputation
	Sourcing scale	Economies of scale (cost/volume) or economies of scope (bulk materials delivery and scheduling)
	Ordering policy	Integrated with supplier information system or not integrated
Supplier and subcontractor development	Supplier relationship management	Develop supplier/subcontractor or look for new sources.
Scope of construction activity	Degree of integration	Build/self perform vs. subcontracting

TABLE 2.3 Construction of Sourcing Strategy Framework

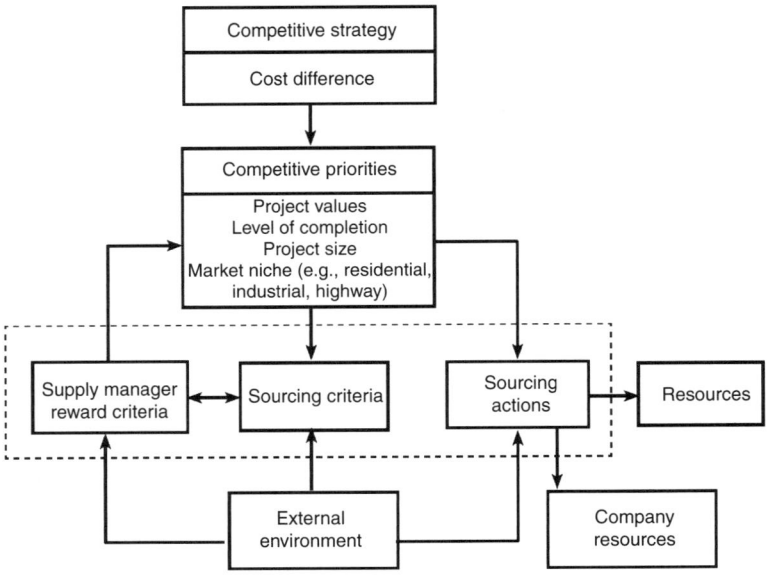

FIGURE 2.3 Components of sourcing strategy.

be useful for day-to-day decision making in a typical construction organization. The competitive strategy is articulated in terms of competitive priorities. Key environmental factors must also be considered.

As an example, low-margin strategies generally imply a more standardized project, less flexibility in responding to customer demands, fewer options, acceptable quality, and a continuous processing technology. A low-cost strategy is mostly concerned with residential markets, which includes many competitors. On the other hand, a project differentiation strategy is concerned with creating barriers to entry, which implies complex engineering capabilities, strong financial capabilities, and higher material and equipment costs.

Supply Chain Strategy

As competitive forces increase, project owners expect high-quality projects, on time completion, increased service, and decreased costs. As construction organizations become more competitive, a rippling effect is experienced by the suppliers and subcontractors. As a result of more competition and the increased cost of subcontracting and materials, the supply chain management concept has emerged as a competitive weapon. Other secondary reasons for supply chain management are the increased use of technology and the concept of continuous improvement.

These new supplier/subcontractor prime contractor relationships require trust and commitment by all supply chain parties, which is in direct contrast to their historical relationships which have been far from cooperative. Traditional subcontracting attitudes have always encouraged arm's-length relationships with price as the dominant buying factor. Today, supply chain management culture looks for a more cooperative attitude between parties. Although many construction organizations are claiming to be interested in the supply chain management concept, the effectiveness of these proposed arrangements is just beginning to be studied in the construction industry. In reality, a single construction organization could participate in the supply chain in a variety of roles, as a supplier, subcontractor, or prime contractor.

The Project Sourcing Plan

The sourcing plan for an awarded contract must be explicit and complete. Several key elements must be considered for the materials, equipment, and subcontracting sourcing, and an equipment plan should be included. The final step in the sourcing plan involves the issuance of either a purchase order or a contract. See Fig.2.4 and Table 2.4.

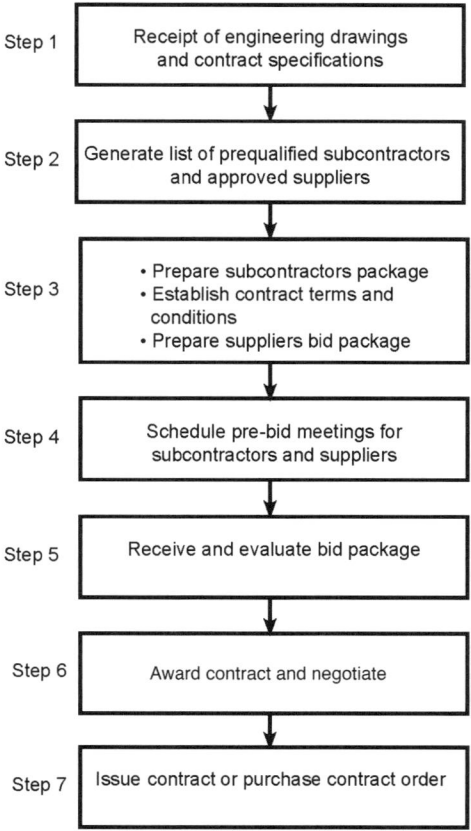

FIGURE 2.4   The project sourcing plan.

	225 CAT Excavator	Dump Truck1	Dump Truck2	Bob CAT Loader	Demonstrator	Compactor
Cost	$165,000	$93,000	$55,800	Rent $1800/month	$19,000	Rent $350/month rent $125/week
Financement						
Cash	7.0%	7.0%	7.0%			
Borrow	$149,000					
Period	60 months	60 months	60 months			
Interest rate	8.5%	9.0%	9.0%		8.5%	
Fuel cost	$4.15/gallon	$4.15/gallon	$4.15/gallon		$4.15/gallon	
Repairs	$18,560	$2,500	$5,000		10% of new cost	
Insurance	$4,250	$8,250	$8,250		$500	
Service cost	$40	$2,400	$2,400			
Horsepower	150			74	74	
Haul capacity		8 CY	8 CY			
New tires		$275 each	$275 each		$200 each	
Tire repair		$100/call	$100/call		$100/call	
Useful life of truck tires		50,000 miles	50,000 miles			

TABLE 2.4 Water Line Project Equipment Requirements Plan

Purchase Order

A purchase order is a binding contract between the construction organization and the supplying organization. It serves as an offer to the supplying organization that is accepted once the supplier signs the actual purchase order. In some instances, a supplier may send a confirmation of acceptance rather than sign the purchase order. (This mode of acceptance can be problematic if there are disputes later and can cause what is known as a "battle of the forms" conflict.) At any rate, the purchase order memorializes the terms and conditions that govern the transaction and supersedes any negotiations. For this reason, the construction organization must take extra care in preparing and wording the purchase order. The "front" side of the purchase order includes a description and specifications for the material, quantities, delivery schedules, and shipping requirements, including who pays for the shipment. The payment term also appears on the face of the purchase order. It frequently offers the buyer an incentive for early payment. For example, 2/10 net 30 means that payments made within 10 days will be discounted by 2 percent, whereas payments made within 30 days must be the full amount. If engineering drawings or any related documents are part of the purchase order, they must be specifically incorporated by reference. In general, the purchase order should include all the information required by the construction organization to ensure acceptable performance and should be clear and unambiguous. In addition to custom provisions, the back of the purchase order will include standard boilerplate terms and conditions. Boilerplate provisions usually cover terms such as arbitration, third party assignment, applicable state law, force majeure general warranties, and order cancellation.

The typical distribution procedure for a purchase order includes the following:

- An acknowledgement copy is sent to the supplying organization.
- A copy is sent to the construction organization's accounting department.
- A copy is sent to the project manager on the jobsite.
- A copy remains in the supply sourcing department.

A copy remains with the supply manager for the project as an open purchase order. See Fig. 2.5. The purchase order file should include the following information:

1. The executed purchase order, change orders, back charges, claims, invoices, and payment records.
2. Specifications and design changes.

Chapter Two

Purchase Order Hoosier Pride Construction, Inc.				Project Name _____ Purchase Order No. _____ Page ____ of ____ Date _____ Prepared by _____		
To:				Telephone No:		
				Facsimile:		
Attention:				E-Mail:		
Confirmed to:				Date:		
Details of Purchase Order:						
Item No.	Quantity	General Description	Code/Equip #	Unit Price	Extension Value	
Confirming order placed with:				Total Value $		
Invoice instructions Send ___copies to: _____ _____ _____			Payment Terms_____ Seller hereby accepts and agrees to all terms and conditions on the back of this purchase order. Accepted by:_____			
The attachments below are herby made part of this purchase order:			Title_____			
_ General Terms and Conditions _ Construction Plans _ Specifications _			Company_____ Date_____			

FIGURE 2.5 Purchase order.

3. The original bid drawings and modifications.
4. Written communications and records of oral communications between the contracting organization and the supplier.
5. Performance reports on deliveries, shortages, and damages.
6. The minutes from the original evaluation and reward committee.

TERMS AND CONDITIONS

1. By shipping the described goods or by acknowledging receipt of this order, Seller agrees to the terms and conditions of sale set forth herein as well as those on the reverse side hereof. These terms and conditions constitute an offer by Purchaser and may only be accepted on the exact terms set forth and no other terms and conditions shall be controlling: and these terms and conditions supersede the terms and conditions of your proposal or acknowledgment form, if any.

2. Seller agrees and warrants that the items or articles furnished hereunder will be in strict accordance with the principal contract and the contract documents, including plans and specifications, and with Seller's samples, if any, previously approved by Purchaser. This warranty shall remain in effect so long as the Purchaser is bound to make corrections of any defects under its contract with the owner of contractor. Seller will bear all cost of reworking or replacing any items or articles which are found to be detective during such warranty period, and all costs incurred by the Purchaser involving damage to and the reworking of other work caused by any such defect in Seller's items or articles.

3. Unless otherwise specified, prices and terms are firm for duration of indicated project.

4. This order is subject to modification or cancellation by the Purchaser in the event of fire, act of God, public enemy, earthquake, flood-strikes, labor troubles, or any other cause beyond Purchaser's reasonable control.

5. Seller shall make no substitutions or changes in this order without written authority executed in the same manner and on the same terms as the original order.

6. If invoices subject to cash discount are not mailed on date of shipment, discount period will be calculated from the date invoice is received by the Purchaser. Invoices incorrectly or incompletely executed with regard to the terms and conditions of this purchase order will be returned for correction or completion and discount period shall not commence until invoice is received properly executed.

7. Shipments or deliveries shall be made at the time and in the manner specified. Time is therefore of the essence. If deliveries are not made at the time agreed upon, Purchaser reserves the right to cancel or to purchase elsewhere, and hold Seller accountable therefore. On all shipments the Seller shall promptly notify the Purchaser with respect to the shipping point and the initial carrier; and if the Purchaser is to assume freight charges, routing must be secured before shipment is made.

8. Unless otherwise specified on the face hereof, all packing and cartage charges, including tax, shall be assumed and paid by Seller and will not be allowed by Purchaser. If deliveries are so far behind the schedules specified in this order as to make it necessary for Purchaser to request Seller to make shipments by other means, it is understood that Seller will allow the increased transportation cost. The risk of loss from any casualty to the goods, regardless of the cause thereof, shall be on the Seller until the goods have been delivered to Purchaser.

9. In the event that the goods ordered hereunder require, in connection with the installation thereof, the services of a supervisor or expert connected with the Seller's company and Seller agrees to furnish the same, either without charge or at a specified rater per day, it is understood that such supervisor shall not, while performing his duties with respect to the goods covered by this agreement, be deemed an Agent or Employeeof the Purchaser and the Seller will assume full responsibility for all acts and omissions of such party.

10. In the event of any proceedings by or against the Seller, voluntary or involuntary, in bankruptcy or insolvency or for the appointment of a receiver or trustee, or an assignee for the benefit of creditors, or the property of the Seller's company, or in the event of a breach by the Seller of any of the terms hereof, including any warranties made in connection with the goods ordered hereunder, the Purchaser shall have the right to cancel this and any or all other orders or contracts between this Seller and the Purchaser or to reduce the quantities of goods to be delivered hereunder.

11. Any articles made according to Purchaser's design or developed for Purchaser at Purchaser's direction, or any designs supplied by Purchaser or copies thereof, shall not be furnished to others without Purchaser's consent.

12. Seller agrees to hold Purchaser harmless from, and to defend and indemnity Purchaser against all loss, liability, damage, and expense (including in the case of litigation, reasonable attorneys' fees and disbursements) arising from or suffered or incurred in connection with (a) any claim or injury to person or property caused in whole or in party by any act or omission by Seller, Seller's agents or employees while executing this order or making delivery hereunder or (b) any claim, with respect to any of the merchandise called for by this order or arising out of the use of such merchandise, or infringement of any patent, copyright, trademark, trade name, brand or slogan, or of unfair competition or any adverse claim of statutory or nonstatutory rights or (c) any litigation based on any claim referred to above. Purchaser agrees to give Seller reasonable notice of the commencement of any such litigation.

13. The Seller agrees to comply with all federal, state, and local laws, executive orders, codes, and regulations effective where this Purchase Order is entered into or to be performed. Where required by applicable law, rules, regulations or executive orders, equal opportunity provisions, shall be included herein as a part of this Purchase Order.

CERTIFICATION OF NONSEGREGATED FACILITIES: The Seller, by execution of this Purchase Order, certifies that he does not maintain or provide for his employees any segregated facilities at any of his establishments, and that he does not permit his employees to perform their services at any location, under his control, where segregated abilities are maintained. The Seller agrees that a breach of this certification is a violation of the Equal Opportunities clause in this contract. As used in this certification, the term "segregated facilities" means any waiting rooms, work areas, test rooms, and wash rooms, restaurants and other eating areas, time clocks, locker rooms, and other storage or dressing areas, parking lots, drinking fountains, recreation or entertainment areas, transportation, and housing facilities provided for the employees, which are segregated by explicit directive or are in fact segregated on the basis of race, creed, color, or national origin, because of habit, local custom, or other.

14. This order is expressly made subject to the contract of the Purchaser with its customer and Seller agrees that should any change in such contract make it advisable or necessary that work be discontinued under this order, Purchaser shall have the right to rescind this order by notice in writing. Seller is to receive, however, payments in the event of rescission, for material purchased and work in process and finished work on hand, to the extent that Purchaser is compensated therefor by its customer.

15. The Seller shall give the Purchaser full assistance and cooperation in the preparation by Purchaser of Form PR-47, U.S. Department of Transportation, Federal Highway Administration, Bureau of Public Roads, as revised from time to time.

16. The laws of the State of Ohio shall govern as to all questions arising under Purchase Order.

FIGURE 2.5 Purchase order. (*Continued*)

The Subcontract Document

The subcontract defines the allocation of risks and responsibilities as between the prime contractor and the subcontractor. In many ways, the subcontract is like a private statute that rules the relationship. Many subcontract relationships begin when the prime contractor solicits either a formal or informal request for quotations. The subcontractor responds with a quotation that sets out the price, scope of work, when the work can be performed, and any other special details. The quotation may also include the payment terms that the subcontractor wants if he or she gets the job. In short, the quotation can be as long or short as the subcontractor sees fit. The prime contractor accepts the quotation and then prepares the subcontract which supersedes the original quotation.

The transformation of the quotation into the subcontract can be the death knell for some subcontractors. The subcontractor always makes sure that the price is the same as what was quoted. However, they do not always make certain that the other terms, that were important to the subcontractor and were stated in the quotation, such as the number of mobilizations are actually written into the subcontract. Additionally, the subcontract usually contains a clause that automatically incorporates provisions from the master agreement between the prime contractor and the project owner. In short, the subcontractor should know exactly what he or she is agreeing to, including provisions in agreements to which the subcontractor is not privy.

As in the case of the purchase order, the subcontract is a legal contract document between the construction organization and the subcontractor once it is signed. For this reason, both parties must take extraordinary care in preparing and wording the subcontract in one case, and reading and interpreting it in the other. Any significant errors in the subcontract can result in bankruptcy. To promote fairness among the supply chain entities, it is suggested that the construction organization select one of the accepted *standard agreements* discussed in Chap. 1 and modify it to reflect the specific construction documents and scope of work. A permanent contract file should be set up similar to the purchase order file that includes the six elements listed earlier. For information about AIA Document A 401—2007 "Standard Form of Agreement Between Contractor and Subcontractor" see http://www.aia.org/docs_purchase. Additionally, CONSENSUSDOCS 750, "Standard Form of Agreement Between Contractor and Subcontractor," is available at http://www.consensusdocs.org/information.html.

The Sourcing Cycle

The sourcing of construction materials ranges from nails, plywood, and small tools to structural steel, turbine generators, and customized design related items. At any rate, there is a general framework for construction sourcing. The construction sourcing cycle is as follows:

1. Recognition of need during design stage
2. Determination of the appropriate design related needs
3. Prequalification of desired skilled capabilities based on the design stage

The Construction Supply Sourcing Process and Procedures 43

4. Requisition generation
5. Solicitation of bids or quotes
6. Evaluation of bid proposals and award
7. Generation of purchase order, lease, or subcontract agreement
8. Submission of sample materials by supplier and the preparation and submission of shop drawings by subcontractor.
9. Review and acceptance of shop drawings by general contractor, architect, or engineer
10. Fabrication by subcontractor or supplier
11. Tracking and expediting
12. Shipping and traffic
13. Delivery and inspection
14. Staging to site location
15. Installation operations
16. Testing based on specifications
17. Acceptance of rejections
18. Warranties and corrections

This generic sourcing cycle above has been highly oversimplified for presentation purposes. For residential contractors, most of the sourcing steps are condensed; however, consider the magnitude of the construction sourcing process when resource inputs are transformed to build a complex span bridge, a skyscraper or football stadium. Since much of the steel for these projects is sourced from Japan, the costs can be impressive and the shipping times can be lengthy. Shop drawings for a span bridge could take up to 2 years to complete. As can be seen, the construction sourcing process can easily become diverse as the complexity of the project increases. At each stage in the sourcing cycle, there are excellent opportunities for cutting project costs and improving quality.

Construction Sourcing Documents

The typical construction sourcing documents are the prime contract, purchase order, subcontract agreement, and lease agreements.

Prime Contract

The prime contract is the exclusive controlling contract awarded by a project owner to a general contactor to perform the requested work according to specifications.

Purchase Order

The purchase order is the short form of a contract issued by the general contractor for purchasing materials, equipment, supplies, and, in some cases, professional services. See Fig. 2.5.

Subcontract

The subcontract is a contract between the prime contractor and a lower tiered contractor. Depending on the complexity of the project, subcontractors may also be held liable for some or all of the provisions in the prime contract, that are incorporated by reference to the subcontract.

Leases and other Agreements

A lease agreement is used to source temporary items that are not consumed by the project. Construction and office equipment are sometimes controlled by lease agreements.

Subcontracting versus Materials Purchasing

There is a vast difference between purchasing materials and subcontracting. Routine materials purchasing is usually transactional. Subcontracting is a complex joint relationship between the prime and subcontracting firms. If the prime contractor and supply manager cannot describe what is needed, either it hasn't been precisely or completely designed or the work methods have not been fully developed. The project owner initially seeks to source technical expertise that will evolve into the desired specified structure or service. Considering the dollar value and complexity of some construction-related subcontracts, the successful project owner and prime contractor will spare no effort to ensure that the very best subcontract source is selected. In routine materials purchasing, if a selected source fails to perform, the materials supplier's contract can easily be cancelled. On the other hand, selecting the wrong subcontractor may be irreversible. The critical nature of the subcontracting sourcing process cannot be taken for granted. As can be seen, there are major differences between purchasing materials and subcontracting services.

The Subcontracting Sourcing Process

The subcontracting sourcing process is driven by the following elements:

1. An efficient planning and control system
2. A precise list of expected deliverables

3. A system for the prequalification of subcontractors (see Chap. 5, Fig. 5.3)
4. An effective progress control system

After these four stages have been formalized, the subcontracting sourcing process can proceed as shown in the three steps outlined as follows:

1. *The request for quotations:* Requests for quotations are driven by the complexity of the scope of work. A newspaper advertisement may be sufficient for a simple project. On the other hand, some complex bid proposals include the following documents:
   - Specifications
   - Drawings
   - Scope of Work
   - Bills of Materials
   - Notice to Bidders
   - Proposal Form
   - Contract Form
   - Terms and Conditions
   - Shipping Instructions
   - Schedules
   - Insurance Requirements
   - Special Requirements
   - Affirmative Action Certification
   - Payment and Performance Bond Form

2. *Bid receipt and evaluations:* Government agencies sometimes conduct public pre-bid meetings and bid openings, whereas private owners are less formal. In some cases, both governmental and private owners furnish the bidders with comparative bid tabulations. Governmental agencies are required by law to select and negotiate with the lowest responsive bidder. Private owners have the discretion to select and negotiate with any of the bidders.

3. *Award and preparation of documents:* Governmental agencies must formalize the contract award by distributing a public "Notice of Award." For materials purchasing, a purchase order is issued to the successful bidder. Performance and payment bonds are usually required to ensure that the low bidder will execute and complete the project and pay the subcontractors and material suppliers. See the miscellaneous subcontract documents in App. B.

Materials Purchasing

The minimum level of materials purchasing expertise must include the following:

1. Competent purchasing personnel
2. Accurate documentation for the requested scope of work
3. A well-documented supplier evaluation system
4. An in-depth understanding of the negotiations process
5. A well-documented quality control system
6. An action plan for implementing an efficient continuous improvement system
7. A just-in-time system for delivering materials and equipment to the jobsite
8. A control system for acknowledging the receipt of materials on the jobsite
9. A well-documented plan for securing materials and equipment on the jobsite
10. A system for job cost accounting for materials and equipment usage
11. An efficient system for tracking back charges

The materials used in the construction industry are produced by highly skilled engineers and production workers. Construction bulk materials are composed of naturally occurring materials such as wood and stone. The materials also include processed steel, aluminum, and plastics. Processed steel becomes beams, rods, screws, and many other construction related products; aluminum is transformed into windows; and wood is transformed into lumber, plywood, and many other related products. Construction materials such as steel are specified by process (e.g., "hot rolled"), physical properties (hardness and strength), and dimension. A steel buyer who orders by industry specification or standard runs little risk of suppliers misunderstanding what material is required: "One-inch diameter, 1020 cold rolled steel bars, 16 ft long" means the same to everyone who makes steel. Note that, while specifications are unambiguous, the quality of the material produced may fail to conform to the specifications. This is the same problem that was discussed earlier—poor execution of a good design.

Building codes and engineering specifications regulate the use of construction materials. Design engineers and architects are responsible for selecting the appropriate materials while considering the owners request, value, and aesthetics, as well as the structural attributes of the project. The materials specifications phase is the key to building a successful project. Symbols are used to specify materials on the work documents. Written specifications should also be produced for each set of plans. The specifications are usually written in concert with each trade area (i.e., concrete, structural steel, asphalt, mechanical, and others). The specifications and drawings should provide the complete scope of how the project will be built. These documents are key legal instruments between the owner and the contractor. During the estimating and bidding phase of the project, the prime contractor uses the drawings and the specifications to determine costs. If the specifications and drawings are sketchy, it is impossible to accurately determine costs and work methods.

Maintenance, Repair, and Operating Supplies

Maintenance, repair, and operating (MRO) supplies are distinct and are specified in various ways. The keys are quality and uniqueness. Over time, equipment parts are subject to wear and need to be replaced. The original equipment manufacturer expects to resupply these parts during the life of the equipment. Not infrequently, a contract to purchase equipment includes a specified number of replacement parts; periodically, engines are removed for overhaul. Replacement parts are specified by manufactured part number and model number according to the unit in which it is installed. Problems arise when manufacturers discontinue equipment. Replacements will be available as long as sufficient machines are in operation in the field. After that, sourcing and specifications become a problem. Some equipment owners may elect to supply themselves, in which case they must provide complete documentation (specification) of the parts required. The same is true if the parts are purchased externally. Sometimes equipment manufacturers will produce replacement parts if a sufficient number is ordered to make their manufacture profitable. The older the model being maintained, the less current experience the supplier has, and the more difficult the task of specifying becomes.

Maintenance also means the application or renewal of materials such as lubricants and coolants. Periodic maintenance (labor and materials) ensures longevity and satisfactory machine operation. In most cases, these maintenance materials are commodity-like in nature and are specified by industry or association standards. These materials are carried in stock and managed as part of raw materials inventory by purchasing management.

The distinction between maintenance and repair materials is not always clear. In theory, if good maintenance is practiced, events requiring repair will occur infrequently. Repair suggests the unexpected, which means the need to patch up or replace equipment components that are not expected to fail. Usually the parts are not carried as inventory by the equipment manufacturer. The repair material may have to be described in very specific ways, that is, drawings and photographs. Perhaps field engineers from the machine supplier will need to be called. The more common event is that the services of a skilled craftsman to repair failed equipment are more important than specific operating supplies, parts, and materials.

Operating supplies, also called "indirect materials," become part of the end item and are essential for its production, but their unit value or size is too small to plan or control usage unit by unit. A good example is ties used in bridge deck steel. Ties are "counted" by weighing them. Bins of ties are located throughout the jobsite and available to anyone on a "help yourself" basis. Ties are dropped on the deck and so on, without regard for usage. No one would suggest counting ties or holding steel workers accountable for them. Adhesives are another common example. These materials are supplied as needed to assemble components or provide seals between components. Generally speaking, operating supplies are standard items and are specified by manufacturer or industry codes. Nonstandard items should be questioned by the purchasing manager: Is the special item really necessary? Can a standard material be substituted?

Conclusion

Historically, the sourcing of subcontracting services was the most arbitrary element in the construction process. Only when the cost of materials and subcontracting services increased did management attempt to solve sourcing problems. The focus on labor was logical simply because the construction process is labor intensive. Recently, some construction market segments have investigated new technologies and invested in technology-driven construction purchasing systems. Although these new systems are up and running, too frequently they are being operated just like the old construction business models, thus defeating the very purpose the system was designed to achieve. The reality is that technology and advanced management systems are rapidly displacing labor.

The supply sourcing function plays a critical role in the transformation of capital, engineering, labor, bulk materials, work methods, and technology into a completed acceptable project. The efficient and profitable transformation depends on an expert sourcing professional who can ensure the on time delivery of the right goods at a reasonable price. Technology-driven sourcing develops systems to identify, prequalify, select, and evaluate vendors to provide materials, equipment, and services while, at the same time, achieving maximum integration with upstream and downstream supply chain members. The objective is to keep inventory investment to a minimum, maintain good relationships with supply chain members, and develop a culture of continuous improvement.

CHAPTER 3
Construction Supply Chain Relationship Management

> The Power of Partnerships

The supply chain management process is based on the idea of efficient resource coordination and teamwork. Depending on whether a project is a vertical or horizontal construction, an architect or design engineer is selected based on qualifications and experience to develop a design that meets code and other regulations while satisfying the functionality and end-use requirements of the project owner. The relationship between the project owner and the architect in vertical construction is established by the scope of the professional services contract and the complexity of the project. In addition to the typical design services in a vertical construction project, the architect may have varied roles in the construction process and oversight, including advice on the award to a prime contractor, detailed document preparation, construction progress reviews, and other contract administration duties. Project owners with too many projects or not enough in-house expertise sometimes hire, in addition to the architect, what is known in the industry as a *Construction Manager Agent* or a *Construction Manager "At No Risk."* The *CM Agency* serves as the owner's representative, manages the project, and has limited liability. Another alternative for the project owner is to use a *Construction Manager "At Risk."* The *CM At Risk* is essentially a general contractor who is contractually obligated to the owner to deliver the completed project for a guaranteed price and within a set schedule.

In the horizontal public works construction, the design engineer is responsible for preparing plans, specifications, and contract documents.

The project owner's in-house staff may perform the project management and administration function or outsource specific duties, such as inspection. The construction manager designation is less frequently utilized in highway work, although the South Carolina Department of Transportation (SCDOT) employed a similar concept in its "27 in 7" program. Beginning in July 1999, Construction Resource Managers (CRMs) were used to assist SCDOT in managing the design and construction of 27 years of road and bridge projects (about 200 projects) that were built in an unprecedented 7 years at a cost of approximately $5 billion. SCDOT estimates that without the CRM project delivery system, the agency would have had to hire approximately 500 new employees.[1]

Construction Supply Chain Relationship Management

For the purpose of the supply chain relationship discussion, we will assume that the owner and architect or engineer and/or construction manager relationships have been preestablished. (The terms *CM At Risk* and prime contractor will be used interchangeably.) The prime contractor takes full responsibility for coordinating and motivating the supply chain to deliver a high-quality project under budget and on time. The supply chain management approach depends on a prime contractor being guided by the following five fundamental principles:

1. Competing by adding supply chain value and eliminating waste
2. Establishing long-term relationships with subcontractors and suppliers
3. Focus on supply chain value analysis and target costing
4. Development of continuous improvement throughout the supply chain
5. Promotion of upstream and downstream information technology

An illustration of an integrated construction supplier relationship management system is given in Fig. 3.1. Construction supply chain relationships have become increasingly important for a number of reasons. There is a major trend toward contractor specialization away from building an entire project and to more subcontracting of a variety of bid items. However, it should be noted that in some heavy highway markets, 50 percent of the contract value *must* be performed by the prime contractor. In the private sector, the subcontracted value allocation is at the discretion of the prime contractor. In some market segments, it is estimated that 80 percent or more of total project revenue often passes directly to suppliers and subcontractors as payment for labor, materials, and equipment. This incredible transfer of dollars downstream emphasizes the importance and significance of

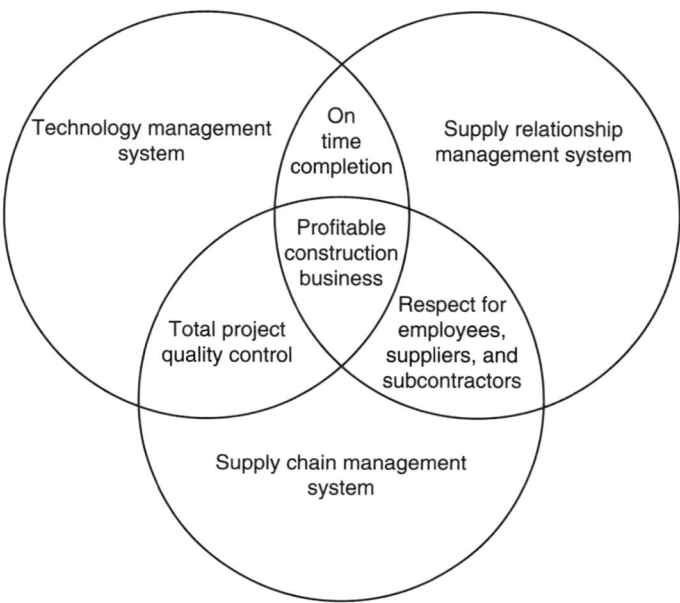

FIGURE 3.1 The integrated supplier relationship management system.

construction supply chain relationship management. For any construction organization to stay competitive in today's aggressive market sector, it is essential that they maintain strong relationships with their best subcontractors and suppliers.

When a construction business subcontracts a large percentage of project activities bid items, the importance of supply chain relationship management cannot be underestimated. Prime contracting organizations experience a great deal of pressure from project owners and from competitors to keep their edge and stay in business by reducing costs, improving project quality, and enacting continuous improvement. Many construction organizations are also reducing the number of subcontractors and suppliers on their list of bidders. The costs of subcontracting and buying materials from a larger number of subcontractors and suppliers, while still managing a relationship with each, may be too great for a company to absorb.

Subcontractor and Supplier Reduction

With the decreasing number of subcontractors and suppliers used by construction organizations, it is more important than ever to maintain strong relationships. Keeping these relationships healthy will secure a source of highly qualified subcontracted capabilities and materials that allow for the possibility of lower costs and higher quality as well as offer the promise of greater market share for the increasingly competitive construction market. Companies that are shifting toward a smaller subcontractor and supply base cannot ignore the role that relationships will play with the remaining subcontracted capabilities and material suppliers. Another reason that construction supply chain relationship management is important is the increasing shortages of skilled capabilities and resources. Many resources and commodity materials are becoming harder to acquire, and in turn, are becoming more expensive to purchase. With rising prices and increasingly scarce materials supply, a construction organization must maintain strong relationships with the subcontractors/suppliers of these materials (work items) to guarantee that they are the first-priority customer of their subcontractor/supplier; no firm can survive if it is unable to have a sustainable source of supply, even for scarce items.

Four Dimensions of Supply Chain Relationships

One model that explains supply chain relationship management includes four behavioral dimensions—the four C's; counterproductive (lose-lose), competitive (win-lose), cooperative (win-win), and collaborative (win-win) relationships.[2] Counterproductive relationships are those in which each firm is so focused on getting what is best for it that each puts the other at a disadvantage. This relationship is undesirable because it does not promote a positive rapport between firms involved and neither firm achieves their goals. Counterproductive relationships also discourage future dealings between firms and create instability in each firm's reputation.

Competitive relationships are those in which firms strive to get the very best arrangement possible in their negotiations and fail to see the benefits of both firms obtaining their goals and objectives. These firms will stop at nothing to make sure that they come out on top and do not care about the other firm's well-being. Typically, the firm that is able to win in a competitive relationship has much more power than the losing firm. The more powerful firm sometimes places its focus on the *present*, not concerning itself with long-term negotiations on future projects. This type of relationship will also discourage an ongoing relationship to the detriment of both firms. There are certain situations in which a competitive relationship is desirable. A competitive relationship is almost always required with transactional/Tier 3 contractors and suppliers and ensures that the construction organization can contract for lower prices to help keep their competitive edge in the market (e.g., commodities are transactional purchases unless there is a monopoly or shortage). It does not matter if the relationship is not strong enough to last because, by definition, transactional suppliers can be easily replaced at any time.

Cooperative relationships recognize the potential value of both firms getting what they want and maximize the potential of having a long-term relationship. Although it is a strong relationship, a cooperative alliance lacks the teamwork that is needed between the various construction organizations to optimize the benefits for all of the members of the supply chain. Cooperative relationships are commonly found within a prime contractor's preferred/Tier 2 subcontractors and suppliers list.

In comparison, collaborative relationships, usually found with firms' strategic/Tier 1 suppliers, include the team component that is missing in a cooperative relationship. In collaboration, the two firms truly realize the benefits of working together to optimize outcomes for both firms. The two firms work together to develop a strategy to deliver a high-quality project on time and under budget. Strategic partners frequently share resources and information. However, the sharing of resources and some information may be illegal, as between the prime contractor and its subcontractor or between the prime contractor and disadvantaged business enterprises (DBEs) involved in federally funded highway projects and other public works. As with any industry, contractors throughout the supply chain must avoid any antitrust violations, including any appearance of price fixing or bid rigging. Certain industry customs, such as informally loaning heavy equipment on a jobsite, cannot be practiced in government programs designed to develop minority- and female-owned businesses.

Supplier Relationship Management Segmentation

Many large construction organizations are implementing subcontractor-supplier relationship management programs in their business plans to ensure that they maintain their competitive edge. There are several different ideas on the exact process that a supplier relationship management program should follow, but the general approach is the same. Consider SMS Construction, a large vertical construction organization that is in the process of developing a supplier relationship program. Most supplier relationship management programs begin with some sort of ranking or categorization of potential subcontractors and suppliers. The process of subcontractor/supplier categorization is important for a number of reasons. This process forces the construction organization to communicate cross-functionally to develop some system for ranking subcontractors and suppliers. Two main items that will be considered in the categorization process are the dollar amount of the contract with an individual subcontractor/supplier and their criticality to the construction organization's business strategy.

Once the system is developed, it then forces the various functions in the firm to evaluate which subcontractors/suppliers truly add value. The rankings are aggregated to enable a ranking of all subcontractors/suppliers. The company will then categorize the suppliers into one of three categories: *strategic*, *preferred*, or *transactional*. *Strategic* suppliers are those which are most important to the construction organization. They supply the construction organization with essential materials and capabilities that are not easily replaced. A firm must spend most of its efforts on maintaining and strengthening these relationships.

Preferred suppliers are those which are important to the construction organization, but alternative subcontractors/suppliers could be found with some effort. *Transactional* suppliers are those which provide the general contracting firm with items that are not critical to their core business and that can be easily replaced in a short time. SMS uses the labels: strategic, preferred, and transactional interchangeably with Tier 1, Tier 2, and Tier 3 suppliers and subcontractors. See Fig. 3.2.

Preferred Supplier Relationship Management

There are several ways in which a construction organization can evaluate its preferred subcontractors and suppliers. If subcontractors/suppliers do not meet quality, delivery, and scheduling standards, the construction organization may face delays and will lose money from not being able to meet critical scheduling start times and project demands. It is well known that good standing relationships with subcontractors and suppliers can increase profitability and reduce overhead expenses. Therefore, subcontractors and suppliers must be developed in order to meet standards and contribute to continuous improvement goals. Specific communication strategies including supplier training and education, feedback, and frequent site visits can aid in developing subcontractors and suppliers. The company can evaluate a subcontractor's work methods and supplier's quality performance. By evaluating the work methods and quality process of the supplier/subcontractor, the capabilities can be easily assessed. Performance-based evaluations assess the company after its product or service has been delivered. There are three common performance-based evaluations systems: the categorical method, the cost-ratio method, and the linear averaging method. In each of these evaluations, the analyses of the results are subjective and rely on the judgment of the buyer using the methods. These techniques are illustrated in Chap. 4.

Strategic Supplier Relationship Management

For each strategic subcontractor or supplier, a key contact or an "owner" within the prime contractor's organization must be established to ensure that the relationship is being properly managed. Specific preferred subcontractors and suppliers can also be referred to as strategic subcontractors and suppliers. This person is the individual within the prime contractor's organization that others in the organization should contact for information on the strategic subcontractor/supplier (source). It is possible that each project manager within the organization will be an "owner" for a specific strategic source relationship.

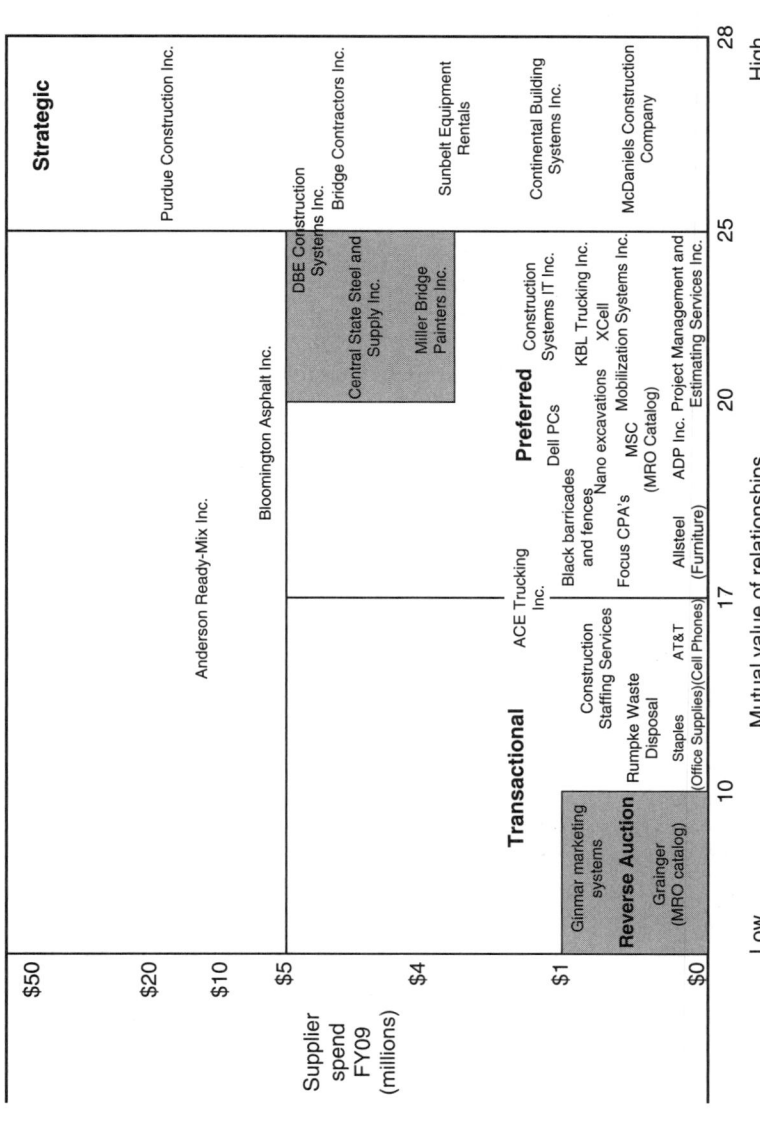

Figure 3.2 Supplier relationship segmentation.

Relationships with strategic sources need to be closely managed. One way to keep up on supplier relationships is for a prime contractor to compile supplier profiles for each strategic source. These profiles should include items such as key management contacts, a company overview, SWOT (strengths, weaknesses, opportunities, threats) analysis, Porter's five key financial figures, information on current contracts, "owners" of the relationship within the firm, and an organizational chart. See the example profile at the end of the chapter.[3] While the process of compiling these profiles should be owned by the supply sourcing manager, the content of the profiles should be owned by all functions of the construction organization. Functional ownership of the content will ensure that all areas within the construction operation that deal with each of the strategic suppliers will have input in the necessary content of the profiles. Ownership of the process by the supply sourcing manager/department makes certain that there is only one source of strategic source profiles for the entire firm. This method also ensures that the supply sourcing manager/department is knowledgeable about all strategic sources and aware of how they are rated by each function. In addition to the strategic source profiles, the construction organization should clearly establish expectations for strategic sources and discuss plans and projects for the future; this is typically done with an annual review period. Public and private project owners may also have their own evaluation system that includes not only the prime contractor but also specific evaluations of all entities within the supply chain.

Strategic Source Performance Review Process

The construction organization should have a process for managing performance and giving feedback to the subcontractors and suppliers. This process is typically accomplished by asking the subcontractor/supplier for a performance self assessment and then communicating to the strategic source subcontractor/supplier exactly how the prime contracting firm rates its performance. Most often there is some sort of reward and punishment system put in place by the construction sourcing organization to further encourage excellent performance. SMS has addressed the feedback and performance management phase.

An overview can be beneficial in developing a clear idea of the supplier performance review process. A performance review is a set of expectations and measurements for controlling long-term relationships with existing strategic subcontractors/suppliers. It includes consistent measurements for establishing positive relationships with new strategic sources and evaluating current performance of the existing ones, according to the expectations of SMS. The SMS review process has a standard template that is used as a guideline for informing a customized review process with criteria specific to each strategic source.

The performance review template includes a personal meeting with the prime contractor's manager or superintendent. Having the project manager in the performance review of a strategic source is beneficial for the prime contracting firm and fosters cross-functional communication. By getting input from the person directly responsible for each strategic source, a more complete review of performance is possible.

The general review process should take approximately 2 work days to complete. The first step is to schedule a review process for each individual strategic source; the review date is established when the contract is signed. Approximately 5 days before the review date, an SMS-developed questionnaire specific to their needs and those of the strategic source is sent. The strategic source is then required to complete the questionnaire and return it to SMS no later than 2 days prior to the meeting. After an internal review is completed, a final analysis of the project relationship expectations is communicated to the strategic source. Within the next few days, meetings are held between them, where all of the action items are recorded. The final step is the distribution of the minutes from the meetings between SMS and the strategic source and the official publication of action items. See Fig. 3.3.

SMS has various review categories that are used to fully assess their strategic sources. Quality is a very important review category. SMS requires their strategic sources to meet or exceed their performance standards and proactively initiate quality process improvements. Customer service is expected to be proactive and flexible, and delivery performance needs to be optimized. The most important attributes that SMS seeks are high quality and on time completion. Technology and innovation are important in order to stay ahead of or at pace with competition and help keep SMS at the top of their field. It is necessary for SMS to have suppliers who are open about their total costs. Cost reduction and continuous process improvement is necessary in order to keep costs down and create trust with strategic sources. The last category is very important from an ethical standpoint for SMS and anyone with whom they work. Every supplier must have formal environmental, health, operational, and safety programs. In addition, they should put forth the effort to reduce, reuse, and recycle when possible. These categories, as well as others, are used in the development of the questionnaire for each source.

Strategic Supplier Relationship Scoring System

The scoring system for each strategic source is done on a scale from 0.0 to 4.0 (where 4.0 is the highest possible score), meaning that there are five different ratings that range from exceptional to unacceptable. The weaker the score, the more often the supplier needs to be evaluated. When a subcontractor/supplier rates between 2.5 and 4.0, (exceptional and very good strategic sources) there are annual evaluations.

Hoosier Pride Construction, Inc.
Minutes of
Meeting Report

Project No. _____
Project Name _____
Project Location _____
Date _____
Page 1 of _____
Compiled by _____

Meeting Subject _____

Meeting Location _____ Date _____ Time _____

Name	Title	Representing	Comments

Item No.	Minutes/Description	Action By	Action Required Date

Remarks: _____ Distribution: _____

FIGURE 3.3 Minutes of meeting report.

A good strategic source rates between 1.5 and 2.49 and needs to be evaluated semiannually. A marginal source has a rating of 1.0 to 1.49 and needs to be evaluated every quarter. When a strategic source is unacceptable, it is given a rating between 0.0 and 0.99, which means it is necessary to develop a new source. Once an investment in developing

Benefits to Owner	Benefits to Prime Contractor	Benefits to Suppliers	Benefits to Subcontractors
• Decreased project cost	• Decreased project costs	• Locked-in business	• Locked-in business
• Increased project quality	• Decreased delays	• Ability to increase skill	• Ability to increase capabilities
• Faster project completion	• Increased profitability	• Less uncertainty	• Less uncertainty
Risks to Project Owner	**Risks Prime Contractor**	**Risks to Suppliers**	**Risks to Subcontractors**
1. Supplier base becomes smaller (sole source)	1. Supplier base becomes smaller (sole source)	1. Limited opportunities for new business	1. Limited opportunities for new relationships
2. Increased supplier development costs	2. Increased supplier development costs	2. Lower pegged prices	2. Locked capacity

TABLE 3.1 Benefits and Risks of Construction Supply Chain Relationships

supply chain relationships is made, construction organizations must actively manage these relationships. Strategic construction supply chain relationships, however, do not come without risks to the project owner, the prime contractor, and the subcontractors/suppliers. See Table 3.1.

Conclusion

Construction organizations cannot afford to ignore subcontractor/supplier relationship management. Competitive advantages can be gained through their superior management. Given the competitive nature of the current business environment, a firm could potentially go out of business if it neglects proper management of strategic subcontractor/supplier relationships. The supply chain management approach encourages a prime contractor to compete by adding supply chain value and eliminating waste. Establishing long-term relationships with strategic subcontractors and suppliers is one of the most important principles of the supply chain paradigm. True information sharing can only be accomplished with both upstream and downstream information technology. Finally, the theme of continuous improvement must permeate all relationships and activities throughout the supply chain.

Tier 1 Supplier Profile Example

Kim Construction

Key Management Contacts

Doug Kim

Chief Executive Officer (since 1996)

- Mr. Kim started the company Kim Construction in 1996
- His background is in civil engineering

Kevin P. Mendel

Chief Financial Officer (since 2005)

- Kevin Mendel joined Kim Construction in 2002.
- Mr. Mendel is a CPA with more than 25 years' experience in the professional and commercial arena.
- He was initially responsible for the financial control of the heavy highway sector.

Since 2005, Mr. Mendel has been responsible for all financial, treasury, and taxation matters for the group

Contact Information

4446 Envoy Rd.
Indianapolis, IN 47450
Phone: 317-567-9834 Fax: 317-348-9834
www.Kimconstruction.com

Company Overview

- Kim Construction was established in Indianapolis in 1996.
- The founder began the company after working 10 years as a structural engineer for the Indiana Department of Transportation.
- Kim Construction is engaged in structural steel fabrication and refinery fabrication.
- The company operates in America and Europe.
- It is headquartered in Indianapolis and employs about 200 people.

Strengths
- Capable workforce
- Experienced engineers

Weaknesses
- Working significantly above effective capacity level

Opportunities
- Will be great supply chain partner
- Also partners with some of our competitors

Threats
- Participates in significant number of projects with primary competitor

Industry Competition
- U.S. Fabricators Construction
- Sanford Limited Construction
- Wilbur Construction
- Bean Construction

Significant Supplier Changes
- Recently prequalified in new market niches in INDOT market

Primary Service
- Horizontal and vertical steel fabrication

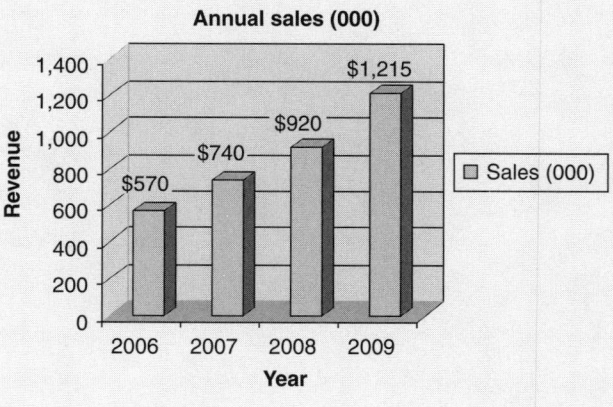

References

1. "27 in 7" Peak Performance, South Carolina Department of Transportation, 2002, www.scdot.org/inside/financing.shtml and Case Study—SIB, South Carolina: "27 in 7" Peak Performance, United States Department of Transportation, Federal Highway Administration, www.fhwa.dot.gov/innovativefinance/ifp/cssc.htm.
2. Trent, Robert J., "Why Relationships Matter," *Supply Chain Management Review*, November 2005, pp. 53–59.
3. Porter, Michael, *Competitive Advantage: Creating and Sustaining Superior Performance*, New York Free Press, New York, 1985.

CHAPTER 4
Construction Supplier Selection and Evaluation

> Milestones for Success

The materials selection process is one of the most important steps in the design phase of the construction process shown in Chap. 2, Fig. 2.1. Concrete and masonry, which are relatively abundant, are two of the most widely used construction materials. Small quantities of concrete can be made manually, whereas large quantities are made at computerized mixing plants. Masonry (clay, brick, and tile) is made in small units, thereby providing the architect with the opportunity to use a variety of designs and patterns. Ferrous metal products have a broad range of applications that are used in the design process. Wood, plastics, and composites are also commonly used by construction organizations. Asphalt is a predominant material in horizontal construction. In addition to the materials component, most complex construction projects require a number of equipment suppliers (e.g., pumps, compressors and blowers, conveyors, cranes and hoist, and testing equipment).

In today's aggressive sourcing environment, construction organizations must select suppliers based on their value-added capabilities and not purely on the competitive process. The current trend in construction materials purchasing is to reduce the supplier base. At the same time, more construction organizations are increasing their percentage of purchased materials. Therefore, in order to select suppliers who continually outperform the competition, suppliers must be carefully analyzed and evaluated. When making these critical material and service decisions, the key issues that a supply manager faces can be classified as either mistakes or success factors.

Construction Purchasing Mistakes

- In most cases, construction organizations are not proficient at identifying the capabilities of their suppliers. They sometimes rationalize materials supplier decisions based on convenience.
- They wait too late to assess the value added by suppliers and service providers.
- They do not recognize the impact of the economic changes on bulk materials prices. There are also continuously new competitors with new technologies entering the construction materials market.

Construction Sourcing Success Factors

- Perform a realistic assessment of the capabilities and expertise of each potential supplying firms. If the core competencies exist, what happens if a key supplier goes out of business? Can the supplier be easily replaced?
- Evaluate alternative strategic supplier arrangements and select appropriate suppliers.
- Share information with all strategic suppliers and request their input.

It is much easier to describe the supplier selection problem than it is to design and implement the selection process. This chapter integrates the materials supplier selection process into the construction supply chain management environment. In the case of the sole sourcing of some bulk materials, such as asphalt, some of the supplier selection concepts may not be applicable.

Material quality, delivery dependability, and price are the most critical criteria for supplier selection in the construction industry. However, the degree of importance that individual firms place on the three criteria varies. The supplier selection process begins with choosing potential suppliers for each material type needed for a specific project. The selection process is usually based solely on past performance. Once a pool of potential sources is formed, requests for quotations (RFQs) are sent out, negotiations are conducted, and specific suppliers are selected.

High-quality materials are expected from every potential supplier. If a supplier has shown the ability to supply a quality product in the past, it is assumed that it will continue to do so. In most cases, there are no formal measures taken to ensure that high-quality materials have been delivered. Visual material inspection is undertaken and any piece of material that is not visibly damaged is accepted and used. However, materials such as steel beams or concrete require a more formal inspection to ensure that they conform to specifications. In the case of steel materials, plant visits may be made by a representative of the buying firm during testing procedures to ensure that the architect's specifications are being met. For example, concrete core samples are sometimes tested to confirm that they are of the desired consistency. In addition, a representative of the supplier will sometimes be present at the construction site in order to ensure that the materials are being placed properly. Although quality is a very important aspect to the buying firm, it may not play a large role in the selection of one supplier over another. Quality is rarely a problem in the construction industry, simply because the buying firm provides the supplier with specifications and the supplier must comply. If a supplier cannot provide adequate quality, it will not receive consideration for future business from the contractor. Therefore, after the potential suppliers have been selected, considerations of delivery dependability and price play a more important role in actually selecting one supplier over another.

Delivery dependability is obviously vital in today's fast-track construction industry, where construction is often begun before the architects' final designs are completed. If delivery deadlines are missed, the result can be costly for both the owner and the contractor. *In the construction industry, time really is money.* If a project is not completed by its deadline, the loss of potential profits increases with each day past the due date. In the construction industry, suppliers must be able to deliver materials to the contractor when promised. If one company can supply a contractor considerably faster than another supplier, the faster company will have an advantage. Delivery considerations are the most important criteria used in selecting suppliers for the construction industry.

Price also has a significant effect on the process selection. Price, however, cannot always overshadow all other criteria. The trick is to strike a balance between price and the other factors considered in the process. Premiums often may be required for rush deliveries. The company must weigh the desire for expected deliveries with the resulting higher prices. Through negotiation, the buyer and supplier must reach a price agreement that is satisfactory to both parties.

While quality, delivery dependability, and price play the most vital roles in selecting a supplier, they are not the only considerations. Depending on the project and the specific types of materials required, other factors may play an even more important role. For example, a supplier must be financially stable in order to ensure the buyer that it will be around to fulfill the negotiated agreement. Warranties may also play an important role when buying roofing materials, wooden doors, and cabinets. Finally, advantages in the areas of customer service or supplier location also may sway a buyer in the direction of a particular supplier.

Sources of Supplier Information

Searching for an appropriate supplier for a specific material or service is a strategic issue in itself. In the new fast-paced and volatile buying environment, the construction organization must know where to look for required materials or equipment services. Materials and service buyers must become experts on the construction industry and in specific bulk materials or equipment services. There are many sources for the buying organization to consider when seeking out potential suppliers. Traditional buying sources—the local chambers of commerce, the Yellow Pages, trade shows, the Internet, the Association of General Contractors, and public libraries—are excellent sources of supplier data.

Strategic Selection

The project manager should have a clear understanding of the strategy of the entire organization and have a specific project sourcing plan that complements and aids the overall strategy execution. Purchasing, logistics, materials management, and construction are functional areas that are linked closely together under the construction supply chain management umbrella. These functions must work as cohesive strategic competitive units where each one complements the other. It is from this perspective that the selection of strategic suppliers should take place.

For example, if a firm's strategy is to be differentiated by bidding highway work, then price will be secondary. Specifications, innovation, technology, and quality dominate the way the firm stays competitive and in compliance. This places a requirement on the project manager to be flexible and capable of change. Therefore, a supplier should be chosen who can adapt to the change that is mandated by the operating needs and contract change orders in the field. A "strategic match" is needed between the construction organization and supplier so that they can work in harmony as far into the future as they are compatible. The selection of suppliers should not be based solely on past performance but on the anticipated capabilities of the future. In order for good communication to exist between buyer and supplier, common ground should exist in management styles, control systems, quality philosophies, and technological abilities (e.g., engineering, design, and supply chain integration). The supplier selection decision should be viewed as an extension of the construction organization's strategy.

Criteria for Supplier Evaluation

There are two main categories of supplier evaluations: *process-based evaluations* and *performance-based evaluations*. The *process-based evaluation* is an assessment of the supplier's production or service process. For strategic suppliers, the construction organization will conduct an audit at the supplier's site to assess the level of capability in the supplier's operating systems. Process flowcharts can be developed to identify the non-value-added activities that should be eliminated to improve business efficiency. In addition, large construction sourcing organizations are increasingly demanding that their suppliers become certified through third-party organizations.

The *performance-based evaluation* is an assessment of the supplier's actual performance according to a variety of criteria, such as delivery reliability, cost, and quality defect rate. It is a tactical assessment which measures the day-to-day performance of the supplying firm; hence, it is an after-the-fact evaluation. The performance-based evaluation is more common than the process-based evaluation, perhaps because objective data are readily available and easier to measure. Benefits of objective measurement schemes include reduced perceptual bias and a means for benchmarking a supplier's performance. Three common performance-based supplier evaluation systems are described in the next section.

Three Common Supplier Evaluation Systems[1]

The three general types of supplier evaluation systems used today are the categorical method, the cost-ratio method, and the linear averaging method. In general, the guiding factors in determining which system is best are ease of implementation and overall reliability of the system. It should be noted that the interpretation of the results from any of these three systems is a matter of the buying organization's judgment.

Categorical Method

The categorical method involves categorizing each supplier's performance in specific areas defined by a list of relevant performance variables. The buyer develops a list of performance factors for each supplier and keeps track of each area by assigning a "grade" in simple terms, such as "good," "neutral," and "unsatisfactory." At frequent meetings between the buying organization and the supplier, the buyer will inform the supplier of its performance. See Table 4.1.

The categorical method is a simple and informal system in the sense that detailed performance achievements or shortcomings are not measured. Instead, it is primarily used as a basic evaluation tool between top managers in the buying organization and the selling organization, while still permitting the discussion of past performance,

Supplier	Cost	Material Quality	Speed	Total
A	Good (+)	Unsatisfactory (−)	Neutral (0)	(0)
B	Neutral (0)	Good (+)	Good (+)	+ +
C	Neutral (0)	Unsatisfactory (−)	Neutral (0)	−

TABLE 4.1 Performance Characteristics

future expectations, and long-term plans. The advantages associated with implementing this sort of evaluation program are that it can be implemented almost immediately and is the least expensive of the three systems discussed here. This method's major disadvantage is its dependence on the judgment of its users. The system is largely dependent on the memories of personnel to explain what "unsatisfactory" or "good" means. With this method, there is no concrete supporting data.

In the construction industry, establishing performance factors and measures is a relatively simple task for management so that some type of quantitative system can be developed to gauge improvement. However, design consultants are perhaps the most difficult to measure. When measuring service businesses, data must be collected on supplier attitude and response time to requests for assistance, quality of technical assistance, and qualifications of support staff. It is normal, therefore, to have a relatively simple rating scheme for services, such as outstanding, acceptable, and poor, along with explanations regarding specific incidents to explain the ratings.

Experience is essential when using any category-based managerial evaluation system. For example, a simple pass/fail approach to supplier rating will work when a construction organization is reducing its supplier base, but should be replaced when the supplier base becomes more manageable. In other words, the initial improvements are easier and less expensive than future evaluation methods.

Cost-Ratio Method

The cost-ratio method evaluates supplier performance using standard cost analysis. The total cost of each purchase of materials is calculated as its selling price plus the buying organization's internal operating costs associated with the quality, delivery, and service elements of the purchase. Calculations involve a four-step approach. The first step is to determine the internal costs associated with quality, delivery, and service. Next, each element is converted to a cost ratio, which expresses the cost as a percentage of the value of the purchase. An example of quality costs follows:

Supplier: AA	
Elements	**Costs**
Site visits	$200
Sample approval	$25
Incoming inspection	$75
Reworking costs	$225
Paperwork inaccuracies	$100
Lost time due to rejected materials	$375
Total additional quality costs	$1000
Total value of purchase	$100,000
Quality-cost ratio (total quality cost/ total purchase)	1%

The third step is to sum the three individual cost ratios (quality, delivery, and service) to obtain an overall cost ratio. Finally, the overall cost ratio is applied to the supplier's quoted unit price to obtain the net adjusted cost figures. See Table 4.2.

The net adjusted cost figure is used as the basis for performance comparison among other suppliers. When applying this evaluation method, all costs of conducting business with the supplier are assessed as a penalty. The best supplier is selected as the one with the lowest net adjusted cost. The main advantage of the cost-ratio method is that the results are cost oriented. However, the associated costs must be known. Therefore, the cost of implementing this method may be expensive when compared to the categorical method. Moreover, this method does not take into account other aspects of supplier performance.

A hybrid of the cost-ratio method is the "total cost-of-ownership rating." It includes five performance factors: quality (maximum of 30 points), delivery (25), technology (20), price (15), and service (10). A perfect supplier would receive a score of 1.00. This is calculated by

Company	Quality Cost Ratio	Delivery Cost Ratio	Service Cost Ratio	Total Penalty	Quoted Price/Unit	Net Adjusted
AA	1%	1%	1%	3%	$86.25	$88.84
BB	2%	2%	3%	7%	$83.24	$89.06
CC	3%	1%	6%	10%	$85.10	$93.61
DD	2%	1%	2%	5%	$85.00	$89.25

TABLE 4.2 Cost Comparison Utilizing Cost-Ratio Method of Supplier Rating

deducting the amount of points received (100 if perfect) from 100, dividing by 100, and adding 1. The idea is to give a simple numeric rating to the so-called hidden cost of ownership—the additional lifetime cost to the organization. A score of 1.20, for instance, means that for every dollar the buying organization spends with that supplier, it spends another $0.20 on everything from delays to added service costs.

Linear Averaging

The linear averaging method is probably the most commonly used evaluation method. Specific quantitative performance factors are used to evaluate supplier performance. The most commonly used factors in goods purchases are quality, service (delivery), and price, although any one of these factors named may be given more weight than the others. Quality is most important for a builder of complex bridge projects. Price might be given equal or greater weight in an evaluation system used by the highly competitive residential housing market. An example of the linear averaging method follows.

The first step is to assign appropriate weights to each performance factor, such that the total weights of each factor add up to 100. For example, quality might be assigned a weight of 50, service a weight of 35, and price a weight of 15. The assignment of these weights is a matter of judgment and top management preferences. These weights are subsequently used as multipliers for individual ratings on each of the three performance factors. After the weights have been assigned, the individual performance factor ratings are determined. This is done by summing the scores for each factor. The third step is to multiply each performance factor rating by its respective weight as a percentage. In this example, a quality rating of 95 would be multiplied by 0.50, if quality had a weight of 50. Finally, the results from step three are added to give a numerical rating for each supplier.

Example

Prime contractor A wishes to rate its suppliers on quality, service, and price, and has assigned each a weighting factor of 50 for quality, 35 for service, and 15 for price. For this example, quality is rated as a direct percentage of the number of acceptable bulk lots received in relation to total lots received. The service rating is a direct percentage of the lots delivered on time in relation to total bulk lots received. In rating price, the lowest price obtained from any supplier is used as the base price, and prices from other suppliers are rated as a ratio of the base price. Two suppliers would thus be rated as follows:

	Supplier 1	Supplier 2
Material quality (weight = 50)		
Acceptable bulk lots	50	35
Total bulk lots received	58	40
Quality rating	86.2	87.5
Service (weight = 35)		
On-time deliveries	52	38
Total bulk lots received	58	40
Service rating	89.7	95.0
Price (weight = 15)		
Lowest price	$75	$75
Price submitted	$75	$82
Price rating	100	91.5
Total performance rating	89.5*	90.7†

*89.49 = (.5 × 86.2) + (.35 × 89.7) + (.15 × 100)
†90.7 = (.5 × 87.5) + (.35 × 95.0) + (.15 × 91.5)

In this situation, Supplier 2 is the more satisfactory supplier. The advantage of this type of system is that it is relatively easy to implement once all the performance factors and their weights have been determined. Another advantage is that this system provides the construction organization with a great deal of flexibility in determining the performance factors to be measured. The example above consists of only three factors (quality, service, and price), but any number of factors can be used. For different product classes, different factors, weights, and measures can be used to reflect the relative importance of each item to the buying organization. Finally, these types of systems produce reliable data and are relatively inexpensive to implement.

The primary objective of the construction organization's purchasing department is to provide for a continuous improvement operation by ensuring the availability of bulk materials and equipment services. In a competitive environment, the purchasing function must ensure on-time delivery of the right goods at a reasonable price. There is a general consensus that quality, service, delivery time, and price are the key buying criteria for competitive firms. Implicit criteria such as managerial expertise, financial stability, and relative supplier location are important in the supplier selection process. Firms must also have a complete understanding of economic trends, innovations, and challenges in the construction industry. Correct supplier selection will be an important factor in determining whether a construction organization is profitable.

Single versus Multiple Sources

Much debate has taken place concerning the number of suppliers a firm should use. One side of the debate is the multiple-sources side, which involves the use of two or more suppliers. The other side of the debate is the single-source policy, in which only one supplier is used to supply a particular lot of bulk materials.

The goal of both policies is to provide the buying organization with the best value of a supplied lot of bulk materials. Many attributes contribute to the value that the buyer receives. They include risk, quality, material price, total cost, delivery, quality, reliability, and service (design capabilities, productivity improvements, research and development).

Advantages of Multiple Sourcing

The main arguments for multiple sourcing are competition and assured supply. It is commonly believed that competition between suppliers for similar materials will drive costs down as suppliers compete against each other for more of the buying organization's business. This sense of competition is at the very root of American thought because competition is the basis for capitalism and the backbone of Western economic theory.

Multiple sources also can guarantee an undisrupted supply of bulk materials. If something should go wrong with one supplier, such as a strike or a major breakdown or natural disaster, the other supplier(s) can pick up the slack to deliver all the needed materials without a disruption.

Multiple sourcing also can provide other benefits such as improved market intelligence and improved supplier appraisal effectiveness. Contact with many suppliers will allow a firm to keep abreast with new developments and new technologies as they emerge across the field. In addition, greater contact with suppliers will increase the effectiveness of evaluating a supplier's ability and progress by comparing cost and production data from among suppliers.

Advantages of Single Sourcing

The major arguments in favor of single sourcing are that, with the certainty of large volumes, the supplier can enjoy lower costs per unit and increased cooperation and communication to produce win-win relationships between buyer and seller. Naming a certain supplier as the single source and providing it with 100 percent of the contract requirements greatly reduces the uncertainty that the supplier will lose business to another competitor. With this contract guarantee, the supplier is more willing to change its business/operating methods to accommodate the construction buying organization. By reducing duplication in operations in areas such as setup, single sources of bulk materials should be able to provide lower costs per lot compared to multiple sources. Spreading fixed costs across a larger volume should also result in an accelerated learning curve. Cooperation and communication is enhanced between buyer and seller with a single-source agreement because of the fewer number of people involved when compared to multiple sourcing.

Advantages of Dual Sourcing

The advantages of multiple sourcing can be viewed as the disadvantages of single sourcing and vice versa. The best scenario would be one that included the advantages of both. This might be done by applying significant pressure to single-source suppliers or by providing significant certainty to suppliers in a multiple-sourcing environment. This may be accomplished through the use of supplier usage limits. Changing suppliers on projects regardless of single or multiple suppliers can be used as a form of punishment; in some instances, using the same suppliers on all projects can be viewed as a reward.

Long-term contracts for specific projects can provide the stability needed to produce single-source results while still using more than one supplier. By servicing several projects, two suppliers (a single source on each project) may be able to achieve the economies of scale comparable to that of one supplier. When spreading volume over fixed costs, materials savings experience diminishing returns. If the volume is great enough, two firms may eventually get the returns diminished enough so they are comparable in price to one firm. The advantage can be attributed to the "economies of scale" that may occur with a single source supplier.

Long-Term Relationship Issues

Single sourcing advocates may want to address certain issues regarding long-term impacts of single sourcing. In the long run, if everyone undertakes a reduction in supplier base, there will be fewer suppliers to deal with and overall competition will decrease. Supplier consolidation will give suppliers more power in the long run.

Finally, many more tasks are being performed by single sources in areas such as engineering and design work. In what is known as "outsourced supply contracts," the construction organization assigns a completed work category or service to a supplier and it is the supplier's responsibility to design and produce it. The project owner and construction organization are only concerned with the completed work item. These types of situations may enable suppliers to become so specialized and to obtain so much expertise that the construction organization cannot effectively compete with its suppliers. Construction organizations must be careful not to let too much of the value-added portion of their product be delegated to suppliers or else the construction organization's power will be reduced.

Cross-Sourcing

The single-sourcing/multiple-sourcing issue does not have to be viewed as a "yes or no" type of a decision. A hybrid approach can be used that is known as cross-sourcing. With this method, the supplier base is expanded without increasing the actual number of suppliers. For example, if supplier A can supply materials on projects 1, 2, 3, 4, and 5 and so can supplier B, the advantages of both single and multiple sourcing can be achieved if supplier A supplies materials for projects 1, 3, and 5 and supplier B supplies for projects 2 and 4. If anything happens to supplier A, supplier B can pick up the slack because B has the capability to supply projects 1, 3, and 5 as well. Neither supplier suffers because overall volume remains the same. The reverse also can be done if supplier B fails to perform.

Supplier Reduction

Regardless of one's final analysis of the single/multiple debate, reduction of the supply base is recommended. If the perceived benefits outweigh the risks, and after careful analysis of both short-term and long-term needs, a single source may be appropriate. However, for operations that would be financially damaged if a supply stoppage occurred, then the use or development of a second source is wise. Assuming that it is desirable to reduce the number of suppliers, the question becomes "which one(s)?" The grade and hurdle methods are used to guide the supplier reduction analysis.

Grade

"Grade" methods are those that are based on a score or grade given to the supplier by the buyer for some attribute. The most common attributes are quality, price, and delivery. The supplier's performances in the past are kept on record and the suppliers receive a "report card" for performance compared to other suppliers. Many additional attributes can be added such as frequency of delivery, but the method remains the same—for each attribute and purchase transaction, the supplier is given a grade. These attributes can be weighted equally or used to emphasize what is more important to the buying firm.

When implementing a policy of supplier reduction, it is often recommended to use the report card, which is usually computerized, to rank the suppliers and then go with the best one(s). One of the drawbacks of this method is that, many times, qualitative information cannot accurately be incorporated into the system—for example, if a design change or traffic congestion caused a shipment to be delayed.

Another drawback of grade methods is that supplier performance is the only element used to resolve the cause of the problems. One major flaw in grade methods is that they assume that the best performance in the past will be the best performance in the future. In a way, it forecasts which suppliers will be able to best meet supply needs even though a construction organization's needs may be different in the future. Computerized supplier performance reports (grade methods) may be of better use if futuristic criteria were used and the criteria were very comprehensive and exhaustive.

Hurdle

The second group of methods used to reduce the number of suppliers a firm uses is what is known as "hurdle" methods. In this situation, suppliers are required to "jump" over higher and higher hurdles to win the buying organization's business. Usually this is done through some sort of supplier certification program.

Certification

Supplier certification programs are very useful tools for evaluating the quality capabilities of a supplier. Because quality is one of the biggest concerns to many construction organizations, this is a good way to control supplied material quality. Basically, certification involves the setting of criteria regarding quality levels as demonstrated through the use of statistical process control and such elements as process capability studies of a supplier's equipment, record-keeping abilities, and so forth. If a supplier meets some but not all of the criteria, it may reach a "preferred" status and will remain on the construction organization's bidders list. If a supplier meets all the criteria and has demonstrated that it can sustain these levels, then it may be granted "strategic" status and be placed on the construction organization's bidders list. By using these methods, buyers can reduce their supply base by only awarding business to those suppliers who can become certified or by rewarding the suppliers who become certified first. Some of the suppliers will not be able to become certified due to their inabilities; thus, the supply base will be reduced.

The certification criteria can be changed and updated as recertification is required. Thus, the "hurdle" can be raised higher and higher until there are only one or a few suppliers left. The price and productivity hurdles can also be used in combination with certification. Construction organizations can add criteria to make it more difficult to be a preferred or strategic supplier.

Certification programs are only as good as their design. The attributes that determine certification must be well thought out and realistic. Part of the single-source philosophy is that, through cooperation and input from the construction organization, suppliers will be able to reduce the project's materials costs. When designing a certification program, careful attention should be paid to the selection of criteria. Good certification should include issues regarding equipment capability, quality assurance, financial health of the supplier, production scheduling methods, value analysis abilities, and cost-accounting methods.

Conclusion

Construction organizations are not proficient at identifying the capabilities of their suppliers and often rationalize decisions for the selection of materials suppliers based on convenience. This integral function—materials supplier selection process—should be integrated into the supply chain management environment so that the availability of bulk materials is ensured. The mistakes made by many organizations in supplier selection can be avoided with three factors for success. Prime contractors should assess the core competencies and capabilities of each supplier and then ask if that supplier could be replaced. Since firms exit the market for various reasons, prime contractors should be prepared to establish alternative partnerships. Lastly, the prime contractor should share information with all strategic suppliers and request their input.

Reference

1. Benton, W. C., *Purchasing and Supply Management*, McGraw-Hill/Irwin, New York, 2007.

CHAPTER 5
Purchasing Subcontracting Services

> Nothing Happens until You Decide

Construction is a project-driven industry that requires many skilled specialties. Historically, the prime contractor served as the master builder who purchased materials and used its own labor to construct a project. Over time, the industry has evolved so that today the prime contractor performs almost none of the work itself, but instead acts as the construction manager who coordinates and administers the project. The actual work is performed by specialty subcontractors. Electrical, mechanical, trucking, structural steel, bridge painting, and roofing services are just some of the many work items that are routinely subcontracted. Because the capabilities of subcontractors are so specialized, sourcing subcontractor services differs significantly from the purchasing of bulk construction materials and equipment. Agreements between prime contractors and materials suppliers or equipment vendors are routine, transactional, and arms-length unless the supplier is a strategic partner. On the other hand, the prime-subcontractor relationship requires *continuous* or, at a minimum, *intermittent* cooperation among many levels in the construction and subcontracting organizations. For example, the design specifications for a bridge project require meticulous coordination and execution between the prime contractor and the structural steel subcontractor. In design-build projects the owner seeks expeditious completion of the project, yet continuous design changes mean that the prime contractor is unable to initially specify some work items and quantities needed. In the fast track environment of design-build, experienced subcontractors are vital links in the construction supply chain. The critical nature of the subcontractor's role is not limited to time sensitive design-build environments. The dollar magnitude of subcontracting, as much as 80 percent of all dollars on some projects, is motivation for the supply chain management-oriented construction organization to spare no effort to ensure that the most adaptable subcontractors are selected.

Technically, because there is no contract between the owner and subcontractors, subcontractors do not have a formal relationship with the project owner. The prime contractor is entirely responsible for the relationship with the subcontractor as demonstrated by a generic project organization chart. See Fig. 5.1.

Practically speaking, however, there are many connections between the owner and subcontractors based on legal project administration requirements. In most jurisdictions, subcontractors have a relationship with the prime contractor because of mechanics' lien laws. Liens attach directly to a piece of property that is the subject of the work. If the owner pays the prime contractor who, in turn, never pays the subcontractors, then the owner is still responsible for money owed to the subcontractors even though the prime contractor has been paid. In order to enforce lien rights in some states, a subcontractor must notify the project owner that work has begun within so many days of starting the project. This notification is frequently referred to as a notice of furnishing or a pre-lien. In the case of public projects, a subcontractor does not lien a road or public building, but instead has the

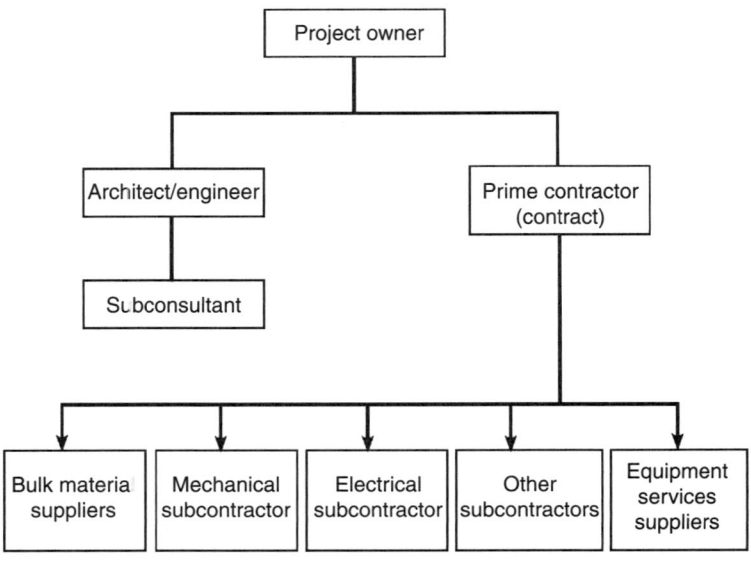

FIGURE 5.1 Generic project organization chart.

right to claim an equitable lien against the funds owed to the prime contractor. This is commonly referred to as an attested account. Similar to a pre-lien in the vertical building market, some state departments of transportation (DOTs) require the prime contractor to file a list of subcontractors before beginning work.

There are other nexuses between the project owners and subcontractors. Some government and private owners may require that subcontractors be prequalified before they are eligible to quote prime contractors who work on public and private projects. Prequalification is intended to determine a firm's financial capacity and experience building a particular work item. A prequalification application from a government agency can be extensive and may require compiled, reviewed or audited financial statements, equipment inventory, resumes of key employees, and a list of completed and ongoing projects. This information is evaluated to set a dollar limit and work category that a contractor is capable of performing; for example, prequalified for $25 million in concrete base pavement and resurfacing. In addition to what project owners require, prime contractors may also have their own subcontractor prequalification process which is discussed later in this chapter.

Insurance and bonding requirements also connect project owners with subcontractors. In the current environment, it is not unusual for a subcontractor to have to list both the project owner and prime contractor as additional insureds on its commercial general liability insurance policy. Where the owner has an in-house engineering staff and conducts its own inspections, subcontractors may have an opportunity to interact directly with the owner. Partnering meetings that include all of the supply chain entities present another opportunity for subcontractors to have some interaction with the project owner.

Affirmative action programs for woman- and minority-owned businesses administered by federal, state, and local government agencies are another instance where project owners must deal directly with a small subset of program eligible subcontractors. For example, the Federal Highway Administration's program for disadvantaged business enterprises is administered by the state DOTs. Based on 49 CFR 26 and other federal and state regulations, state DOTs determine if a business owner is socially and economically disadvantaged. After a business is certified as a disadvantaged business enterprise (DBE), then the firm is listed in a directory with other DBE firms and may be solicited to meet the DBE goal required on some federal aid highway contracts. After a contract is awarded in the DOT market, the agency tracks the field operations of both DBEs and prime contractors to ensure compliance with regulations governing the DBE program.

The depth and number of contacts between the project owner and subcontractors are more than tenuous. The linkages between owner and subcontractors are already significant and may help advance the implementation of construction supply chain management concepts.

Preliminary Subcontracting Planning

Planning for subcontracting is an important phase of the subcontractor selection process. Some of the inputs are:

- Subcontractor data file
- Subcontractor strengths, weaknesses, opportunities, and threats (SWOT) analysis
- Subcontractor capacity analysis
- Performance data
- Economic trends
- Field intelligence

Subcontract planning can account for improved supply chain performance, thereby substantially increasing the probability of a successful project. Prime contractors should not wait until they receive bid proposals to evaluate subcontracting expertise.

Subcontracting Source Selection

Open bid subcontractor selection is the accepted contracting approach for most federal, state, and local government contracts. See Fig. 5.2. Taxpayer's money is being spent on public works contracts; therefore, there must be comprehensive oversight, transparency, and accountability. Most open bid contracts are competitively bid. Prime contractors usually select subcontracting firms based on expertise and costs. A formal treatment of the open contractor approach follows. The open bidding approach is used extensively for vertical building and horizontal projects. The written contract must specify the rights and obligations of both the prime and the subcontractor. The subcontract contains the same terms and conditions as reflected in the contract between the project owner and the prime contractor.

For complex, high dollar-value projects, the selection of the right subcontractors for the construction supply chain is important and should not be taken lightly. In large construction organizations, contract management has the primary responsibility in subcontractor selection, but input is also needed from the superintendent and project manager.

Preparation of the Bid Package or Request for Quotation

The prime contractor must have a thorough understanding of the project specifications before compiling the bid package for the potential subcontractors. *Written specifications* and *construction plans* are two of the most important documents in the bid package. One document

Purchasing Subcontracting Services

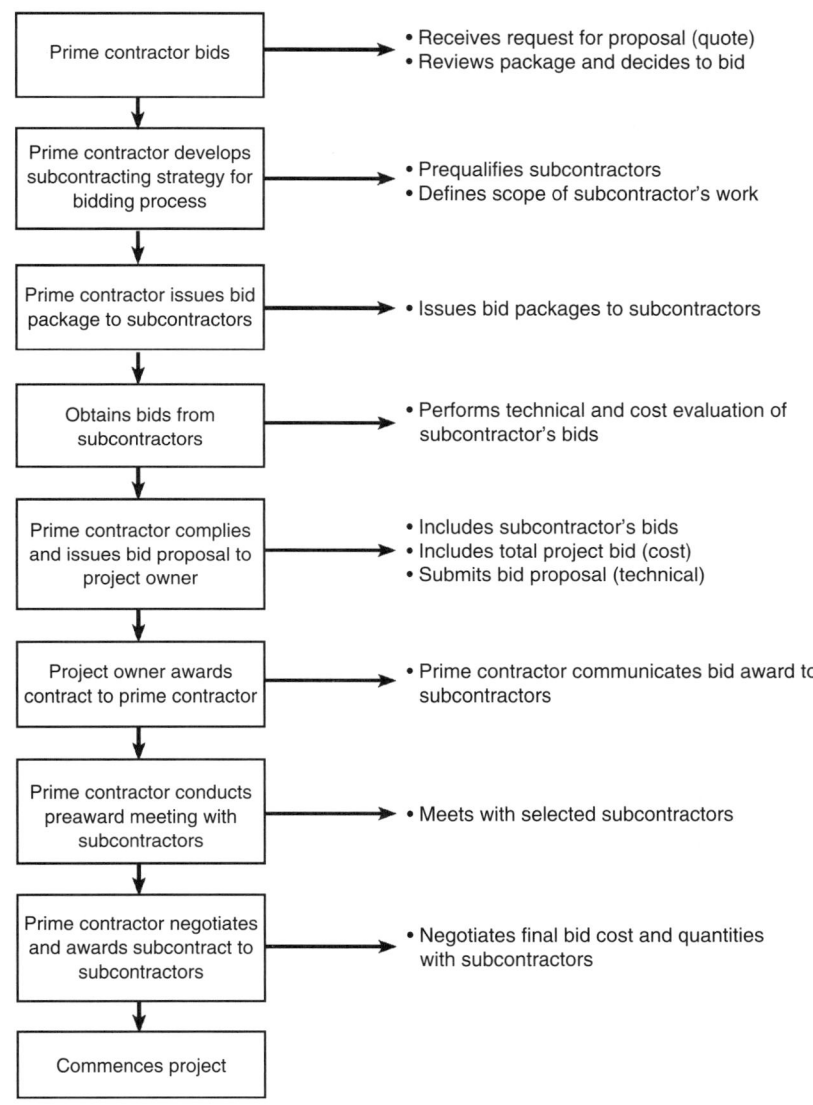

FIGURE 5.2 The subcontractor selection process.

without the other is meaningless. The contracting manager, the architect/engineer, the estimator, legal, and the perspective project manager should have input in the preparation of subcontractor bid package. Ultimately, the purchasing/contracting manager should have the responsibility for making sure that the bid package information is accurate, complete, and current.

Chapter Five

After the bid package has been finalized, the prime contractor must evaluate the project schedule, determine the deadline for the evaluation process, and set a target date for awarding subcontracts. Next, the prime contractor must prequalify the perspective bidders' list. The subcontractors' qualification data should be collected from each potential bidder in the form of a completed questionnaire and database sheet prior to releasing the subcontractor bid package. See Fig. 5.3. The list of qualified subcontractors should be updated annually.

```
                                           Project No. _____
         Hoosier Pride Construction, Inc.  Project Name _____
                                           Project Location _____
              Subcontractor                Date _____
              Database                     Prepared By _____
                                           Page _____ of _____
```

Organization

Name of Company _____

Street Address _____

City and State _____ Zip Code _____

Telephone No. _____ Fax No. _____

1. Indicate type of business organization.

   ☐ **Corporation.** List names of officers.

      President _____ Secretary _____

      General Manager _____ Treasurer _____

      State of incorporation _____ Date _____

   ☐ Limited Liability Company/ List names of members.
      _____
      _____
      _____

   ☐ Partnership/ Names of partners_____ ☐ Sole Proprietor /Name_____

2. Names of owners (stockholders holding over 10% of stock):
   _____
   _____
   _____

3. Principals of company (officers' names, titles, qualifications, experience, and years):
   _____
   _____
   _____

4. Subsidiaries (indicate whether wholly owned or percent controlled):
   _____
   _____

5. Number of years in business under your present name: _____ years.

6. The company is _____ % minority owned.

7. Indicate the number of permanent employees currently on payroll:

   Management _____
   Engineers _____
   Draftsmen _____
   Office admin. Staff _____
   Field supervisors _____
   Field labor force _____
   Total _____

FIGURE 5.3 Subcontractor database and prequalification questionnaire.

Hoosier Pride Construction, Inc.

Subcontractor Database (page 2)

Project No. _____
Project Name _____
Project Location _____
Date _____
Prepared By _____
Page _____ of _____

CLASSIFICATION OR TYPE OF WORK PERFORMED

1. Check type of construction work your company employees perform.

☐ Architectural	☐ H.V.A.C.	☐ Piping systems
☐ Carpentry	☐ Inspection & testing	☐ Plumbing
☐ Concrete	☐ Insulation/heat tracing	☐ Roofing
☐ Conveyors/Elevators	☐ Lap equipment installation	☐ Sheet metal
☐ Demolition/Relocations	☐ Landscaping	☐ Site preparation
☐ Electrical	☐ Masonry/brick	☐ Sprinkler
☐ Excavation	☐ Mechanical	☐ Structural steel
☐ Fencing	☐ Millwright	☐ Tunnelling
☐ Fire protection	☐ Painting	☐ Others (List)
☐ Glass/glazing	☐ Paving	_____
☐ Hazardous waste removal	☐ Pile driving	_____

2. Percent of work performed as a general contractor _____%
3. Percent of work performed as a subcontractor _____%
4. List type of work usually subcontracted to others _____

WORK HISTORY

1. List the important projects completed by your organization within the last 5 years including contract value.

Name of client	Person to contact	Project title and scope of work	Contract value	Year work performed

FINANCIAL

1. Submit last three annual financial reports and current profit and loss statement (audited report preferred).
2. a. What is the maximum dollar value of a project you believe your company is capable of handling?
   $ _____
   b. Over what period of time? _____
3. Average annual dollar volume of work for the past five years $ _____
4. Is there any litigation now in progress or pending with clients, subcontractors, or suppliers? ☐ Yes ☐ No
If yes, give details. _____

FIGURE 5.3 Subcontractor database and prequalification questionnaire (*Continued*).

Components of the Bid Package

The generic bid package includes the following components:

- The name and address of the project owner, prime contractor, and potential subcontractor (bidder), the bidding schedule including time and date that the bid is due and the time and date of bid opening.

Chapter Five

```
                                          Project No. _____
        Hoosier Pride Construction, Inc.   Project Name _____
                                           Project Location _____
                Subcontractor              Date _____
              Database (page 3)            Prepared By _____
                                           Page _____ of _____
```

5. a. Do you have an established bonding company? ☐ Yes   ☐ No
   b. If yes, name of bonding company _____
      Address _____
      Contact _____ Telephone no. _____ Bonding capacity $ _____
6. Indicate banking references _____
   _____

CONSTRUCTION EQUIPMENT AND MACHINERY

1. List owned construction equipment with capacity, age, type, and attachments.
   _____
   _____

LABOR AND UNION AFFILIATIONS

1. Does your organization perform work as an open shop? ☐ Yes   ☐ No   Closed shop? ☐ Yes   ☐ No

   If both, is work performed under same name? ☐ Yes   ☐ No   If different names, please list both.
   _____
   _____

2. Do you have any union national agreements? ☐ Yes   ☐ No   If yes, with which crafts?
   _____

3. If you are signator on local agreements, indicate the following:
                  Craft and Local   Holder of your bargaining rights
      _____   _____

SAFETY AND INSURANCE INFORMATION

1. Person responsible for safety program _____
   Title _____ Phone no. _____
2. Person to be contacted for matters involving insurance _____
   Phone no. _____ Fax no. _____
3. Insurance agent's name and address _____
   _____

	Last year	Previous 5 yrs.
4. a. Number of lost workday cases (injuries involving days away from work)		
b. Number of cases with medical treatment only		
c. Number of fatalities		

This statement was completed by:
Name _____ Title _____
Signature _____ Date _____

FIGURE 5.3 Subcontractor database and prequalification questionnaire (*Continued*).

- The scope of work, including specifications, construction plans, completion date, and quality and reliability requirements set forth by the specifications and document updates.
- General provisions of the contracted work item(s), indicating the anticipated contract type in boiler plate form or a sample contract.

• Outline contents of bid package and describe each section
• Identify all referenced documents
• Include flow-down of terms and conditions
• Identify where to obtain plans and specifications
• Identify price and quantity submittal information
• Identify due date, time, and submittal requirements
• Include scope of work (quantity) confirmation required before bid
• Resolve any qualifications, exceptions, or scope differences

TABLE 5.1 Bid Package Development Checklist

- Special provisions that are additions and revisions to the standard and supplemental specifications that are pass-down provisions in DOT contracts and that describe the conditions for a particular project.
- Special instructions for preparation and submittal of proposals, such as the number of copies, delivery instructions, separation of price and technical submittals, and DBE goals (if applicable).
- Direct costs, overhead, and pricing forms, if applicable for negotiated contracts.

Prior to releasing the bid package, the contracting organization must obtain approval from legal, the owner, the project manager, and the superintendent. If there are errors or omissions, it is much easier to correct the bid package before it is mailed to the potential subcontractors. A checklist can be useful in developing a bid package. See Table 5.1. See App. B for a sample subcontractor's bid package and pre-bid invitation.

Pre-Bid Conference

If the project is large, complex and includes security concerns, it may be desirable to require a *mandatory* pre-bid meeting in order to answer any questions related to the bid package. Mandatory pre-bid meetings, even for prime contractors, are rare in most markets, especially heavy highway. When a pre-bid meeting is mandatory, potential bidders must attend or they are precluded from bidding. The pre-bid conference ensures that all potential subcontractors have the same interpretations of the requirements. In most cases, pre-bid conferences will result in lower prices, especially when there are several potential bidders. The prime contractor must make every attempt to be objective at the pre-bid meeting. There are certain technical questions that involve work methods and engineering processes that could bias the bidding and should *not* be answered during the pre-bid conference.

Purchasing/Supply Management (Large Construction Organizations)

The contracting manager should be the *only* point of contact for communication with the potential bidders. There should never be any communications between the potential bidders and other personnel from the contracting organization, (i.e., the prime contractor's project manager). All potential subcontractors should be treated fairly during the solicitation period. Bid package amendments should be disseminated to all bidders in writing via both e-mail and a confirming letter. Amendments may take the form of changes in the terms and conditions, changes in material quantities, and clarifications requested from competing subcontractors. The contracting manager must ensure that no proprietary information is disclosed during the evaluation process. Competition in subcontracting can be assured by preparing identical bid packages and treating subcontractors equally in the selection process.

Evaluation of Bid Packages

The bid evaluation process and criteria should be established before the bids are submitted. If the evaluation process is based on a point system, the weighting method must be set up before evaluating the bid proposals. The evaluation committee should consist of the project manager, superintendent, legal, and the contracting manager.

Submitting Bids by E-mail, Facsimile, and Telephone

In some instances the prime contractor will allow subcontractors to submit bids via facsimile or telephone on the bid due date. See Fig. 5.4. Upon receiving these bids, the contracting manager will call the most competitive bidders and discuss the scope of work. See Fig. 5.5. The contracting manager will then compare the subcontractor bids and select the most competitive and qualified subcontractor. This subcontractor selection approach is risky if the prime contractor does not have a relationship with the successful subcontractor. The selection approach also requires detailed documentation. After all of the responsive subcontractor bids are collected, a bid analysis is performed. See Fig. 5.6.

To eliminate bid shopping and bid pedaling, California law requires that in public contracting, prime contractors must name or

Hoosier Pride Construction, Inc.

Subcontract Bid
Telephone Confirmation

Project No. _____
Project Name _____
Project Location _____
Date _____
Page _____ of _____
Prepared By: _____
Report No. _____

Date: _____ Revision: _____ Time: _____

Owner _____
Subcontractor's name _____
Address _____
Telephone no. _____
Contact _____
Title _____
Fax no. _____
Bid reference no. _____

Scope of work _____		Yes	No
_____	All taxes in bid	☐	☐
_____	Freight	☐	☐
_____	Plans & spec	☐	☐
_____	MBE/WBE contractor	☐	☐
_____	Shop drawings	☐	☐

Addenda no's. included in bid _____
Value: $ _____

Exclusions and omissions to bid: _____
_____

Bid value: $ _____
Alternatives: A. _____
$ _____
B. _____

$ _____
Information received by _____ (Date/time) _____
Information from: _____

Note: Subcontractor must confirm bid price in writing within 24 hours.

Comments: _____
_____
_____

FIGURE 5.4 Subcontractor telephone bid confirmation.

"list" subcontractors who will be used on the project and indicate the portion of work that each subcontractor will perform.[1] Prime contractors bidding on The Indiana Department of Transportation projects are required to list all DBE subcontractors by name, work item, price, and quantity and are bound by this commitment if the contract is awarded.

Hoosier Pride Construction, Inc.

Subcontractor
Verbal Quotation Record

Project No. ______________
Project Name ______________
Project Location ______________
Date ______________
Page ________ of ________
Prepared By ______________

Subcontract ☐	Material/equip. ☐	Services ☐	Verbal quotation ☐

If material, FOB point: __________	Via ship	Via air	Via truck	Via rail	Type of work: ________

Subcontractor or vendor:	Telephone no.	Fax no.	Date

Address ______________	Name of person contacted/title

Equipment/Materials or Services Required

Item No.	Description	Quantity	Unit	Unit Price	Amount

Number of days that bid is valid (______ days)	**Total Bid Value**	**$**

Vendor assistance to be furnished by ______________

Date delivery commenced	Date delivery to be completed	Delivery to be made at ________Items per____

Items Missing	**Yes**	**No**	**N/A**	**Exclusions/Exceptions**
Engineering costs				
Bonds				
Sales taxes				
Complete scope of work				
Freight				
Escalation				
Price is firm				

Remarks: ______________

Confirmation being sent by: Fax ☐ Letter ☐	Quotation received by: ______________

Figure 5.5 Subcontractor verbal quotation record.

Contract Types

The choice of contract type is closely related to the magnitude of risk associated with the specific work item. Overall project risks can mean inherent risks for the subcontractor. The subcontractor's risks include increases in materials, labor, and fuel costs. To assess the technical

Hoosier Pride, Inc.		Contract Work Scope _____				Project No. _____ Project Name _____
Subcontractor **Bid Analysis**		Contract Cost Code _____ (Unit Price, Lump Sum, Cost Plus, etc.)				Location _____ Client _____ Date _____ Page _____ of _____

	Subcontractor Bidding Details						
Description	Subcontractor AJ&S	Subcontractor Pioneer, Inc.	Subcontractor Crayton, Inc.	Subcontractor B&B, Inc.	Subcontractor Plina, Inc.	Subcontractor Thompson, Inc	**Budget** **Estimate**
Total all-inclusive price							
1. Adjustments made:							
2. Adjustments made:							
3. Adjustments made :							
Price adjustments made resulting from letters of clarification and faxes							
Price used for comparison/evaluation (lump sum or unit price contracts)							
Selected Bid							
Remarks:							
Signatures of Approval:							

Figure 5.6 Subcontractor bid analysis.

risk, one must analyze the complexity of the specific work item, the accuracy of design specifications, the scope of work, the availability of historical pricing data, and prior work item completion experience. Technical risks are reduced as the work methods, productivity rates, and pricing data become more defined and the specifications and scope of work become more predictable.

Think, for example, of the risk involved in the construction of the Cumberland Gap Tunnel, a pair of 4600-foot-long, two-lane tunnels that were bored through the Cumberland Mountain, one of the principal ranges of the southern Appalachian mountain chain. In the course of the 17-year construction project, the borings revealed underground springs that would result in the leakage of 450 gallons of water per minute. To eliminate the leakage, the tunnels were lined with a thick PVC layer that ensures that they stay dry. The construction of the tunnel, an engineering feat, cost $280 million, almost double the original estimate.[2]

The major construction contract types are discussed in the following sections.

Lump Sum Contracts

The lump sum contract is an agreement to pay a subcontractor a fixed price upon completion, regardless of the costs incurred. Because the subcontractor assumes certain project risks, lump sum contracts are best suited to situations where the scope of work and specifications are well defined and understood by both parties. In a lump sum contract, there is a direct correlation between a subcontractor's work methods and productivity and the actual profits or losses incurred. The subcontractor is motivated to manage and complete the work efficiently. The subcontractor is responsible for proposing a fixed price that anticipates the worst conditions and price increases. Changes in the contract requirements requested or caused by the owner or prime contractor may be used to modify the fixed price.

Lump sum contracts are used in all types of construction. When a lump sum contract is employed, it is important that the subcontractor has been prequalified. The bid package is released to the prequalified subcontractors as stated earlier. In the bid package, the subcontractor submits a lump sum bid based on the scope of work outlined in the bid package. In most cases the contract is awarded to the lowest responsive bid. The major disadvantage of lump sum contracts is that sometimes changes requested by the prime contractor may lead to disputes, cost increases, and significant delays.

Unit Price Contracts

In a unit price contract, the owner assumes the risk of predetermining the amount and type of work to be done. Unit pricing is very common in the heavy highway market and is well suited for items like excavation. The breakdown of a unit price submitted by a subcontractor includes direct costs, indirect costs, and profit. See Fig. 5.7. This contracting method also works best with prequalification because the prime contractor knows in advance that all bidders have the same capabilities to perform the work. The most competitive subcontractor is usually selected. The estimated quantities are usually plus or minus the final quantities. The subcontractor is paid for the final installed quantities.

Cost-Plus Contracts

By definition, cost-plus contracts are used where the scope of work is uncertain and the costs can easily become out of control. In some cases, such as emergency projects, where cost plus agreements are employed, the owner wants to begin construction even though the plans and specifications are ill defined and incomplete. In this arrangement, the owner pays the prime contractor for costs incurred in construction plus some sort of additional fee.

The written agreement between the prime contractor and subcontractor must specify which costs are reimbursable. Typically reimbursable costs include all field and project costs including, labor, materials, equipment, overhead, insurance, and bond premiums. On the other hand, a contractor's corporate office operations are not usually included in cost-plus agreements. In addition, the agreement should specify what costs should be considered when computing additional fees. Contract modifications and change orders can easily consume the budget. These cost overruns require either a diminution in quality in certain tasks, total elimination of certain aspects of the project, or the need for an additive change order to increase project funding. Cost-plus contracts can be expensive compared to lump sum contracts. The project owner is at a disadvantage with cost-plus contracts. The various hybrids of cost-plus contracts are described in the following sections.

Cost-Plus Fixed Percentage

The contractor is paid actual costs plus a percentage of the total project costs. The contract must clearly state what costs are reimbursable.

Cost-Plus Fixed Fee

The customer agrees to reimburse the contractor's actual costs, regardless of amount, and to pay a negotiated fee that is unrelated to the amount of the actual costs.

Cost-Plus Fixed Fee with Guaranteed Maximum Price Contract and/or Bonus or Sharing Any Cost Savings

There are several variations of the cost-plus fixed fee agreement. A *cost-plus fixed fee with guaranteed maximum price* is used when the contractor is paid for the total project cost plus a negotiated fee, but the

06-092 Unit Price Construction Contract Misc. Pavement Const. Reconst. Services, March 22, 2006

COMPANY NAME:		Walton Construct	Cather & Son's Const.	Dickey & Burham, Inc	Schmieding Concrete Pavers, Inc
REPRESENTATIVE:		Claude L. Walton	Thomas Petsch	Steven N. Burham	Robert Schmieding / Michael McCullough
ADDRESS:		5100 N. 48th St.	PO Box 29199	PO Box 22555	4101 N. 40th / 12303 Hwy. 6
CITY,STATE,ZIP:		Lincoln, NE 68504	Lincoln, NE 68529	Lincoln, NE 68542-2555	Lincoln, NE 68504 / Waverly, NE 68462
TELEPHONE NO.:		402-464-5797	402-464-2113	402-421-6000	402-464-7367 / 402-786-5900
FAX NO.:		402-464-8793	402-464-6759	102 121 6021	402-464-2375
E-MAIL ADDRESS:			catherandsons@futuretk.com	steve.burham@dickey-burham-inc.com	rschmieding@neb.rr.com / pavers@paversinc.com
Item Description	U/M	Unit Price	Unit Price	Unit Price	Unit Price
Schedule I - Concrete Work					
1 Type "B" Sawing - Portland Cement Concrete Pavement	L.F.	$5.00		$5.75	$5.00
2 Type "C" Sawing - Portland Cement Concrete Driveways	L.F.	$5.00		$5.50	$5.00
3 Miscellaneous Asphalt and Concrete Removal	C.Y.	$25.00		$1.40	$150.00 / $70.00
4 Concrete Sidewalk, 4" Thick	S.F.	$3.75		$4.75	$3.00 / $4.00
5 Concrete Bikeway, 5" Thick	S.F.	$4.00		$4.95	$3.25 / $5.00
6 Concrete Driveway, 6" Thick	S.F.	$4.75		$5.25	$3.50 / $5.75
7 Concrete Driveway, 8" Thick	S.F.	$5.00		$6.30	$4.00 / $7.00
8 Remove & Replace Concrete Sidewalk, 4" Thick, Complete	S.F.	$4.00		$6.60	$4.75 / $6.00
9 Remove & Replace Concrete Bikeway, 5" Thick, Complete	S.F.	$4.50		$6.95	$5.00 / $6.60
10 Remove & Replace Concrete Driveway, 6" Thick, Complete	S.F.	$5.00		$7.70	$5.25 / $6.75
11 Remove & Replace Concrete Driveway, 8" Thick, Complete	S.F.	$6.00		$8.00	$5.75 / $8.00
Schedule II - Asphaltic Concrete Work					
1. Type "A" Sawing - Asphaltic Concrete Pavement	L.F.	$5.00	$4.50		$5.00
2. Type "D" Sawing - Asphaltic Concrete Surface Course	L.F.	$5.00	$3.50		$5.00
3. Miscellaneous Asphalt and Concrete Removal	C.Y.	$30.00	$9.00		$70.00
4. Non-woven Pavement Overlay Fabric, In Place	S.Y.	$30.00	$2.25		$2.50
5. Asphaltic Concrete Curb	L.F.	$14.00	$9.00		$6.50
6. Remove & Replace Asphaltic Concrete Curb, Complete	L.F.	$20.00	$12.00		$9.00
7. Concrete Curb	L.F.	$15.00	$15.00		$30.00 / $20.00
8. Remove & Replace Concrete Curb, Complete	L.F.	$18.00	$20.00		$35.00 / $22.00
9. Asphaltic Concrete Pavement Class 2, Non-Arterial	S.Y.	$18.00	$14.40		$25.00
10 Asphaltic Concrete Resurfacing	Ton	$60.00	$68.00		$50.00
11 Paint Pavement Marking, white or yellow traffic paint, not					
11.a. With Glass Beads	L.F.				$3.00
11.b. Without Glass Beads	L.F.				$2.00
Schedule III - Mobilization Cost (per site)		$2,000.00		$350.00	$780.00

FIGURE 5.7 Unit prices for miscellaneous pavement construction.

total does not exceed an agreed-upon upper limit. A bonus can be added to this compensation if the project finishes below budget, ahead of schedule, and so forth. This contract arrangement would be a *cost-plus fixed fee with guaranteed maximum price and bonus contract*. If the project comes in under budget, the contractor might also share in any cost savings in contract known as *cost-plus fixed fee with agreement for sharing any cost savings contract*.

Design-Build Contracts

Design-build is a turn-key project delivery system. The project owner says I need a new office building on January 10, 2011. In a traditional design-bid-build arrangement, the owner first contracts with a design professional to prepare construction plans and specifications, which are later used to solicit competitive bids for construction. In design-build, a single entity is selected to do both the design and construction of the building. While price may be a factor in the selection of the design-builder, other factors are also evaluated. The design and construction may proceed simultaneously. The advantages of design-build are cost savings for the project owner since typically no change orders are allowed and potentially early completion of the project. The downside of design-build is that the owner gives up control. Because design-build is fast track and turn-key, the owner must also be certain of the project requirements before the project begins.

Negotiated Contracts

In rare instances the prime contractor may forego a formal assessment process in lieu of selecting a subcontractor. This decision is usually based on a schedule constraint. Negotiated contracts are priced as lump sum or cost-plus based on the complexity of the work items. When the work items are straightforward, a *lump sum* contract is negotiated. However, if there is uncertainty associated with the work item, a *cost-plus* contract is negotiated.

Contract Negotiations

Bargaining and negotiation are important components of the contractor subcontractor relationship. In the process of constructing a building or bridge, negotiations must take place between all of the supply chain partners to arrive at a mutually satisfactory agreement for performing the work items. Whenever the terms of construction contract agreements are determined or project modifications are settled, bargaining is likely. In a sense, each supply chain member becomes a bargainer at one time or another. Bargaining takes place when two or more parties have divergent interests or goals and communication between the parties is possible. Three additional conditions also must exist in order for bargaining to occur. (1) Mutual compromise must be possible. If one of the parties must choose between total victory and complete loss, no bargaining occurs. Bargaining situations require intermediate solutions for the parties involved. (2) There must be a possibility for provisional offers made by those involved in the situation. (3) The provisional offers must not determine the outcome of the situation until the terms are accepted by all parties. A bargaining situation can be defined as an interaction where parties with certain disagreements confer and exchange ideas about a possible solution until a compromise is reached or the bargaining is terminated. This definition of bargaining is referred to as *explicit bargaining*. In the construction industry, distributive bargaining occurs between two parties who possess resources that the other one desires.

While bargaining sometimes occurs in what has been referred to as multiopponent bargaining situations—where the prime contractor shops several subcontractors when purchasing subcontracting services or where a contractor negotiates bulk material purchases with several alternative suppliers—this approach cannot be productive in a supply chain environment. Instead, the emphasis should be on bargaining in a *bilateral monopoly* system. This does not rule out the influence of other constituencies on the two bargainers, but it does limit the bargaining to just two parties. The total gains from the situation must be "distributed" between the two parties involved and each party usually wants as much as it can get. However, if either party is too greedy, an agreement will not be reached. In dealing with distributive bargaining, the influence of both parties must be considered. Discussion, understanding, and agreements are vital to distributive bargaining. By the very nature of the prime subcontractor relationship, cooperation is important. Without some degree of cooperation, either party can block trading and reduce individual gain to zero.

In a varying-sum schedule bargaining situation, the profits (and/or losses) of the respective bargainers, when added together, need not always equal the same fixed amount, thus the term *varying sum*. While the payoff schedules are usually inversely related—if one gains, the other must lose—there can be some situations where both parties realize a gain (or loss) not in direct proportion to what happens to the other bargainer. In the zero-sum bargaining situation, the profits (and/or losses) of the respective bargainers always sum to the same fixed amount. The term *zero-sum* means that what one bargainer gains, the other loses, and the gains (and/or losses) net out to be zero.

Both of these bargaining situations exist in the construction industry. The varying-sum schedule is often found in customer service situations where the bulk material supplier is at or above the 90 percent service level. To go from the 90 percent to the 95 percent level, an improvement of only 5 percent for the prime contractor can mean a doubling of the costs to the supplier to attain that increased level. The zero-sum schedule is usually found in situations where the subcontractor's cost structure is relatively fixed. The less the prime contractor agrees to, the less profit there is for the subcontractor almost on a dollar-for-dollar basis. A successful construction supply chain relationship requires that both the prime contractor and subcontractor make concessions. To simplify matters, the following bargaining conditions are assumed to exist:

1. Each subcontract negotiation is an independent event.
2. The bargainers are honorable people.
3. The decisions are binding.
4. No arbitration or third party is available to assist bargainers.
5. Any party can break off the negotiation and continue as before.
6. The setting and language are not important.

Subcontractors and prime contractors tend to have conflicting bargaining goals. The aim of the prime contractor is to influence the subcontractor's actions to its advantage. This goal is effectively communicated and reinforced by the prime contractor's cost structure. Subcontractors often agree to conditions and terms that do not consider their company's total cost structure. Logic dictates a similar objective for power imbalances between the prime contractor and the subcontractor.

Awarding Major Subcontractors

In major high-value subcontracts a pre-award meeting between the prime and the subcontractor is important to ensure that the scope of work, technical requirements, and scheduling requirements are fully understood. See Fig. 5.8. The subcontractor's managerial capabilities and financial health should also be reviewed and confirmed. After the pre-award assessment process is complete, the contracting manager recommends the subcontractor to the project manager. The complete subcontractor data file is submitted by the contracting manager to the project manager. The contracting manager should then brief the project manager on the subcontractor's technical, managerial, quality, and field support capabilities. The final step in the award process is to issue a letter of intent to inform the successful bidder that he or she has been awarded the contract. See Fig. 5.9. The purpose of the letter of intent is to signal to the subcontractor to plan for the forthcoming mobilization. A notice is also sent to the unsuccessful bidders. See Fig. 5.10.

Subcontractor and Supplier Quality Assurance and Quality Control Expectations

The materials suppliers and subcontractor quality assurance (QA) systems must be consistent with the project quality requirements and

---

Hoosier Pride Construction, Inc

To: _____

_____

_____

Subject: _____

_____

Project No. _____
Project Name _____
Contract No. _____
Purchase Order No. _____
Project Location _____
Page 1 of _____

Dear Sir or Madam:

In accordance with the terms and conditions of the above referenced subcontract, please forward the following:

☐ Submittals and current insurance certificate_____

_____

☐ Bonding certificate: _____

_____

☐ As-built drawings: _____

_____

☐ Other: _____

_____

This information is required no later than _____.

If you have any questions or comments, please contact us at your earliest convenience

Sincerely,_____

Distribution: _____	Action: _____
_____	

FIGURE 5.8 Letter requesting information.

specifications. Thus, the stated targets and expectations of the project must meet the level of performance specified by the architect or engineer. In cases where the quality target expectations are not achieved, the construction supply chain must be programmed to rapidly respond in order to return to the specified quality targets. Construction QA is the verification that the suppliers and subcontractors have conformed to the plans and specifications. The construction quality control (QC) is concerned with the monitoring and inspection process associated with

Purchasing Subcontracting Services

Hoosier Pride Construction, Inc.

To: _____
_____
_____
Subject: _____
_____
_____

Project No. _____
Project Name _____
Contract No. _____
Purchase Order No. _____
Project Location _____
Page 1 of _____

Dear Sir or Madam:

Your company _____ was the successful bidder on bid packet #___. (A brief description of the project should be given here.)

This letter of intent is contingent upon Hoosier Pride and _____ agreeing to the forthcoming subcontract.

The subcontract is being prepared and will be forwarded to you on or before _____. The subcontract will include any modifications and agreed adjustments that were made during our post-bid meetings or discussions. Prior to your commencement of the contract/subcontract, we will require satisfactory proof of insurance, together with the following:
_____
_____

When you receive our contract/subcontract, please sign and return to this office:
Attention _____.

If you have any comments or questions, please contact us as soon as possible.
Sincerely,

_____

| Distribution: _____ | Action: _____ |

FIGURE 5.9 Letter to successful bidder.

---

the installation of materials and work methods. The materials and work methods must be in compliance with the architect/engineer's plans.

In the heavy highway market, the QC function is efficient because the project owner/agency has a well-trained engineering staff in-house. The resident engineer and a team of inspectors in the agency's district offices regularly inspect the work performed by the contractor's workforce. This open system of communication at the field level is a valuable attribute of the horizontal supply chain. See Fig. 5.11.

Hoosier Pride Construction, Inc.

To: _____ Project No. _____
_____ Project Name _____
_____ Contract No. _____
_____ Purchase Order No. _____
                                 Project Location _____
Subject: _____ Page 1 of _____
_____
_____

Dear Sir or Madam:

The subcontract for the contract number referenced above has been awarded to _____. We would like to take this opportunity to thank you for your bid. We look forward to working with you on future projects.

Sincerely,

_____

Distribution: _____ Action: _____

FIGURE 5.10 Letter to unsuccessful bidder.

Strategic Construction QA and QC

Material quality and work methods are the most critical components in a construction project and require extensive quality assurance requirements. In addition, quality assurance strategy generally involves one or more of the following criteria:

- Supplier and subcontractor participation in the construction supply chain strategy
- A high level of systems integration for complex projects
- Planning for delays and change orders

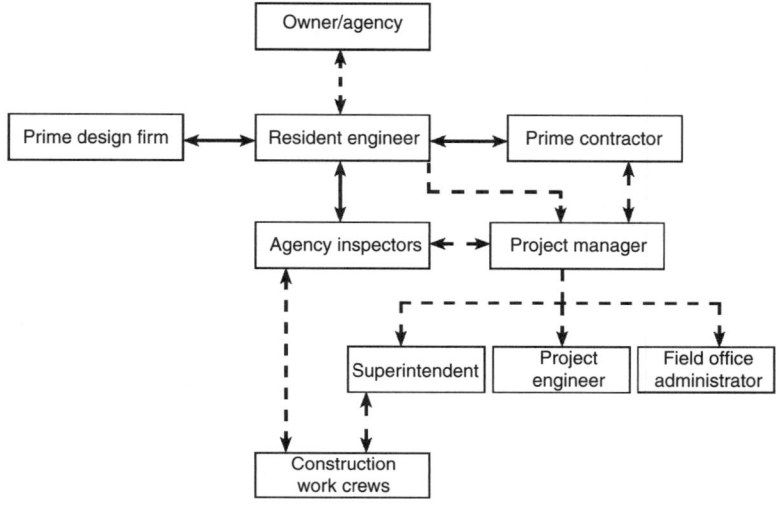

FIGURE 5.11 Quality control organization and information flow for heavy highway supply chain.

- Long lead time for fabricated items
- Planning and coordinating materials testing requirements
- Careful monitoring of the critical path

The approval of the shop drawings, materials, and work methods form the basic foundation for effective construction QA/QC programs. This system of approvals must be strategically planned and systematically executed. See Fig. 5.12.

Change Orders

It is not uncommon for construction contracts to require modifications in design and engineering specifications. The construction manager must communicate these changes in writing to all suppliers and subcontractors in the form of a change order. See Fig. 5.13. Changes in contracts are significant on complex projects. The majority of construction change orders causes are as follows:

1. Design errors (e.g., inconsistencies and discrepancies)
2. Technology changes (e.g., improved materials and discontinued materials)
3. Scope of work changes by the project owners
4. Differing site conditions

100 Chapter Five

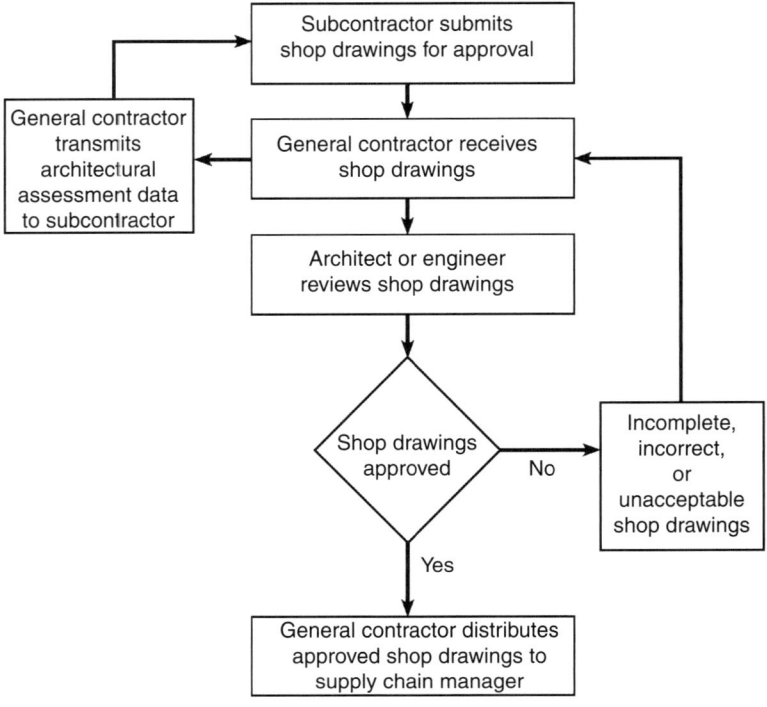

FIGURE 5.12 Shop drawing approval cycle.

5. Improved work methods
6. Discrepancy in the contract documents that is counter to the intended design
7. Changes in the local building codes
8. Final conditions with equipment installation and project utilization

Change orders may be raised by any member of the construction supply chain although only the project owner can authorize a change order.

Conclusion

Planning the use of subcontractor services can account for improved supply chain performance, thereby substantially increasing the probability of a successful project. Prime contractors should not wait until they receive bid proposals to evaluate subcontracting expertise. The dollar magnitude of subcontracting is motivation for the supply chain management-oriented construction organization to ensure that the

Hoosier Pride Construction, Inc.

Change Order

Project No. ____________
Project Name ____________
Prepared by ____________
Contract Number ____________
Change Order No. ____________
Page ________ of ________
Date of issue ____________

Issued To: ____________

The above referenced contract is hereby amended to provide for the following described change(s) upon the terms set forth below. Subcontractor shall provide (scope of work)

Cost Code Number	Description of Work	Add/Deduct	Value

Comments		
	Original contract price:	$ ________
	C.O. #1 thru C.O. _____ (increased) (decreased) (no change)	$ ________
	This change order: (increases) (decreases) (unchanged)	$ ________
	New Total Contract Price is:	$ ________
	Contract duration will be (increased) (decreased) (unchanged) ( ) Delete where necessary	________ days

Subcontractor: ____________	Hoosier Pride: ____________
By: ____________	By: ____________
Signature: ____________	Signature: ____________
Title: ____________	Title: ____________
Date: ____________	Date: ____________

FIGURE 5.13 Change order.

appropriate subcontractor is selected. The subcontractor selection process involves the many important factors including the evaluation of a subcontractor's capacity and performing a SWOT (strengths, weaknesses, opportunities, and threats) analysis. An equitable bid submission and evaluation process, along with mutually satisfactory negotiations set the tone for sound relationships with subcontractors once the project begins.

References

1. Subletting and Subcontracting Fair Practices Act (California Public Contract Code 4100 et seq.).
2. Longfellow, R., "Back in Time," The Federal Highway Administration, Infrastructure Library, Highway History. Accessed at http://fhwa.dot.gov/infrastructure/backintime.htm. Last accessed date is July 1, 2009.

CHAPTER 6

Construction Equipment Planning, Purchasing, and Leasing

> Profitable Innovations

The acquisition of capital equipment is a major decision in most construction firms from an organizational standpoint and in terms of the impact on the firm's financial health. Equipment investments can require substantial expenditures and are made with the expectation that the returns will be extended over several years or multiple projects. The tax planning process is also an important factor in the equipment acquisition decision. The timing of both the expected returns and the tax effects are critical and can contribute favorably to the bottom line of a successful construction company. Depending on the size of the organization, most high-value capital equipment purchases are processed at the superintendent level and above. However, the purchasing/supply manager still serves a critical role in the equipment acquisition process. In most large construction organizations, there is typically an equipment buyer with expertise in the construction industry. Most equipment costs are pegged to the construction industry norms. Sometimes it is more cost-effective to purchase equipment at auctions rather than from traditional sources. The purchasing department should be familiar with these sources and continuously look for effective equipment purchasing opportunities because equipment investment decisions are not easily reversible once they are made.

Chapter Six

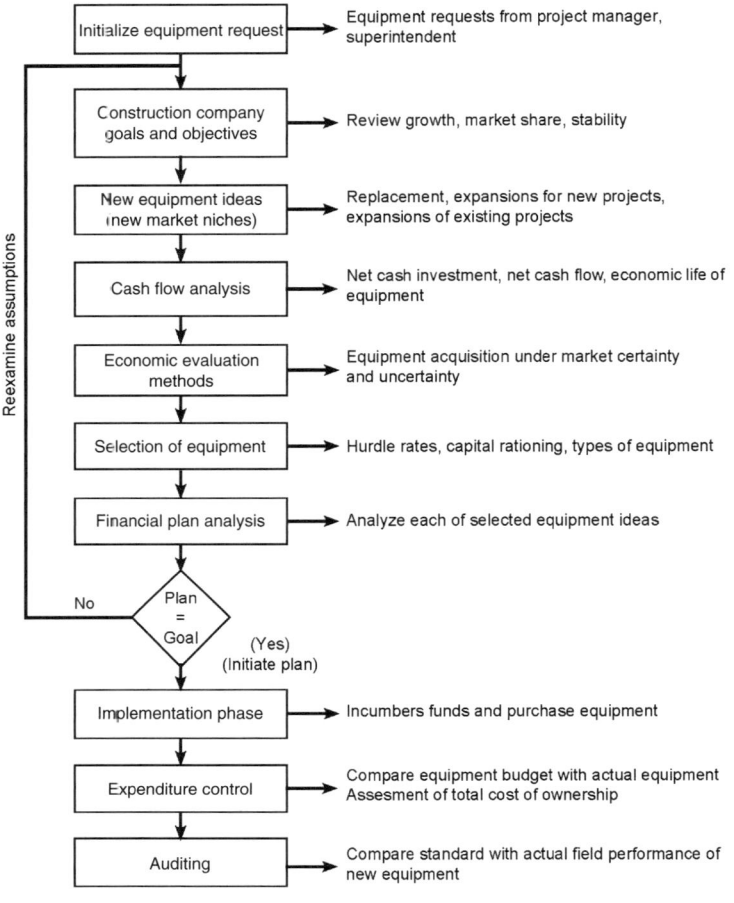

FIGURE 6.1 The construction equipment acquisition process.

The acquisition process can be shown with a construction capital equipment acquisition flow diagram. See Fig. 6.1. Depending on the equipment category and the economic environment, the process may be slightly modified. Short-term equipment investment decisions depend on the estimated work quantities on specific projects. An effective "rule of thumb" for the short-term equipment investment decision is that if the equipment will be utilized at least 1500 hours per year and it pays for itself, it should be purchased. Otherwise a lease or rental option may be more appropriate. On the other hand, long-term equipment investment decisions are sometimes driven by the tax effect of acquiring equipment now rather than later. There are numerous steps in the construction equipment acquisition process. Each cross-functional step is a subsystem of the entire process, which is closely related to a variety of other subsystems in the process.

Requisition

The capital acquisition process is initiated with a company officer or owner requesting equipment replacements in order to expand into new market niches. This step requires the authorization of the company owner, the superintendent, the project manager, or the executive in charge of a specific project. The requisition process is sometimes initiated by a "specific project," or a low-cost financial projection. Without special approval, a monetary limit is usually placed on equipment acquisitions. As an example, some of the larger construction organizations place a limit of $25,000 for general "job specific" acquisitions. Capital purchases in excess of $25,000 require the owner's or superintendent's approval. Typical corporate policies might allow a project manager to purchase miscellaneous equipment (i.e., compressors, generators, trench pumps, fire pumps, etc.) in the regular course of business, whereas a request for a backhoe or rubber-tired vehicle might have to first be recommended by the owner or superintendent. The process must have built-in control mechanisms.

For example, an equipment purchasing requirements plan for a water line project includes details for the purchase of an excavator and two dump trucks. The information in the equipment purchasing requirements plan will be used as input to the equipment pricing component of the final bid package. See Chap. 2, Table 2.4, and Fig. 6.2. The hourly rate for the excavator in this example and the decision to rent the loader and compactor are all based on information obtained from the requirements plan. See Fig. 6.3.

Company Goals and Objectives

The next step in the process is to compare the acquisition request with the overall long-term objectives of the construction organization. These objectives will be the basis for evaluating proposals for making alternative equipment selections. The strategic plan and market analysis of the construction organization are important input data simply because any major equipment purchase will probably affect the segmented work category, the effective company capacity, the capabilities, and the company competitive priorities for many years in the future. Company goals may be slightly different across the construction industry, but all *competitive* construction organizations must eventually maximize profitability and minimize avoidable risk.

New Market Niche Ideas

The capital acquisition process for construction projects must follow a well-designed process of specification, construction bidding, contractor selection, and the actual construction phase. This process is

	225 CAT excavator	Dump truck1	Dump truck2	Bob CAT loader	Demonstrator	Compactor
Cost	$165,000	$93,000	$55,800	Rent $1800/month	$19,000	Rent $350/month
Financement						Rent $125/week
Cash	7.0%	7.0%	7.0%			
Borrow	$149,000					
Period	60 months	60 months	60 months			
Interest rate	8.5%	9.0%	9.0%		8.5%	
Fuel cost	$4.15/gallon	$4.15/gallon	$4.15/gallon		$4.15/gallon	
Repairs	$18,560	$2,500	$5,000		10% of new cost	
Insurance	$4,250	$8,250	$8,250		$500	
Service cost	$40	$2,400	$2,400			
Horsepower	150			74	74	
Haul capacity		8 CY	8 CY			
New tires		$275 each	$275 each		$200 each	
Tire repair		$100/call	$100/call		$100/call	
Useful life of truck tires		50,000 miles	50,000 miles			

FIGURE 6.2 Water line equipment requirements plan.

Crane & B/H machine 225 D CAT excavator	
Rubber tired vehicle machine - unit cost	$165,000
1- Depreciation 5 years	33,000.00
2- Interest, taxes, insurance	
Interest borrowed	6,332.50
Cost of $ invested	1,120.00
Insurance	4,250.00
P.P. Taxes	2,875.00
2875/year	
3- General repairs	18,560.00
4- Tire replacement	
5- Tire repair	
6- Fuel costs coeff = .042 1500 hours	10,867.50
7- Service cost 21 days/month 8 months	6,720.00
8- Cutting edges	
9- Fuel man	
Estimated use 1500 hours/year	**Total cost 83,725.00** 55.82/hour

FIGURE 6.3 Hourly excavator rate.

guided by well-defined planning and scheduling methods. In large organizations, the equipment acquisition team includes personnel from engineering, finance, management, and purchasing. The equipment acquisition team approach is an excellent example of a cross-functional purchasing supply chain strategy. In any progressive construction firm, the marketing plan provides a continuous stream of attractive capital equipment opportunities. The company owner/superintendent must spend many hours brainstorming, analyzing, and carefully planning for their firm's projected equipment needs. The classification of the various capital equipment requests must be based on certain common characteristics. Equipment acquisitions are frequently grouped according to the following categories:

- Replacement equipment
- Expansion (new market niches)
- Expansion (existing market niches)
- Others

The *replacement* of old equipment is often motivated by a need to increase quality, reduce operating expense, and provide more efficiency. Construction organizations can easily conduct in-depth cost savings and efficiency studies. Construction organizations on a growth pattern fueled by technology acquire new equipment to expand into *newly introduced market segments.* Technology-driven equipment acquisitions can become a formidable competitive weapon. Investment in construction equipment for expansion purposes should increase incremental revenue. Sometimes construction organizations are interested in expanding the output of *existing* market niches, which is usually an alternative to replacing the current equipment. Expanding existing equipment is also a way to increase capacity.

Cash-Flow Analysis

If a long-term equipment request survives the new market niche ideas step, cash flow estimates must be considered for each equipment investment idea. The after-tax cash inflows and outflows of each equipment acquisition alternative must be evaluated on an incremental cash-flow basis. Three criteria should apply to the cash-flow analysis:

- The net cash investment
- The net cash flow
- The economic life of the project

In other words, the construction organization must consider net cash outlays and the total implementation costs. Net cash flows are net economic benefits generated from the equipment purchase. The net incremental cash flows from the purchased equipment should be measured. The economic life of the equipment investment versus the physical life of the purchased equipment investment must also be considered.

Life cycle costing is an evaluation method used to assess alternative equipment purchasing proposals. Life cycle costing is based on the total cost of ownership (TCO) over the expected life of the purchased equipment. The total cost components are given as follows:

- Research
- Development
- Productivity
- Operation
- Maintenance

There are numerous testimonials regarding the use of life cycle costing for both capital equipment and systems acquisition. Consider a construction organization that currently spends an average of $1,500 per month to maintain a 1996 Caterpillar Motor Grader. Recently the company purchased a 2004 Caterpillar Motor Grader at an auction for $100,000 based on the life cycle costing concept. The average monthly maintenance cost for the 2006 Motor Grader is $220 for the remaining life of the 2006 Caterpillar Motor Grader. The efficiency and cost of operating also will have a significant effect on the construction equipment acquisition. Productivity, dependability, and durability are the principal operating variables that must be investigated.

Economic Evaluation

The five most commonly used methods for an economic evaluation of individual projects are *payback, average rate of return, net present value, internal rate of return,* and *profitability index*. These methods can be used to measure the financial performance of individual equipment purchases. Prior to applying a particular method, the construction organization must set a predetermined required rate of return based on its business plan. To illustrate the concept of economic evaluation, consider the Motor Grader example.

Example: Motor Grader

Suppose Hoosier Pride Construction, Inc., is considering purchasing the used Motor Grader mentioned herein. Assume the complete stream of *estimated after-tax cash flows (EATCF)* is

Year	0	1	2	3	4
EATCF($)	−100,000	40,000	40,000	30,000	30,000

These data will be used to illustrate the five economic evaluation criteria.

Payback

Payback is the best known investment criterion. Payback is the number of years it takes to repay the initial investment. Using the Motor Grader example and given that the cash flows are constant and positive

$$\text{Payback} = 40,000 \text{ (year 1)} + 40,000 \text{ (year 2)} \\ + 20,000 \text{ (.67\% of year 3)} = 2.67 \text{ years}$$

Suppose that Hoosier Pride predetermines that the maximum payback period is 3 years. In this case, the Motor Grader is a candidate for acceptance. On the other hand, if the standard payback period were set at 2 years, then, the Motor Grader would be rejected.

Average Rate of Return

The average rate of return (ARR) is the average cash flow after tax divided by the initial investment:

$$\text{ARR} = (\Sigma \text{EATCF}/\text{economic life})/\text{initial investment}$$

$$\text{ARR} = [(40,000 + 40,000 + 30,000 + 30,000)/4]/100,000$$

$$= 35\%$$

If ARR > the required ARR, accept the Motor Grader.

If ARR < the required ARR, reject the Motor Grader.

This method ignores the timing of the cash flows: What if most of the cash flows ($140,000) in the example problem were all lumped into 1 year? The ARR would still be 35 percent. Even so, the ARR is the most popular evaluation criterion used today.

Net Present Value

The net present value (NPV) recognizes that a dollar today is worth more than a dollar tomorrow because the dollar today can be invested and begin earning interest immediately. This NPV is calculated by taking the present value of all expected cash inflows from the project minus the initial investment. If the NPV is greater than zero, then the investment should be made. But if NPV is less than zero, then the investment should not be made. This evaluation method is applied to the example of the purchase of a Motor Grader.

$$\text{NPV} = \sum_{t=0}^{m} \frac{\text{EATCF}}{(1+k)^t}$$

where k = Motor Grader's required rate of return and m = Number of periods

$$\text{NPV} = \sum \left(100,000 + \frac{40,000}{1+k} + \frac{40,000}{(1+k)^2} + \frac{30,000}{(1+k)^3} + \frac{30,000}{(1+k)^4} \right)$$

Year	0	1	2	3	4
EATCF ($)	<100,000	40,000	40,000	30,000	30,000
Discount factor ($)	1,000	0.909	0.826	0.751	0.683
Present value ($)	−100,000	36,300	33,040	22,530	20,490

NPV = −100,000 + 36,360 + 33,040 + 22,530 + 20,490 = 12,420

The investment decision is

If NPV > 0, accept the Motor Grader

If NPV < 0, reject the Motor Grader

Notice the difference between the ARR and NPV methods is the timing of the various EATCF cash flows. In other words, as the EATCF increases, the project becomes more attractive.

Internal Rate of Return

Using the internal rate of return (IRR) method, a project is considered a good investment if the opportunity cost of capital is less than the internal rate of return. If the cost of capital is equal to the IRR, the project has zero NPV. On the other hand, if the cost of capital is greater than the IRR, the project has a negative NPV. The IRR will give the same answer as the NPV. The IRR is defined as the discount rate that will make the NPV of the project equal to zero.

$$\sum_{t=0}^{m} \frac{EATCF}{(1+IRR)^t} = 0$$

For example

$$\sum (100,000) + \frac{40,000}{(1+IRR)^1} + \frac{40,000}{(1+IRR)^2} + \frac{30,000}{(1+IRR)^3} + \frac{30,000}{(1+IRR)^4} = 0$$

For a discount rate of 20 percent the NPV= −$7060. Using a trial and error approach, the IRR can be determined. If the EATCF was $40,000 for each of the 4 years, the IRR would be approximately 22 percent. Since the EATCF for the last 2 years is $30,000 per year, the discount rate should be decreased. We calculated a negative NPV of −$7060 at a 20 percent discount rate; thus, we must lower the discount rate to let us say, 16 percent. At a 16 percent discount rate, the NPV = $138.90. Thus, the IRR is approximately 16 percent.

If IRR > k, accept the Motor Grader.

If IRR < k, reject the Motor Grader.

where k = Required rate of return and m = Number of periods

If it is assumed that the cost of capital is 10 percent, the project will be accepted.

Profitability Index

The profitability index (PI) is defined as the present value of future flows divided by the initial investment:

$$PI = \left[\sum_{t=1}^{m} \frac{EATCF_t}{(1+k)^t}\right] / \text{Initial investment}$$

Since the future cash flows are typically positive,

$$PI = \left[\frac{40{,}000}{1.10} + \frac{40{,}000}{(1.10)^2} + \frac{30{,}000}{(1.10)^3} + \frac{30{,}000}{(1.10)^4}\right] / 100{,}000$$

$$PI = (36{,}360 + 33{,}040 + 22{,}530 + 20{,}490)/100{,}000$$

$$PI = 110{,}243/100{,}000 = 1.12$$

The decision rule is

If PI > 1, accept the Motor Grader (*ceteris Paribas*).

If PI < 1, reject the Motor Grader (*ceteris Paribas*).

Like the NPV and IRR methods, the PI method accounts for timing.

Selection

The final selection is an accept—reject decision based on these evaluations. See Table 6.1. The hurdle rate may be based on the cost of capital, the opportunity cost, and other conceptual standards. In any case, each proposal must compete for limited funds.

Financial Plan Analysis

At this stage, a comprehensive comparison of the selected alternatives is performed. The planned equipment selections are then measured against Hoosier Pride's initial goals and objectives. Equipment acquisitions can be financed in a variety of ways. For the purpose of the purchasing professional, two methods will be considered: traditional loans and leases. The leasing method has become very popular in the last 20 years and can be used to finance almost any kind of fixed asset. The lease-versus-purchase decision requires many considerations, some of which are listed as follows:

Method	Good Features	Bad Features
Payback	Easily understood Easy to calculate Provides a crude risk screen	Doesn't account for the time value of money of pre-payback cash flows Completely ignores post-payback cash flows
ARR	Easily understood Easy to calculate Considers past-payback cash flows	Doesn't account for the time value of money of any of the cash flows
NPV	Relatively easy to calculate Best method for mutually exclusive ranking problems Tied for best method for accept—reject decision problems (with PI)	Hard to understand May not work well in capital rationing problems
IRR	Easily understood Has intuitive economic meaning Works okay on *simple* accept—reject problems, which are most common investment problems	Can be tedious to calculate May not work well on complex accept—reject problems (multiple rates), mutually exclusive choices, or capital rationing problems
PI	Relatively easy to calculate Best method for one-period capital rationing problems Tied for best method for accept—reject decision problems (with NPV)	Hard to understand May not work well in some mutually exclusive choice situations

TABLE 6.1   Evaluation Methods for the Acquisition Decision

- *Tax effect*: Lease payments are expenses that can be written off against income immediately. Loans are depreciated over a longer period of time. One major advantage of leases over loans is the impact leases have on land use. When a firm leases land for its operations, it can deduct the lease expense from the income burden. Purchased land, on the other hand, cannot be deducted from tax obligations.
- *Effects on future financing*: Leasing versus purchasing can also free up cash needed for other purposes or alternative projects. There is a positive balance sheet effect of leasing simply because operating leases are not recorded either as debt or as an asset. Operating leases (discussed later in this chapter) are

considered "off balance" sheet transactions where lease payments are simply reported as an expense. A leasing arrangement can actually increase a firm's borrowing capacity. Most loans require the borrower to place a reasonable down payment. Leases generally do not require an initial down payment beyond the first and last monthly payment.

- *Risk of obsolescence*: In the case of fast-moving technology, it is possible for the lessee to shift the risk level to the lessor. Computer technology is a good example of the risk of obsolescence.

- *Salvage value*: The lessor is responsible for the salvage value of the leased assets. If the expected salvage value is high for leased equipment, the cost of ownership to the lessee may be lower. In this case, the lessee should write a contract that will enable it to buy the fixed asset at the end of the lease term.

- *Maintenance*: In most lease agreements the responsibilities and risks for each party are spelled out in detail. If the lessor assumes the costs of maintenance, insurance, and taxes, it will usually pass the expense to the lessee in the form of increased lease payments.

- *Discount rate*: The after-tax borrowing rate is commonly known as the discount rate. Both leasing and buying involve cash outflows over an extended period. Since the lease payment is fixed and other costs associated with the lease (salvage value, operating expenses, and interest rates) are uncertain, it is important to evaluate the implicit interest rate for a lease-versus-buy decision.

Lease versus Borrow and Purchase

When does it make more sense to buy equipment? When does it make more sense to lease? The lease-versus-buy decision can be made quickly for some companies. In fact, in the construction industry, the rent/lease-or-own decision is routine when acquiring new or used equipment. Equipment leasing is a popular option for construction firms that need new equipment. The buying and leasing of equipment is a profitable business. There is a tax advantage for the leasing company if it has a high tax liability. On the other hand, the lessor can also structure the lease arrangement so that some or all of the tax savings are passed on to the lessee in the form of lower lease payments. There are three types of leases:

Sale and Leaseback   The seller-lessee sells the property to the buyer-lessor who in turn leases it back to the seller-lessee. The effect of the transaction is that the buyer has title, receives rent from the seller and earns a specified rate of return. The seller-lessee has use of the property and also an immediate cash infusion from the original sale. The buyer-lessor earns a specified rate of return on the investment.

Operating Lease   The operating lease makes it possible for a company to use assets such as computers, trucks, automobiles, and furniture. In this type of agreement, the lessor maintains and services the equipment. The lessee also can cancel the agreement before the term if not satisfied. The lease term is usually shorter than the life of the capital asset. At the end of the lease term, the lessee returns the property.

Capital Lease   Because of their favorable "off balance sheet" treatment, operating leases are preferred. To keep firms from reporting all leases as operating leases, the Financial Accounting Standards Board has ruled that a lease should be treated as a capital lease if anyone of these four conditions is met:

1. If lease life exceeds 75 percent of the life of the asset
2. If there is a transfer of ownership to the lessee at the end of the lease term
3. If there is an option to purchase the asset at a "bargain price" at the end of the lease term
4. If the discounted present value of the lease payments exceeds 90 percent of the fair market value of the asset.

A capital lease is maintained by the lessee. The lease cannot be canceled because it is fully amortized. The lessee is leasing from a third party lender, typically a bank. In short, the capital lease is somewhat like a purchase.

Lease-versus-Buy Decision

The lease-versus-buy method can be used to compare (1) the purchase price and lease payments, (2) income tax effects, and (3) present values. These steps are shown in the *detailed tutorial* that illustrates the construction equipment lease-versus-buy decision.

Hoosier Pride has two choices: (1) buy a used Motor Grader or (2) lease a used Motor Grader for 3 years. The Motor Grader has a useful life of 5 years and costs $100,000. The Monroe County Bank is willing to loan Hoosier Pride $88,000 at 6 percent interest and requires a down payment of $12,000 and annual payments of $20,891, which are due at the end of each of the next 5 years. Since Hoosier Pride does not have the proper maintenance facilities, the bank will require Hoosier Pride to sign a maintenance contract with ACME Caterpillar. The contract, good for 5 years of maintenance, requires annual payments of $5,000. ACME made Hoosier Pride a proposal that competes with the bank's offer. ACME is willing to lease Hoosier Pride the same Motor Grader for 3 years. Since the Hoosier Pride's cash situation is very tight, ACME structured the lease with the $30,917 payment due at the end of each year. In addition, ACME agreed to:

- Perform all of the maintenance during the lease period.
- Give the contractor the right to purchase the Motor Grader at the end of 3 years for the prevailing market price (estimated to be $35,000).
- Allow the organization to buy a maintenance contract for two years on the Motor Grader for $6,000 annually, paid at the end of years 4 and 5.

Step 1: Comparing Purchase Price and Lease Payments The first step in a lease-versus-buy analysis is listing the purchase price and lease payments. See Table 6.2.

The "Today" row in the example shows that purchased equipment must be paid for upon delivery. This payment may be from cash reserves or from money borrowed from a lending agency, but it must be paid to the bank up front. The first lease payment, at least in this example is shown as 1 year from today. The purchase option must include interest payments, depreciation, and maintenance expense that also must be paid by the contractor. ACME assumes these costs for the first 3 years of the lease option. At the end of year 3, a final payment of $35,000 is made to ACME.

Step 2: Comparing Income Tax Effect One of the most important economic differences between leasing and buying equipment is the way each is treated for income tax purposes. Since the value of these tax benefits varies greatly among individuals and corporations, it is important to calculate potential benefits on an individual basis. The marginal tax rate is the rate of tax that must be paid on each additional dollar of income.

	Buy ($)	Lease ($)
Today	12,000	
1 year from today	20,891	30,917
2 years from today	20,891	30,917
3 years from today	20,891	30,917
4 years from today	20,891	—
5 years from today	20,891	—

TABLE 6.2 Comparison of Lease-versus-Purchasing Payments

Construction Equipment Planning, Purchasing and Leasing

Different tax rates are applied to different levels of income. As income rises, it is taxed at a higher rate. The marginal tax rate determines how much a tax deduction will actually reduce taxes owed. Individuals or corporations with high incomes may have marginal tax rates of 35 percent or more, while those losing money will have tax rates of 0 percent. The higher the marginal tax rate, the more a tax deduction is worth. The value of a tax deduction is determined by multiplying it by the tax rate. Using this rule, a $10,000 tax deduction is worth nothing if the tax rate is 0 percent, $1,500 at 15 percent, and $2,800 at 28 percent.

The situation is relatively simple with leases. Each lease payment is a tax deduction for the company leasing the equipment. Its value can be determined by multiplying the marginal tax rate by the lease payment. If the buy option is chosen, depreciation on a Motor Grader must be taken over a 5-year period. Both straight-line and accelerated methods are possible, and either can have its advantages depending on Hoosier Pride's tax situation. In this example, straight-line depreciation of $20,000 for each of 5 years will be used. Hoosier Pride has a 40 percent tax rate, so the tax savings will be calculated:

$$\text{Tax savings} = 40\% \times (\text{interest payment} + \text{depreciation} + \text{maintenance})$$

If the lease option is chosen, the tax savings will be calculated as follows:

$$\text{Tax savings (years 1–3)} = 40\% \times \text{Lease payment}$$

$$\text{Tax savings (years 4 and 5)} = 40\% \times (\text{lease payment} + \text{depreciation} + \text{maintenance})$$

The table from Step 1 can now be rewritten to include taxes. See Table 6.3.

Step 3: Comparing Present Values   While the after-tax values of leasing compared with purchasing the Motor Grader have been considered,

	Tax Deduction Expense	
	Buying Option ($)	Leasing Option ($)
Today		
1 year from today	30,280	30,917
2 years from today	29,343	30,917
3 years from today	28,350	30,917
4 years from today	27,298	25,500
5 years from today	26,183	23,500

TABLE 6.3   Comparison of the Income Tax Effect

the time at which these costs are incurred has not been taken into account. Ignoring the timing factor can lead to an invalid decision because money has a time value. Time value is evident every time money is invested for a period of time to earn interest or borrowed for a period of time in exchange for interest payments.

The time value of money affects leasing or buying because the farther into the future the cost becomes due, the fewer of today's dollars it will take to repay. How many of today's dollars it will take to pay a cost due in the future depends on the level of interest rates. Interest rates are used to choose present value factors, which are, in turn, used to convert future costs into today's dollars. A future cost, expressed in terms of today's dollars, is called a present value. The interest rate chosen is either that at which money can be borrowed or that at which money can be invested.

In the case of Hoosier Pride, a 6 percent rate is used. The present value factor table is used to find the *present value* factors for today through 5 years from today. Hoosier Pride must now multiply the present value factors (PV = $1/(1+k)^t$) by the *net cash outflows*. See Tables 6.4 and 6.5. Hoosier Pride then uses the same factors to find the present value of the after-tax costs of leasing. A complete Motor Grader analysis is then finalized. See Tables 6.6 and 6.7.

The borrow purchase option is slightly better than the lease option. However, it is easy to see that the two options are not significantly different. The three-step method is an effective tool, but legal and accounting advice must be added to any economic analysis before a decision on leasing is made or capital equipment purchased.

Implementation

During the implementation stage, companies encumber funds for accepted equipment investments. The approval process usually ends

	Net Cash Outflows for Purchase Option ($)		Factor	Present Value ($)
Today	12,000	×	1.0000	= 12,000
1 year from today	13,779	×	0.9434	= 12,999
2 years from today	14,154	×	0.8900	= 12,597
3 years from today	14,551	×	0.8396	= 12,217
4 years from today	14,972	×	0.7921	= 11,859
5 years from today	15,418	×	0.7473	= 11,521
Total present value cost				73,193

TABLE 6.4 Net Outflows of Purchase Option

	Net Cash Flows for Leasing Option ($)		Factor	Present Value ($)
Today	0	×	1.0000	= 0
1 year from today	18,550	×	0.9434	= 17,500
2 years from today	18,550	×	0.8900	= 16,510
3 years from today	18,550	×	0.8396	= 15,575
3E years from today	35,000	×	0.8396	= 29,387
4 years from today	(3,400)	×	0.7921	= (2,693)
5 years from today	(3,400)	×	0.7473	= (2,541)
Total present value cost				73,738

TABLE 6.5 Net Outflows of Lease Option

with the owner making the decision. This stage in the process is basically a rubber stamp. The purchase order procedures are consistent with the approaches outlined in Chap. 2. However there is a need to check the status of affirmed equipment purchases, which is achieved through equipment status and delivery reports. See Figs. 6.4 and 6.5.

Expenditure Control

The time between approval of the capital and completion of the equipment acquisition is the critical scheduling stage. At this stage, the equipment acquisition should stay within budget and corrective action should be taken if the budget is violated.

Audits

The equipment acquisition process is complex and leads to many assumptions and estimates. The entire project should be audited to analyze the differences. The audit stage also will identify mismanagement and flaws in the equipment acquisition process. If the process has been unsatisfactory, it should be revised or replaced.

Disposal of Capital Equipment

The disposal of capital equipment is becoming more complicated. The United States Environmental Protection Agency has developed specific guidelines for disposing various types of obsolete equipment. The purchasing function is usually charged with the task of scrapping or selling retired equipment. In some cases, the business is able to trade in the obsolete equipment for new purchases which transfers the burden of disposal to the equipment supplier. If the equipment is

Year	Payment ($) (1)	Interest ($) (2)	Reduction ($) (3)	Principal ($) (4)	Depreciation ($) (5)	Maintenance ($) (6)	Tax Deductible Expense ($) (7 = 2 + 5 + 6)	Savings ($) (8 = 7 × TR)	Net Cash Outflow ($) (9 = 1 + 6 − 8)	PV Factor (10)	PV of Purchase ($) (11 = 9 × 10)
Beg.	12,000		12,000	100,000 88,000					(12,000)	1	(12,000)
1	20,891	5,280	15,611	72,389	20,000	5,000	30,280	12,112	(13,779)	0.9434	(12,999)
2	20,891	4,343	16,548	55,842	20,000	5,000	29,343	11,737	(14,154)	0.8900	(12,597)
3	20,891	3,350	17,540	38,301	20,000	5,000	28,350	11,340	(14,551)	0.8396	(12,217)
4	20,891	2,298	18,593	19,708	20,000	5,000	27,298	10,919	(14,972)	0.7921	(11,859)
5	20,891	1,183	19,708	0	20,000	5,000	26,183	10,473	(15,418)	0.7473	(11,521)
	116,454	16,454	100,000		100,000	25,000	141,454				(73,193)

Tax rate (TR) = 0.4
Discount rate = 0.06
Interest rate = 0.06
Lease rate = 0.06
Borrow and purchase

TABLE 6.6 Motor Grader Analysis purchase Option

Year	Payment ($)	Depreciation ($)	Maintenance ($)	Tax Deductible Expense ($)	Savings ($)	Net Cash Outflow ($)	PV Factor	PV of Purchase ($)
	(1)	(5)	(6)	(7 = 1 + 5 + 6)	(8 = 7 × TR)	(9 = 1 + 6 − 8)	(10)	(11 = 9 × 10)
1	30,917			30,917	12,367	(18,550)	0.9434	(17,500)
2	30,917			30,917	12,367	(18,550)	0.8900	(16,510)
3	30,917			30,917	12,367	(18,550)	0.8396	(15,575)
3E	35,000					(35,000)	0.8396	(29,387)
4	0	17,500	6,000	23,500	9,400	3,400	0.7921	2,693
5	0	17,500	6,000	23,500	9,400	3,400	0.7473	2,541
	127,751	35,000	12,000	139,751				(73,738)
	4.21236379							
	2.67301195							
	26,417							

Tax rate (TR) = 0.4
Discount rate = 0.06
Interest rate = 0.06
Lease rate = 0.06
Borrow and purchase

TABLE 6.7 Motor Grader Analysis Lease Option

Hoosier Pride Construction, Inc.

Equipment Purchasing Status Report

Project No.__________
Project Name__________
Location__________
Date__________
Page1 of__________
Prepared By__________

Equipment Item No.	Description	Requisition No.	Specifications to Purchasing *Schedule/Actual*		Out For Bid	Bids Due/Rec'd		Bids To Eng.	Technical Evaluation Complete *Schedule/Actual*		Award Date	P.O. No.	Comments

FIGURE 6.4 Equipment purchasing status report.

Hoosier Pride Construction, Inc.

Equipment Delivery Status Report

Project No _____
Project Name _____
Project Location _____
Date _____
Page 1 of _____
Prepared By _____

P.O. No.	Supplier Contact Name	Equipment/ Item	P.O. Date	Supplier Location	Shipment Dates					Comments/Actions Taken
					P.O. Date	Revised Delivery Date?	Current Delivery Date	Actual Date (Now)	Revised (*Expedited*) Date	

Figure 6.5 Equipment delivery status report.

useable, there may be an active dealer that may purchase the used equipment. In general, most firms have not yet designed a clean process for the disposal of used equipment.

Purchasing New versus Used Construction Equipment

Despite today's competitive markets, it may not be cost-effective to purchase new equipment. Depending on the purpose and expected use of the purchased equipment, it may be more cost-effective to buy used equipment. In this section the guidelines for purchasing new versus used equipment are discussed.

New Construction Equipment Purchases

When a company purchases new construction equipment, there is no uncertainty regarding the performance to stated specifications. The buying firm must first determine the number of hours per year that the equipment will be employed. The construction organization must pay close attention to the theoretical usage levels of certain equipment. As an example, the life expectancy of construction equipment is easy to predict given the normal operating conditions. Construction equipment is usually purchased new. In cases where significant demand or uses already exist for a particular piece of equipment, the purchase of new equipment is appropriate. The technological advantages of new equipment also may increase productivity in these situations. In the case of backhoes, dump trucks, and other rubber-tired vehicles, it may be more cost-effective to purchase new equipment. However, if an older model is adequate for the expected use, significant savings could occur. Remember, new equipment requires less maintenance than used construction equipment. This is perhaps the strongest argument for considering only new equipment. For example, after a Motor Grader is used for more than 10,000 hours, a new $30,000 scraper is usually required. The maintenance record must be considered when deciding to buy used equipment.

Specifications must be carefully considered when purchasing major construction equipment. It is a simple task to compare new equipment. It is next to impossible to compare different models of used equipment. Sometimes low equipment prices may lead to purchasing construction equipment that is ready to be scrapped. However, if the used equipment dealer is willing to offer a reasonable warranty and other guarantees, purchasing a specified piece of used equipment may be justified.

Used Construction Equipment Purchases

Low cost is usually the only reason to purchase used equipment. The determination of the true value of used equipment is extremely difficult. A review of the historical maintenance record should be the first step in the acquisition of used equipment. In some cases, used equipment may provide a good short-term solution to a construction organization's production problems. The company must also consider the trade-off between long-term financing costs and short-term maintenance costs. In this case, financial efficiency is more important than maintenance costs. A thorough inspection *must* be performed when buying used equipment. It is a sad reality that some used car dealers are experts when it comes to cleaning and painting severely damaged equipment. Likewise, some used equipment dealers are disreputable and will do whatever it takes to mislead an unsuspecting buyer. The selling terms are usually "as-is" and net cash with no warranty.

Conclusion

The capital equipment acquisition is a specialized function for the purchasing department.

A step-by-step capital acquisition process includes (1) requisition, (2) company objectives, (3) new product ideas, (4) cash-flow analysis, (5) an economic evaluation, (6) a financial plan analysis, and (7) expenditure control. The decision to lease or buy capital equipment requires both analytical analysis and normative judgments. When does it make more sense to invest in construction capital equipment instead of leasing it? Another element of the capital acquisition process is whether to purchase new or used equipment. Equipment investments can serve to replace existing equipment, allow expansion into new markets, and increase market share in existing market niches. But, whatever the reason for the purchase or lease, technology driven equipment acquisitions can be a formidable competitive weapon.

CHAPTER 7
Construction Supply Chain Complexity, Profitability, and Information Sharing

> The Next Generation

The construction supply chain is an operational and strategic cycle that includes labor, materials, equipment, subcontracting, and a finished project. Technology, safety, and communications are the three elements that connect all of the components of the chain. The construction supply chain has even more significance because of the potential for participation in many complex private and public sector construction projects. The concept of the construction supply chain implicitly takes a strategic look at profitability. In the short run, contractors may be able to survive with losses; however, in the long run, *every* construction business *must* show a profit in order to be considered a going concern. Profit or net income is a component of retained earnings on the balance sheet. Retained earnings pay for the future by enabling contractors to buy new equipment and hire, train, and develop more employees. Successful construction organizations must focus on the question: "What is meant by profitability?" Any one of the five approaches listed below or combination of them will increase profits:

- Increase contract revenues through niche marketing.
- Decrease the total cost of construction.
- Decrease overhead.

- Increase other income and decrease expenses.
- Decrease delays in deliveries of materials, equipment, and services to the project site.

Increasing contract revenues alone is not enough to ensure profits. Project owners must be targeted through niche marketing. What category of work should a construction organization consider based on its expertise and skill sets? Is subcontracting an effective approach for marketing construction services? The measurement criteria for a good niche are the profitability and predictability of the project outcome. In other words, if a company can *consistently* deliver a specific type of high-quality project ahead of schedule and under budget, this may be an optimum project for the firm. Once a firm makes a commitment to a particular item of work and type of project owner, finishing ahead of schedule is critical to increasing the revenues. The old adage in the construction industry is "Get in and get out."

One way to *decrease the total cost of construction* is to increase productivity through better work methods and effective supervision. Two conduits of the construction supply chain, *technology and safety*, are also critical to decreasing the cost of construction. By implementing technology in the field and home office operations, firms can reduce the time it takes to perform certain routine administrative tasks. A safe workplace means no fines, fewer workers' compensation claims or other litigation, and a good reputation in the community. Another effective means for increasing profitability is *reducing overhead*. The home office must be the appropriate size so that it supports the firm's operations; some contractors have too many employees working in the home office. Another approach to increasing profitability is to *increase other income and decrease related expenses*. Efficient billing systems that turn receivables quickly improve cash flow and minimize interest payments for borrowed funds.

Construction Supply Chain Management

The final means of increasing profitability is by implementing supply chain management concepts in order to *decrease delays in delivery of materials, equipment, and services to the project site*. As shown in Chap. 2, Fig. 2.1, construction is unlike any other industry. The industry is composed of many fragmented self-protected entrepreneurs with paranoid attitudes. The industry actually promotes an adversarial culture based on competition and very little information sharing. Unlike the manufacturing sector, each project is based on a uniformed distribution for that specific project with little motivation for continuous learning. In contrast, in the manufacturing sector, units of production are based on a continuous exponential distribution. In spite of the fact that construction is a rich industry—approximately $3 trillion was spent in 2007—it has historically been a slow- to no-learning industry. However, the days of slow learning construction firms are coming to an end. More and more firms in the construction industry are adopting the lessons learned from the manufacturing sector. Progressive firms are now implementing six sigma and lean management initiatives to drive efficiencies for their project operations. This transition has generated the construction supply chain management revolution.

Information Sharing

Construction supply chain execution is the process of purchasing materials, leasing or buying equipment and contracting with subcontractors in order to produce a finished project. Construction purchasing, the central focus of supply chain execution, is responsible for project sustainability and efficiency. The supply chain execution is complemented by the supply chain information model which begins with project requirements that are determined by the owner. The project expectations are communicated downstream. The project owner's requirements ignite a series of information, material and money flows, and the quality of these flows determines the level of supply chain integration. Despite the inherent complexities, on a project-by-project basis, some project managers adequately execute the construction processes. However, if the various processes were more integrated and driven by information sharing, there would be fewer disruptions resulting in continuous improvement on succeeding projects.

There are three aspects of information sharing: information sharing support technology, information content, and information quality.[1] Information sharing support technology includes the hardware and software needed to support information sharing. *Information content* refers to the information shared between the various construction supply chain participants. *Information quality* measures the quality of information shared between the construction supply chain participants.

In the past decade, supply chain management and information technology (IT) management have attracted much attention from construction organizations. Construction supply chain practice focuses on material, equipment, and labor movement, while information sharing focuses on information flow. There are two categories of supply chain practice: construction supply chain network design and supply chain integration. Information sharing is the key driver for construction supply chain integration. During the past decade, the investment in information technology in corporate America has increased significantly. It is estimated that US information technology spending will increase to approximately $497 billion in 2009 and increase again to approximately $511 billion by 2010 (http://www.itfacts.biz). Information technology has had an impressive impact on construction supply chain practice.

Effective supply chain practice and effective information sharing are two sources of construction supply chain improvement. While some construction organizations emphasize on improving supply chain practice, others emphasize on leveraging information sharing among construction supply chain partners. Because these two major approaches are not independent, construction organizations must work on both construction supply chain practice and information sharing simultaneously.

This section is intended to show (1) the relationship between information sharing and the construction supply chain, (2) the influence of supply chain information sharing and supply chain construction projects, and (3) the impact of information sharing and supply chain practice on project delivery performance.

Construction supply chain planning practices are used to process information from project owners, design engineers, construction managers, subcontractors, and suppliers. Construction supply chain planning is driven by two objectives: developing good estimates of project requirements and coordinating the various project activities upstream and downstream.

The importance of the final estimate for the project cannot be ignored. Interaction and coordination within the project supply chain are important because alignment among the supply chain partners is necessary to achieve the project owner's goal. The coordination with materials suppliers and subcontractors is critical and is supported by research that shows the value of the interfirm cooperation and information sharing. The ultimate construction supply chain objective is to complete high-quality projects on time and under budget. The objective is to reduce wasteful activities in a process as a way to improve value added content. The project process must be simplified and the construction resource model must be carefully managed. See Table 7.1.

Construction supply chain management (CSCM) is based on the coordination of materials, information, and money flows between the various project partners. The integration of these flows will increase

Resources	Disruptions
1. Labor	1. Congestion
2. Materials	2. Weather
3. Equipment	3. Sequencing
4. Tools	4. Rework
5. Information	5. Work method
6. Support services	

TABLE 7.1 Construction Resource Model

the probability for a successful project. It is impossible to achieve integration without information sharing. In fact, information is the lifeblood of *all* successful construction projects. There are significant volumes of data generated by each CSCM member. This data must be translated into useable information and shared throughout the CSCM process. Currently, many construction projects are driven by the critical path or project schedule. The shortcoming of driving the project by the *Critical Path Method* schedule is the static nature of the project schedule, while timely accurate information is dynamic. With modifications, most of the supply chain concepts can be recommended and implemented into the construction industry.

However, without strong leadership throughout the complex construction network, the construction supply chain management concepts cannot be properly implemented. Supply chain management initiatives must be implemented in the initial stages of the project because each of the *key strategic* supply chain partners may not have worked together and may not be aware of the project owners or prime contractors' team-oriented goals. Otherwise, the flow of materials, money, and equipment will continue to move inefficiently across the project. The supply chain application for the construction industry must be flexible enough to adjust to project and supply chain partner changes. In the case of the horizontal government model, the project owner is in a strong position to exert supply chain leadership and information sharing. Implementing the supply chain management concepts for heavy highway and other complex public works projects can lead to reduction in delays and claims, as well as continuous improvement through the processing of real-time information by the strategic supply chain partners.

The three stages of supply chain information sharing are: (1) bid preparation, (2) preparation and execution of contractual agreements, and (3) project management and administration.

Bid Preparation

An estimate that matches the skill and other resources of the firm with the needs of the project is at the heart of a project supply chain. A competent and effective estimator is one of the key links in the supply chain operation. The attributes and qualities of a good estimator are:

- A background of construction experience
- Ability to visualize a project from plans and specifications
- Ability to scale and read plans and specifications accurately
- Well grounded in mathematics and geometry
- Adept in using computers
- Understand the importance of visiting the site of a proposed project; visualize step-by-step construction process
- Keep current on construction materials, methods, equipment, and processes

- Familiar with the production rates of bidding firm's labor force
- Understand the difference between overhead chargeable to a specific project and home office overhead
- Check all subcontracts for price and conformity

Knowledge of the construction industry and the item(s) of work, efficiency with technology, and the ability to visualize the project after visiting the site are some of the more important characteristics for an estimator. The comprehensive process of estimating and bidding includes plan reading, preparing and analyzing the work breakdown, and using automated spreadsheet applications. After understanding the documentation, the estimator should feel more capable preparing profit-producing estimates. In short, a good estimator must have strong practical knowledge and exceptional analytical abilities. The primary factors in estimating are:

- Contract documents, construction plans, and specifications
- Materials
- Labor
- Overhead
- Equipment
- Profit

Labor information is the most important of the six factors. The workforce must be well suited for the kind of work that the firm pursues. Contractors are encouraged to never bid 100 percent productivity. The profit margin should be determined based on the perceived risk, complexity, the dollar size of the project, and current capacity. There is no substitute for putting in the time required and commitment necessary to produce an effective estimate. In the estimating stage, information sharing takes place between the design engineer and the project owner, and among the prime contractors, suppliers, and subcontractors.

Contractual Agreements

As much as any element, the contracts used in the construction industry affirm a fragmented, hierarchical, single-interest, and blame-pointing environment. The tone and content of most construction contracts have little in common with supply chain objectives. Information sharing is the least common denominator in traditional construction models. Instead, the industry is dominated by contract documents that prize avoiding liability rather than accepting responsibility.

If the supply chain were a freight train, the project owner would be the locomotive engine with the other freight cars vying to be linked directly to the engine. At two extremes, it is the architect that typically has the closest relationship to the owner and the subcontractors that are more like a caboose. The industry is notorious for the practice of intentionally shifting risk and pushing down potential liability from the project owner to the prime contractor to strategic subcontractors. There is always the issue of how to allocate risks in a way that is commensurate with compensation. Put another way, the transfer of risk is the transfer of wealth. The nexus between firms in the supply chain is based primarily on who pays whom. The prime contractor reports to the project owner through the architect and the subcontractors report to the prime contractor; the second-tier subcontractors report to their respective subcontractor. The ideas of control and rank are pervasive. It is a hierarchy of reporting rather than a linear organization devoted to efficient production processes.

There are at least three major sources of standardized documents in the construction industry. The American Institute of Architects (AIA) is the leading professional membership association for licensed architects. Since 1888, AIA's family of contract documents has been widely used in the construction industry.[1] Consensus DOCS (Designers, Owners, Contractors, Surety), released in 2007, is a new family of contract documents that were developed by 22 associations of owners, contractors, and trade groups. One of the lead associations in the creation of Consensus DOCS is the Associated General Contractors of America (AGC). AGC, and some others, have folded their own association's documents into the Consensus DOCS.[2] The Engineers Joint Contract Documents Committee (EJCDC) is a group of engineering professionals and other stakeholders in the industry that have published standard contract documents for about 30 years.[3]

Even though all of the lead members of the various groups have worked together from time to time, their interpretations are naturally influenced by their respective constituencies. Periodic revisions of these various documents also consider applicable judicial interpretations. Sometimes contracts actually reflect best practices. No disputes or claims could mean that the project was successful. However, contracts seldom go further and mandate new approaches. A contract simply describes the optimum responsibilities and obligations of each party. The question is: Who is in the best position to perform a certain task and pay for it from revenues or insurance if something goes wrong? These well-intentioned industry groups have a limited albeit large objective, and that is to codify an equitable system of allocating risk in the context of existing mores.

In jockeying for proximity to the owner, there can be conflicts upstream between the architect and the prime contractor. The architect is traditionally responsible for design development, construction documents, bidding, and specific aspects of contract administration during construction. Conflicts occur upstream between the architect and prime contractor because of the architect's position as the central figure in the complex project delivery process. As the owner's representative, the architect is an independent observer who undertakes minimal risk with respect to the construction phase. Contractually, the architect is preeminent because the AIA documents require the prime contractor to communicate with the project owner through the architect. AIA document 201—2007, ¶4.2.4, "General Conditions of the Contract for Construction," outlines how communications should be handled throughout the supply chain:

> Except as otherwise provided in the Contract Documents or when direct communications have been specially authorized, the Owner and Contractor shall endeavor to communicate with each other through the Architect about matters arising out of or relating to the Contract. Communications by and with the Architect's consultants shall be through the Architect. Communications by and with Subcontractors and material suppliers shall be through the Contractor.

The lack of direct communication between the prime contractor and the project owner is a significant obstacle to supply chain objectives and tends to supplant the notion of information sharing. The architect's role in the construction process was amplified over the years because the architect was one of the most educated entities on the job site with a coveted professional license. The project owner was financially capable but unfamiliar with the construction process. Thus, the bifurcated roles of the architect-as-designer and -as-contract-administrator evolved. However, the reality is that the construction and business environments that existed during the late nineteenth and early twentieth centuries are radically different today. A construction site in the twenty-first century is likely to include a broad mix of business, engineering and construction professionals. In fact, the evolution and growth model of the construction industry from the general contractor to construction manager supports this thinking. The Consensus DOCS supports the opposite position of the AIA contract documents in that they implicitly allow direct communications between the prime contractor and project owner. CD 240 ¶3.14, Standard Form Agreement between Owner and Architect/Engineer, which treats the architect like the owner's consultant, reads:

> Except as provided in this Agreement or unless otherwise directed by the Owner, the Architect/Engineer shall communicate with the Contractor and Subcontractors only through the Owner.

The Consensus DOCS takes a progressive view of communications between the prime contractor and owner, but falls short when it comes to subcontractor communications. CD 240 ¶3.6 provides:

> Unless otherwise provided in the Subcontract Documents and except for emergencies, Subcontractor shall direct all communications related to the Project to the Contractor.

This provision may work for a transactional supplier, but it does not bode well for a strategic subcontractor (discussed in Chap. 5) who could be critical to the execution of large portions of the work. Communication is the cornerstone of construction supply chain management. The concerns about who speaks to whom and for what reasons seem to be more tied to avoiding claims and litigation than to accomplishing the work. Instead, the thinking should be what can be gained from allowing supply chain entities to share information at all levels. The pecking order of who officially can talk to the owner and who cannot is outdated and not at all useful in today's high technology fast track construction environment. A construction supply chain management environment will not diminish the architect's importance in the supply chain; it will simply elevate other strategic entities to the same level in order to advance the best interests of the project over the interests of individual firms.

The legal arrangements downstream in the supply chain for strategic subcontractors are more like entanglements that are complicated by the lack of communications, the awkward timing of contract negotiations and execution, and the contract terms that establish patterns of blame instead of efficiency. Subcontracting is a means of getting the work performed while transferring risk. Subcontracting also allows the prime contractor to extract a fixed price for the subcontracted portions of work. Practically speaking, the prime contractor controls the money and is responsible for the coordination of the work, while the subcontractor is responsible for executing the work with limited rights and potentially unlimited risk.

The discussion of distributive bargaining in Chap. 5 underscores the lack of real give and take between prime contractors and subcontractors and shows the imbalance of power. The pre-award discussions between the prime contractor and subcontractor center on price, scope of work, and payment terms. During this period, the prime contractor may have similar discussions with more than one subcontractor for the same item of work. The intention of the prime is to influence the subcontractor's actions to the prime contractor's advantage. This goal is effectively communicated and reinforced by the prime contractor's cost structure. Once the prime contractor is identified as the most responsive bidder, the imbalance of power is even more significant because the prime contractor is in a position to dole out the work. In some markets, after the award, the prime contractor will further beat down the price of the subcontractors. By the time both the prime contract award and the subcontract award are made, the subcontractor believes that it has no choice but to agree to terms and conditions that do not consider its cost structure, and worse, terms and conditions that the subcontractor may not have even read.

Hopefully, all subcontractors read the agreements that they sign. What they may not read, however, is the prime contractor's agreement with the project owner that is almost always incorporated by reference in the subcontract agreement. In short, even if they have not read it or have never seen it, subcontractors are bound to the project owner by the same terms and conditions as the prime contractor. These conduit, or "flow-down," terms from the prime contractor's agreement with the owner provide that the subcontract incorporates the prime contract provisions that apply to the subcontracted work. Where these flow-down terms become difficult is when the most onerous provisions are pushed down to the subcontractor; but reciprocal rights, as between the owner and prime contractor, are not always pushed down and included in the subcontractor's agreement. Both the AIA and Consensus DOCS subcontract agreements take the most equitable position and give the subcontractor reciprocal rights, meaning that the subcontractor has the same rights against the prime contractor as the prime contractor has against the owner.[4]

Consensus DOCS specifically requires that the prime contractor provide the subcontractor with copies of the contracts to which the subcontractor is bound.[5] The AIA subcontract states that the prime contractor make available to the subcontractor copies of the agreement between the prime contractor and the owner.[6] Sharing the prime contract agreement with the strategic subcontractor who is bound by its terms may seem basic, but this level of information sharing and transparency is a giant step away from industry practices that seek to cut off the information flow and keep strategic subcontractors in the dark.

In the traditional fragmented project delivery system, there have been some advances in information sharing at critical junctures in the construction process. For example, the project dispute resolution system, at least in Consensus DOCS, is predicated on discussions at the project level of the supply chain entities and then at the executive level of the entities before invoking dispute mitigation procedures. CD 200, "Standard Agreement and General Conditions Between Owner and Contractor, ¶12.2, Dispute Mitigation and Resolution, Direct Discussions" provides:

> If the Parties cannot reach resolution on a matter relating to or arising out of the Agreement, the Parties shall endeavor to reach resolution through good faith direct discussions between the Parties' representatives, who shall possess the necessary authority to resolve such matter and who shall record the date of first discussions. If the Parties' representatives are not able to resolve such matter within five (5) business days of the first discussion, the Parties' representatives shall immediately inform senior executives of the Parties in writing that resolution was not affected. Upon receipt of such notice, senior executives of the Parties shall meet within five (5) business days to endeavor to reach resolution. If the dispute remains unresolved after fifteen (15) days from the date of first discussion, the Parties shall submit such matter to the dispute mitigation and dispute resolution procedures selected herein.

Similar terms are found in CD 750, "Agreement between Contractor and Subcontractor," Section 11.5. The AIA documents provide that the initial decision maker (IDM) will make the first determination about any claims that are made except for claims involving hazardous materials, emergencies, and subrogation. In AIA 201—2007, the parties can agree that someone other than the architect will act as the IDM. A neutral choice for IDM may be advisable since some claims actually involve the architect's role in contract administration.[7] EJCDC—C 700 (2007) requires that, as a condition precedent, most claims must be first referred to the engineer before the owner or contractor pursues any other remedies.[8] Over time, other contract terms have been modified to inspire more balance and parity between supply chain members. Indemnification is one of those provisions. Construction jobsites are dangerous and, unfortunately, can be the scene of serious accidents. When those accidents occur and workers and others are injured, claims and litigation frequently ensue and all of the supply chain members are named as parties. Indemnification or hold-harmless provisions are contractual terms which set forth one party's obligation to assume another party's liability to third parties if there is bodily injury and death, and/or property loss on a jobsite. The types of indemnity provisions are defined below using supply chain entities as the parties.

- *Limited form indemnity* means that the subcontractor will pay for losses that are the subcontractor's fault.
- Intermediate form indemnity means that the subcontractor will pay for losses that are partly the prime contractor's fault.
- Broad form indemnity means that the subcontractor will pay for all losses even though they may be solely the prime contractor's fault.

Not only do indemnity provisions obligate a party to pay for losses, they typically include provisions which require a party to pay attorneys' fees and defense costs incurred by the party being indemnified. Unfair indemnification provisions can lead to the insolvency of individual supply chain entities and adversely impact the solvency of an entire project. Adequate insurance coverage can buffer the impact of paying claims due to contractual indemnification. The indemnity provisions in the industry contracts are generally moving more toward a supply chain philosophy. The AIA, Consensus DOCS, and EJCDC have comparable terms that embrace the more desirable limited form indemnity model for subcontractors and downstream supply chain members. However, AIA and EJCDC contracts could do more for upstream entities by implementing mutual indemnity, as between the owner and the prime contractor. The more impartial individual contract terms in the construction industry have changed over time. But a revised contract in a fragmented, adversarial environment is just that, a revision and not a new way of doing business. More is needed. In order to achieve integration and transparency throughout the supply chain, the contractual documents should be more forthright with respect to communications and information sharing. The content of many provisions should be completely overhauled. More importantly, the guiding principles for the project and management team should be incorporated in the contract so that participants are as committed to principles as they are bound by specific term regarding indemnity. Dispute resolution methodologies should be systematic and require discussions at all levels. The dispute resolution system should reflect more than legal compliance with requirements for notice and time limits. Disputing parties should be held accountable for managing by the numbers and employing project management tools like the "S" curve discussed later in this chapter, which is used to monitor and forecast shortfalls.

CSCM methodologies mandate a fundamental departure from traditional practices and require contractual arrangements that foster the successful project outcomes instead of individual firm successes. The issue becomes how to draft agreements that promote trust, sharing, and openness across all levels of the supply chain, including the project owner, architect, prime contractor, and *all* strategic subcontractors and suppliers who impact delays, quality, and cost. Both AIA[9] and Consensus DOCS have developed contract documents that encourage collaboration among supply chain entities. In October, 2008, the national AIA and AIA California announced the Integrated Project Delivery system to design and build projects. Consensus DOCS has also introduced a collaborative tri-party agreement that is an outgrowth of principles of lean construction. Both document series integrate key stakeholders in a design and construction environment that values information sharing, openness, risk allocation, and transparency. These industry documents are valuable resources as project owners make the wise decision to implement construction supply chain management. But the legal arrangements can never drive change; they can only be a by-product of change that comes from within the industry. See sample sections from CD 300, Standard Form of Tri-Party Agreement for Collaborative Project Delivery in App. C, and AIA Document A 295—2008 Instructions, General Conditions of the Contract for Integrated Project Delivery in App. D.

The Project Management Stage

The management of the project is the last line of defense. If the bid preparation and contractual agreements are adequate, the right prime contractor is selected and the ultimate project budget is reasonable, then a good management effort will deliver a successful project to the owner. A poor management effort will undo the pre-execution achievements. On the other hand, if the project is in trouble when the execution starts, a good project management effort can bail it out and, conversely, a poor effort will put the nail in the coffin. In order to be successful, the project must conform to the plans and specifications and, be on time and within budget.

The duties and responsibilities of the project manager are diversified. The precise duties depend on the construction supply chain organization. The skill and experience of the strategic supply chain partners are the ultimate determinants of delivering a successful project. Two important factors that contribute to success are:

- Adequacy of site operations and management
- Relationship between the strategic supply chain partners

Costs are often divided into two categories, direct and indirect costs, defined as:

- *Direct costs* include materials, labor, and subcontract expenditures associated with the actual implementation [subdivided into various accounting codes to reflect the actual work, the work breakdown structure (WBS)].
- *Indirect costs* are all other expenditures, sometimes referred to as hidden costs.

The tasks involved in a typical complex project are as follows:

- Establish a reasonable budget.
- Know where expenditures are being made.
- Forecast final expenditures.
- Identify problem areas by comparing expenditures and budgets.
- Apprise contractors and strategic supply chain partners of the information early so that actions can be taken to achieve economies.
- Determine total cost of a laborer.
- The productivity must be maximized.
- The field manager must properly balance the indirect costs to achieve the maximum level of efficiency.
- Contractors/managers must be assigned indirect cost center responsibility early.
- Joint reviews of indirect cost must take place on a scheduled basis.
- Use tracking curves or lists to monitor budgeted versus actual costs.
- Work hours must be controlled.

- Establish at least 20 percent productivity improvement over previously established norms for the type of work category in question.
- Labor budgets must be available to the strategic supply chain partners early in the project.
- Measures of actual performance against budgeted performance must be collected accurately. The data must be reliable.
- These data should then be used for decision making.
- Labor productivity, or effectiveness, should be tracked for each of the direct labor accounts.

$$\text{Labor productivity} = \frac{\text{Percent complete}}{\text{Percent of budget labor hours}}$$

Historical plots are useful for tracking labor productivity.

- The subcontract provisions may include both direct and indirect work activities.
  - Direct activities—well-defined scope of work.
  - Indirect activities—work only on necessary activities.
- Changes to the contracts must be strictly controlled and documented. If not documented, what are the possible outcomes?
- See the change order form shown in Fig. 5.13 in Chap. 5.
- Schedule control is essential to the success of any complex project.
- Major projects are a complex effort to mobilize and coordinate large numbers of personnel, materials, equipment, and money.
- Good schedule control is to develop a plan, implement the plan, monitor execution of the plan, and make changes to the plan when necessary in order to meet the target.
- The master schedule is generally a logical network-type schedule that reflects perfect execution plans, the strategy, equipment delivery estimates, and engineering plans. Project milestones must be reviewed and assessed. Also see Chaps. 4 and 5.
- Gantt charts or CPM should be used to assess progress.

Project Execution

In the project execution stage, the flow of materials, money, and subcontracting is shared among the strategic supply chain partners. The transmission of information related to material supply, project progress, project scheduling, and money flows must be accomplished in a timely manner in order to successfully complete the project. The

Construction Supply Chain, Profitability, and Information Sharing

Week	Estimated Completion	Actual Complete
1	3	2
2	10	5
3	14	10
4	20	18
5	30	30
6	45	32
7	60	66
8	78	67
9	90	88
10	100	100

TABLE 7.2 Estimated and Actual Field Measurements

actual progress of a project can be directly compared with the estimated progress as shown in the final bid. The elapsed time can be compared with the estimated activity or project duration. The estimated budget for labor, materials, and equipment can also be compared with the actual recorded productivity. Management judgment and "seat of the pants" measurements are qualitative and less reliable. Field measurements are a more accurate measure. The "S" curve, or cumulative progress curve, is an excellent analytical tool that can be implemented to measure progress. See Table 7.2 and Fig. 7.1.

Shared progress information can be transmitted in many forms, ranging from face-to-face conversations, cellular telephones, e-mails,

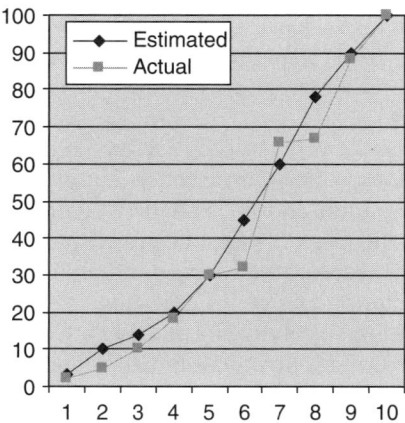

FIGURE 7.1 "S" curve.

and meetings using PowerPoint presentations. The most acceptable forms of information sharing at this stage in the project include CPM diagrams and real-time Internet transmissions. Regardless of the format, an effective information sharing system should consist of the following items:

- *Estimates*: The project or activity estimates based on the plans and the final bid.
- *Actual*: The actual quantities and budget usage to date.
- *Forecasts*: The most accurate expectations of future projects forecasts are usually based on past performance.
- *Variances*: The positive and negative differences between the estimates and actuals. The variances should be reported in relative (percentages) and absolute (money and production) quantities. The construction manager can then assess the magnitude of the variances and share the information both upstream and downstream.

Two pure construction supply chain models will be presented in Chap. 8.

- Horizontal government and nongovernment construction supply chainbusiness models
- Vertical government construction supply chain model

Conclusion

The concept of construction supply chain has gained significance because of the increasing number of potential complex private and public sector construction projects. In the short run, contractors may be able to survive with losses; however, in the long run, *every* construction business *must* generate a profit. Niche marketing, decreasing total costs, and decreasing overhead are traditional means of increasing profits.

In the construction process, costly delays in materials, equipment, and services erode profits. Construction supply chain management through the integration and coordination of materials, information, and money flows between the various project partners resolves delays and offers a new means of increasing profitability. CSCM's emphasis on information sharing and communications fosters cooperation and collaboration among supply chain members. Contract arrangements that promote core values across all levels of the supply chain depart from traditional practices by advancing successful project outcomes instead of individual firm's successes. Project management and execution are the final tests of how well the supply chain is working. Tracking progress in the field ensures that a project will be on-time and under budget and within specifications. Sharing field measurements with all members in accordance with supply chain values is the final predictor of a profitable project

References

1. http://www.aiacontractdocuments.org/
2. Harris, Larry D., and Perlberg, Brian M., "The Advantage of the Consensus DOCS," presented at Winds of Change, the Consensus DOCS, American Bar Association Forum on the Construction Industry, September 11-12, 2008, Chicago, Illinois.
3. http://www.content.asce.org/ejcdc
4. AIA Document A401—1997 ¶2.1, Standard Form of Agreement between Contractor and Subcontractor and CD 750 ¶3.1, Standard Form of Agreement between Contractor and Subcontractor.
5. CD 750 ¶2.3, Standard Form of Agreement between Contractor and Subcontractor.
6. AIA Document A401—1997, Standard Form of Agreement between Contractor and Subcontractor, page 1, Description of project.
7. AIA Document A201—2007 ¶15.2, General Conditions of the Contract for Construction.
8. EJCDC C-700 ¶10.1 Standard General Conditions of the Construction Contract.
9. CD 750 ¶9.1.1, Standard Form of Agreement between Contractor and Subcontractor; AIA Document A401—1997 ¶4.6.1 Standard Form of Agreement between Contractor and Subcontractor; AIA Document A201—2007 ¶3.18.1 General Conditions of the Contract for Construction; and EJCDC C-700 ¶6.20 Standard General Conditions of the Construction Contract.

CHAPTER 8

Construction Supply Chain Management Business Models

> A Road Map for Success

The construction industry has become increasingly more complex. There has been significant growth in construction projects in domestic markets and in emerging free market economies throughout the world. Horizontal and vertical construction projects are increasing at an impressive rate. The construction of bridges, highways, schools, housing developments, hospitals, apartment buildings, manufacturing facilities, and levies has led to an explosion in construction knowledge. What follows is a general categorization of two construction supply chain business models that encompass the various types of construction projects.

Public and Private Sector Heavy Construction and Horizontal Supply Chain Models

Projects in heavy construction or horizontal segment are the most complicated and require the highest levels of technical, financial, and managerial expertise. This market sector also requires sophisticated materials handling and placement methods. The characteristics of the heavy construction supply chain market segment are:

- Dams, bridges, flood control highways, airports, interchanges, and the like
- Large projects—petroleum refineries, nuclear plants, and the like

- Large global market potential
- Requires high levels of engineering
- Accounts for 25 to 30 percent of the annual construction costs in the United States

There is also an increasing international demand for this market segment. The design phase in this sector is controlled by civil engineers. The construction phase is characterized by fleets of heavy equipment: cranes, earthmovers, and trucks, which are used extensively for these projects. Almost all of these projects are publicly financed and inspected by civil engineers who work directly for the project owner, typically a government agency. The prime contractor must be highly qualified in engineering, geology, planning, scheduling, and control. The industrial sector is heavily capitalized with significant engineering expertise. There are only a few companies qualified to operate at this level. For example, Halliburton and Brown-Root both are engaged in infrastructure projects in Iraq.

The heavy highway market is regulated by state departments of transportation (DOTs) and the Federal Highway Administration (FHWA). The DOT is the project owner and contract administrator and FHWA is the custodian of the Federal Highway Trust Fund, which is primarily funded by taxes on motor fuels. The FHWA disburses the gas tax moneys to state governments to fund road construction. The DOTs match the federal funds at a rate of 10 to 20 percent state money versus 80 to 90 percent of federal funds. The FHWA is responsible for oversight of federal aid highway projects. The 1956 Federal Aid Highway Act was the seminal legislation that created the highway trust fund and system for building roads and bridges which has been implemented in all states and the District of Columbia. What makes this sector significant is the similarity in operations and processes across all of the state DOTs. Most DOTs have a corporate and district offices with in-house engineers and staff who play a critical role in contract and project administration. Each DOT has its own standard specifications that apply to its respective projects. Interestingly enough, as between the state DOTs, sections of the standard specification manuals are similar in terms of organization and definitions. The dedicated transportation function within state governments has been replicated on a smaller scale by local municipalities and county governments.

Because of the financial and technical complexities of the heavy highway projects, most states require that prime contractors be prequalified. Prequalification is a measure of a firm's capacity and capabilities based on financial information, equipment, personnel, and relevant past experiences. The heavy supply chain market requires specific engineering expertise and managerial skill. Some states even require that subcontractors meet prequalification standards similar to the

Construction Supply Chain Management Business Models

prime contractors. In reviewing financial information for prequalification, the DOTs tend to value liquidity, that is cash and cash equivalents. In some respects, prequalification is akin to a performance bond and helps the state safeguard the taxpayers' dollars. Annual prequalification is the key to regular bid lettings. Only the contractors who are prequalified in advance—that is, those who are capable of building a particular item and have the financial resources, equipment, and personnel—are permitted to bid.

Because of prequalification, when all the bids are accepted then, generally speaking, the only remaining task is to identify the low bidder.

The Components of the Heavy Construction Supply Chain Model

The key supply chain participants in the heavy construction supply chain model are the project owner, the design engineer, the prime contractor, the subcontractors, the suppliers of materials and equipment, and the banks. See Fig. 8.1. The model shows the upstream and downstream flows of money, work, and information. The success of any construction project is inherently affected by the people who participate. A functional organizational structure is important, as well as sound state-of-the-art management practices. Each supply chain

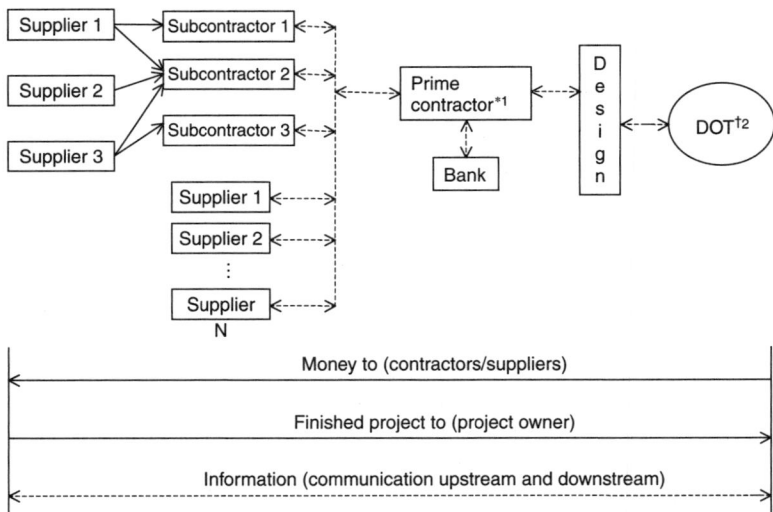

*1. In this model, prime contractor 1 performs at least 50 percent of work
†2. Department of Transportation

FIGURE 8.1 Public sector heavy construction and horizontal supply chain model.

participant must understand its role in the completion of a project so that it is high-quality, under budget, and on time.

The Project Owner (Tier 1 in the Construction Supply Chain)
Responsibilities of the project owner:

1. Determines what is to be constructed. [For purposes of this discussion, the project owner is the Indiana Department of Transportation (INDOT).[1] The funding agency is the FHWA.] As part of its preconstruction responsibilities, the project owner issues the *Federal Environmental Impact Statement* (EIS), which describes the purpose and need for the project. The EIS outlines the various alternatives including the routes that were selected and those that were eliminated. The EIS further describes the environmental consequences and impact, and then discusses measures to mitigate these impacts. *The Record of Decision* (ROD), issued by the FHWA, is the final step in the EIS process. The ROD identifies the preferred alternatives and discusses the means that will be adopted to minimize the environmental impacts.
2. Establishes the date the project must be completed.
3. Establishes the major quality and reliability project construction milestones.
4. Prepares final plans and specifications.
5. Establishes preliminary cost estimates for the project.
6. Prepares bid package.
7. Establishes disadvantaged business enterprise (DBE) participation goals
8. Prepares notices and advertisements for bid letting.
9. Posts notice to contractors. The definitions for the various bid postings are provided at http://www.in.gov/dot/div/contracts/standards/drawings/index.html.
10. Posts electronic bidding system 4 weeks before the opening of bids. This is the electronic exchange that lists the schedule of pay items. The exchange is updated for revisions as needed beginning 10 days prior to the opening of bids.
11. Posts bidder and plan holder lists 14 days before the bid opening, and updates 7 days before and again 1 day before the opening of bids. This information is strategic because the bidders know who will be the competition prior to submitting their bids.
12. Conducts mandatory pre-bid meeting in special circumstances.
13. Receives bids from prime contractors.

Construction Supply Chain Management Business Models 149

14. Opens bids and selects contractor.
15. Prepares contract documents.
16. Awards contract.
17. Conducts preconstruction meeting.
18. Ensures that permits, insurance, performance bonds, DBE goals, and other requirements are in place before beginning the project.
19. May conduct partnering meetings with supply chain members throughout the life cycle of a project.

The major elements of an INDOT project are presented in a flow diagram in the project development process (PDP). See Fig. 8.2.

The Prime Contractor (Tier 2 in the Construction Supply Chain)
Responsibilities of the prime contractor:

1. Reviews the Notice to Contractors found at http://www.in.gov/dot/div/contracts/standards/drawings/index.html. The notice is posted 5 weeks prior to the bid opening; it lists the type of work, location, qualification requirements, and the cost of the bid documents.
2. Reviews contract information booklet, construction plans, specifications, special provisions, and additional contract requirements. In its review, the prime contractor is assessing the project location, special conditions, and completeness of the construction plans and specifications. The prime contractor also considers the type of contract, schedule of pay items and quantities, which can be found at http://www.in.gov/dot/div/contracts/standards/drawings/index.html. The prime contractor's current prequalification capacity and work in progress are factors that affect its decision to bid.
3. Submits new prequalification application at least 21 calendar days before bid opening date to be considered for that bid opening. Renews prequalification annually at least 15 calendar days before bid opening date in order to receive consideration for that bid opening. Prequalification determines what items of work a prime contractor can perform and the dollar value. To be prequalified to perform work over $1,000,000, the prime contractor must submit an audited balance sheet. The classifications of work by type include concrete base-pavement and resurface; bituminous base-pavement and resurface; grading, and bridges. The dollar value of all unearned work, including non-INDOT work, counts against the prequalification limits. The INDOT prequalification application form can be found at http://www.in.gov/dot/div/contracts/standards/drawings/index.html.

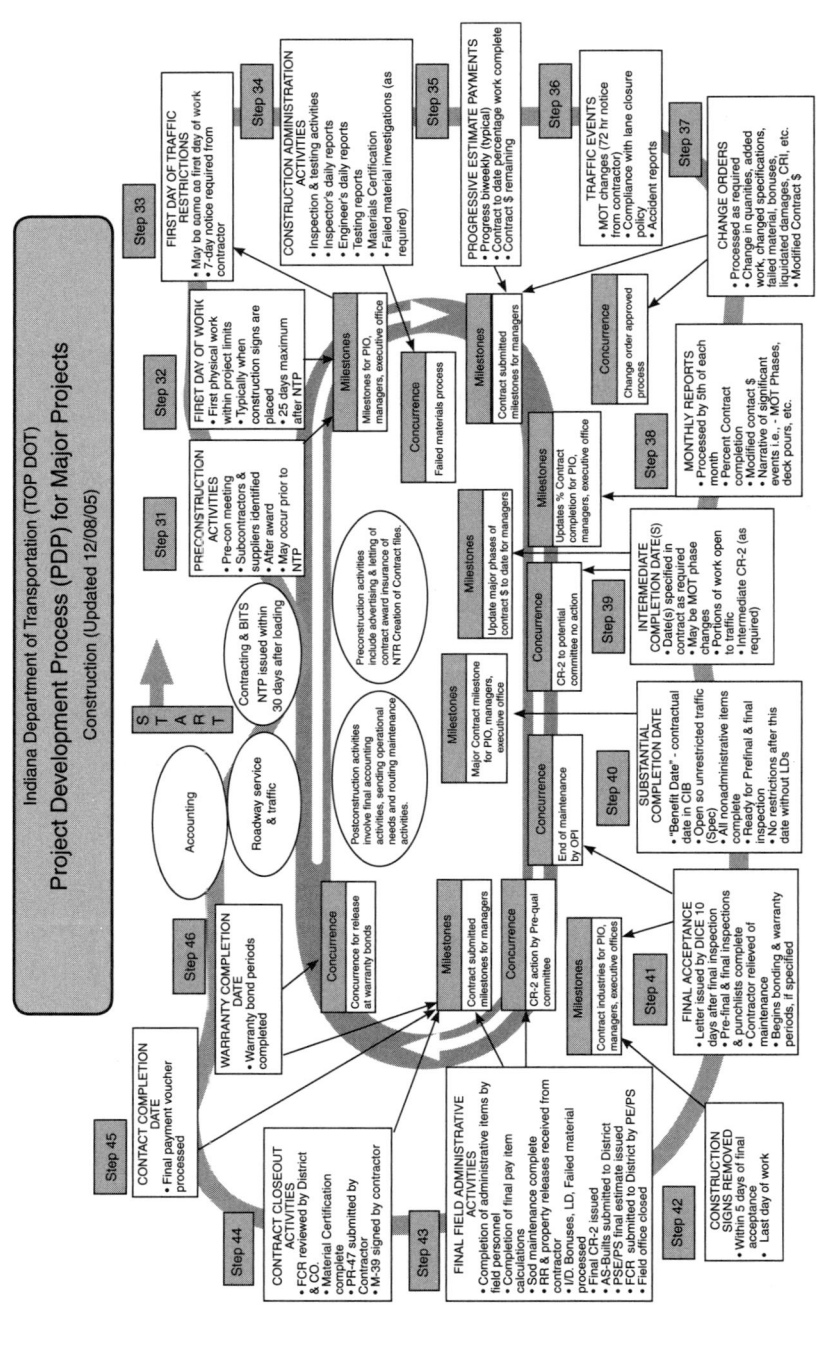

FIGURE 8.2 INDOT project development process (PDP) for major projects.

4. Conducts intensive visit of project site in order to evaluate the characteristics of the site, such as conditions, accessibility, and obstructions. The site visit will also help the prime contractor determine what items will need to be demolished. While at the site, the prime contractor should take photographs and prepare a list of probative questions. The prime contractor should visualize the work being performed at the site and begin to develop a plan for mobilizing and demobilizing labor, equipment, and materials.
5. Receives updated information on bid, such as supplemental notices issued up to 2 weeks prior to the bid opening.
6. Attends pre-bid conference if one is held.
7. Performs a precise analysis of the general requirements, construction plans, specifications, and proposal book. The prime contractor must assess the quality of the bid documents.
8. Determines what items prime contractor will self-perform and then solicit quotes from subcontractors, equipment and material suppliers. Most INDOT jobs require the prime contractor to self-perform 50 percent of the work.
9. Determines DBE participation strategy. The DBE firm must be listed by quantity, work item, and dollars in the bid. The prime contractor includes the *Affirmative Action Certification* sheet in the project proposal.
10. Checks the electronic bidding system that is posted four weeks before the bid opening. The electronic exchange is updated with revisions as needed beginning 10 days prior to the opening of bids. It is the prime contractor's responsibility to check the electronic exchange for amendment files prior to the bid deadline.
11. Checks for bidder and plan holder list which is posted 14 days before the bid opening. This information is updated 7 days before the bid opening, and again, 1 day before. This information is strategic because the bidders know the competition prior to submitting their bids.
12. Registers on INDOT website for valid bidder status. This step is imperative for electronic bidding.
13. Performs final work breakdown and takeoff and generates final bid.
14. Submits bid via electronic medium.
15. Waits for award decision. If the prime contractor is the low and responsive bidder, INDOT will award the contract to transform the construction plans, materials, equipment, labor, and support services into a safe and reliable roadway for the traveling public.

Please see Chap. 5, Fig. 5.2, for a general explanation of the bid preparation and submission process.

The Subcontractor (Tier 3 in the Construction Supply Chain)

In cases where the prime contractor cannot perform or decides not to perform certain project tasks, it will contract with a subcontractor. Subcontracting organization must have the resources and expertise to perform the requested tasks. The subcontracting organization must also share some of the project risk. The prime contractor must self-perform at least 50 percent of the work. There are no second tier subcontractors on INDOT projects.

Responsibilities of the subcontractor:

1. Submits new prequalification application at least 21 calendar days before bid opening date to be considered for that bid opening. Renews prequalification annually at least 15 calendar days before bid opening date in order to receive consideration for that bid opening. Prequalification determines what items of work a prime contractor can perform and the dollar value. To be prequalified to perform work over $1,000,000, the subcontractor must submit an audited balance sheet. Special contracts and subcontract components are the general types of work and classifications given for subcontractor prequalification. The INDOT prequalification application form can be found at http://www.in.gov/dot/div/contracts/standards/drawings/index.html.

2. The subcontractor receives a request for quotation for a specified item of work from the prime contractor. In the INDOT market, the subcontractor can go online and retrieve all of the information required to submit a quote. In addition, the bidder and plan holder's list may be a source of competitive information because it indicates who is a valid bidder and who may not be a valid bidder, but has copies of the plans.

3. Reviews contract information booklet, construction plans, specifications, special provisions, and additional contract requirements. In its review, the subcontractor is assessing the project location, special conditions, and completeness of the construction plans and specifications with respect to the item that it will build. The subcontractor's current prequalification capacity and work in progress are factors that affect its decision to submit a quote.

4. Conducts intensive visit of project site to evaluate the characteristics of the site, such as conditions, accessibility, and obstructions. The site visit will also help the prime contractor determine what items, if any, will need to be demolished. While at the site, the subcontractor should take photographs

and prepare a list of probative questions. The subcontractor should visualize the work being performed and consider the extent and number of mobilizations and demobilizations required.

5. The subcontractor solicits bids from equipment and material suppliers (if applicable).
6. The subcontractor considers any revisions that impact its item of work that are posted prior to the bid opening. The prime contractor requesting a quote will also notify the subcontractor of any changes.
7. The subcontractor does a takeoff and generates the final quote.
8. The subcontractor submits and delivers quote.
9. The subcontractor waits for award decision.
10. If the subcontractor is awarded the contract, the shop drawing process is initiated. (See the shop drawing submittal process in Chap. 5.)

The Construction Material Supplier (Tier 3 in the Construction Supply Chain)

The responsibilities of the prime contractor's purchasing department or purchasing manager are:

1. Review and coordinate with estimating department, the material requirements, specifications, quantities, and time frames. Consider any special fabrication needs. Based on usage in project, classify materials as strategic or commodity.
2. Locate and select possible suppliers for project from the INDOT approved materials list found at www.in.gov/indot/div/M&T/appmat/appmat.htm.
3. Prepare request for quotations that includes specifications, quantities, and due dates.
4. Receive quotations.
5. Organize and participate in the evaluation team for responsive bids from strategic suppliers.
6. Wait for decision on award to prime contractor.
7. Organize and lead negotiating team to finalize price, shipment and delivery, and other terms.

The Construction Equipment Supplier (Tier 3 in the Construction Supply Chain)

Because most complex construction projects require a number of equipment items, contractors are periodically evaluating their equipment needs. The inventory of equipment used on a major construction project goes on and on, from compressors and blowers, to backhoes and dump trucks. Some equipment decisions may be made project-by-project. For example, the company needs to rent an additional crane to install barrier walls. But for the most part, because of the prequalification requirements, equipment decisions are more closely tied to market niches. Firms pursuing grading and earth work are going to buy or lease motor graders and then pursue projects that need this sort of equipment. The INDOT prequalification application requires contractors to list and describe in a detailed schedule all construction equipment, for example, machinery, trucks, barricades, and asphalt plants by type, capacity, and manufacturer and indicate the purchase price, date of purchase, accumulated depreciation, and net book value. The kind of equipment that a firm either owns, leases, or rents is one indicator of which work classifications INDOT will approve. Finally, as part of their annual internal operations review, contractors should develop an hourly rate for each type of equipment. This rate is based on historical usage. If a firm finds that the equipment is not being used at the rate of approximately 1500 hours per year, then the contractor should consider selling the equipment and leasing or renting it as needed. The 1500 hour rule is based on empirical evidence.

Public versus Private Construction Projects

Compliance with the Davis Bacon Act and related statutes is one important difference between public and private projects. Davis Bacon requires that prevailing wages be paid to workers on all federal government construction contracts over $2,000. Prevailing wage laws also apply to construction projects with federally assisted funding. Davis Bacon provides that both prime contractors and subcontractors pay workers employed directly on the site not less than the local prevailing wages and fringe benefits paid on projects of a similar character. Contractors whose workforces have been organized by collective bargaining units work on both public and private projects. However, the Davis Bacon requirement in public works has been one reason that some small contractors work solely in the private sector.

Supply Chain Document Flows

The document flows between supply chain entities include the agreement between the project owner and prime contractor and the agreement between the prime contractor and subcontractors. There may also be contracts between the prime contractor and the material suppliers, and between the subcontractor and material suppliers. Change orders for any supply chain member approved by INDOT are an element in the supply chain document flow. In addition to the formal legal arrangements, the DOTs require bid bonds from the prime contractor when the bid is submitted. Performance and payment bonds are required of the contractor who is the responsive low bidder and awarded the job. Prime contractors sometimes demand that other members of the supply chain also obtain a performance bond.

The proofs of insurance, comprehensive general liability insurance, worker's compensation, and other coverage are typically kept by the prime contractor. There is a trend to name the prime contractor as an additional insured on the subcontractor's policy. This coverage may be overreaching because it gives the prime contractor the same rights under the policy as the insured.

Supply Chain Coordination and Information Flows

In public works markets, there is an abundance of information. INDOT has a public website with information on how and when to bid. The names of potential bidders and plan holders are published periodically before the public bid opening. After the project is awarded, there is a preconstruction meeting with the prime contractor, other supply chain members, and the district engineers and project administrators from INDOT. As the project progresses, the agency will conduct partnering meetings that include all supply chain members. Lower tier supply chain members have their own relationship with the INDOT district officials because prequalified subcontractors are evaluated on each job by the district officials. However, there are practical, if not actual, limits to the contacts with the agency because it is well known among supply chain entities that INDOT's contract is with the prime contractor.

Supply Chain Money Flows

The flow of payments is one of the more attractive features of the INDOT market. The project owner is the state government and not vulnerable to bankruptcy in the same sense as private owners. The source of funding, gas tax revenues, and state matching funds are predictable in good economic times. There is no invoicing system, per se. Instead, the district engineers inspect the work as the project progresses and then issue an "estimate" for payment. The estimates are taken about every 2 weeks. On some projects, inspection is outsourced to consulting engineers. Payments are made directly to the prime contractor who, in turn, pays the subcontractors. The contract provisions between INDOT and the prime contractor require the prime contractor to pay subcontractors no later than 10 business days after the prime contractor is paid.

American Recovery and Reinvestment Act: Federal Economic Stimulus

The state departments of transportation are playing in critical role in the federal economic stimulus plan, 2009 American Recovery and Reinvestment Act. The flow of money and controls from FHWA to the DOTs makes the horizontal heavy construction model ideal for managing the economic stimulus program. The law provides approximately 27.5 billion for highway work and requires that one-half of the funds be obligated by June 30, 2009. The remaining half must be under contract by March 2, 2010. All projects must be completed by February 17, 2012.[1] Vertical construction projects will also be funded through various state and federal agencies under similar conditions. This fast track program provides an unprecedented opportunity for supply chain entities to work together to reduce waste and achieve impressive efficiencies.

Private and Public Sector Vertical Construction Supply Chain Models

The vertical construction sector includes a wide range of projects from apartment buildings, elementary schools, and department stores in the private sector to universities, hospitals, and local, state, and federal office buildings in the public sector. The private projects in this sector are financed by commercial banks. Engineers and architects usually collaborate on the design phase of projects in this segment. The bids are packaged and categorized by system, such as mechanical, electrical, or structural. Typically more than 70 percent of the bid items are subcontracted to specialty contractors. The characteristics of the vertical-non-government construction supply chain market segment include:

- Construction management as the predominant project delivery system.
- An equipment-intensive operating environment.
- Significant material costs (concrete, steel, pipe, and rock).
- Mostly privately financed projects.
- High levels of expertise.
- Pricing based on competitive bidding.
- A dollar volume that accounts for 35 to 40 percent of the all annual construction in the U.S.

Public sector supply chains consist of projects ranging from small retail spaces in airports to hospitals to universities. Each of the projects in this market sector requires engineering and management capabilities. In most cases, the projects are financed by the federal, state, or local governments or some combination of the three. Architects are used to design these projects. Construction managers, general contractors, and subcontractors are used for executing and managing the construction transformation process. Projects in this market sector are highly centered on the actual utilization of the various facilities, which is especially true for hospitals, universities, and schools.

A flow diagram of vertical public sector construction supply chain model shows the upstream and downstream flows of money, work, and information. See Fig. 8.3. Current and future construction projects are driven by technology, information, and continuous

Construction Supply Chain Management Business Models 157

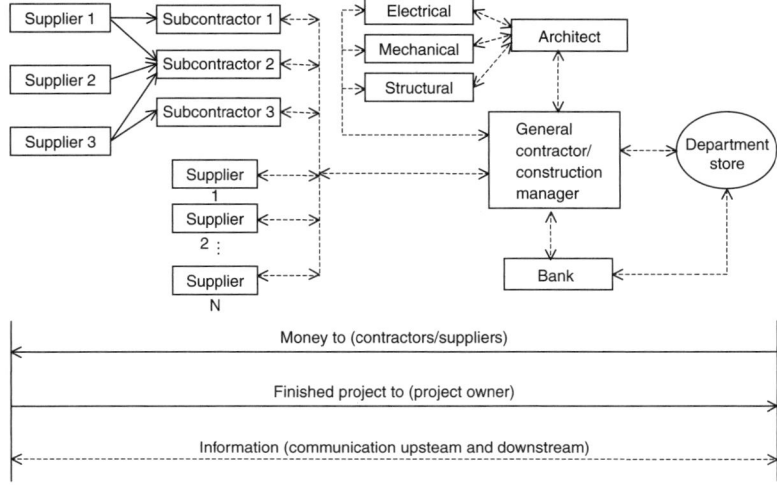

FIGURE 8.3 Private and public sector vertical construction supply chain model.

improvement. Projects are becoming increasingly complex and burdened with extensive governmental regulations. The success of any construction project is inherently affected by the people and work methods. The primary players in this model are the project owner, the construction manager, the design engineer, the subcontractor, the suppliers (materials and equipment), and the funding sources.

The Project Owner (Tier 1 in the Construction Supply Chain)
Responsibilities of the project owner:

1. Determines what is to be constructed and the location. The project owners in this market sector must either be knowledgeable and have civil and design engineers on staff or hire professional expertise, such as a construction manager at risk. The extent of the project owner's in-house capabilities must be considered when selecting a construction manager or general contractor. See an example of a construction management contract in App. E.
2. Establishes the date the project must be completed.
3. Quality and the reliability of project construction milestones.
4. Determines the preliminary scope of work.
5. Establishes a preliminary budget for the project.
6. Establishes the strategy for selecting the architect or construction manager. The architect or construction manager must be experienced, have a capable organization as well as individual resumes, have specialized experience on similar projects,

have technology and other systems for project implementation, and be strong financially.
7. Screens architect and construction manager for the design phase of the project.
8. Recommends short-listed architects and construction managers.
9. Schedules selected architect and construction manager presentations.
10. Selects architect and construction manager.
11. Awards contracts to architect and construction manager.
12. Negotiates with successful architect and construction manager.
13. Conducts project kick-off meeting with architect and construction manager.
14. Ensures compliance with local government permits, insurance, performance bonds, and other requirements are in place prior to beginning the project.
15. Establishes disadvantaged business enterprise (DBE), minority business enterprise (MBE), and women business enterprise (WBE) participation goals if required.
16. Decides on the bid package strategy with the assistance of architect and construction manager.

The Construction Manager (Tier 2 in the Construction Supply Chain)
Selecting a professional construction manager is similar to selecting an architect. The effective construction management organization must have the personnel, capabilities, systems, and experience to complete high-quality projects on-time and under budget. The construction manager should have experience both as prime contractor and as a construction manager on projects of similar size and type. This requirement of specialized experience on similar projects includes knowledge of up-to-date work methods and inspection expertise, the supply chain concept in the vertical sector. Lean construction methodologies coupled with state-of-the-art technology are management systems that the construction manager should implement for the most efficient project planning and control functions.

The construction manager's ability to work with the architect and interpret the design objectives is fundamental to implementing the supply chain concept in the vertical sector. The construction manager's knowledge of the project requirements and owner's ultimate usage of the project should include a keen understanding of the project risks and the local construction labor market. Finally, the construction manager should itself be financially strong and have references that demonstrate honesty and prudent financial management and controls.

Responsibilities of the construction manager:

1. The construction manager works with the architect to complete the plans and specifications.
2. Conducts intensive site visit, which includes evaluating conditions and accessibility. The construction manager takes photographs of the site and makes a list of questions. The construction manager's intent is to identify any concerns early that may cause problems later during construction.
3. In some cases depending on whether the construction manager is operating as an agency entity or is at risk, after completing the design phase, the construction manager assists the project owner in selecting a qualified prime contractor.
4. Performs a precise analysis of general requirements, specifications, and plans. Must also assess the quality of the specifications and drawings.
5. Assists in bid package development. Assist project owner in selecting relevant (subcontractors and suppliers) project team. Set DBE/MBE/WBE participation goals for each package.
6. Solicits bids from subcontractors and equipment and material suppliers.
7. Manages public involvement.
8. Designs quality compliance and oversight.
9. Coordinates environmental responses.
10. Coordinates right of way plan (if applicable).
11. Coordinates utilities.
12. Performs related construction management activities.
13. Implements safety program.

The Subcontractor (Tier 3 in the Construction Supply Chain)
Since subcontracting is used extensively within this construction supply chain model, it is important to prequalify the bidders' list. The supply manager must collect information using a data collection instrument similar to the data collection form shown in Fig. 5.4, Chap. 5. Also see the shop drawings process and sample subcontractor's bid package shown in Chap. 5.

The Construction Material Supplier (Tier 3 in the Construction Supply Chain)
The materials purchasing function is consistent with the public and private sector heavy construction supply chain model discussed earlier in this chapter.

Supply Chain Document Flows

The document flows between supply chain entities include the agreement between the project owner and architect and the agreement between the project owner and construction manager at risk. There are also contracts between the construction manager at risk and the subcontractors and material suppliers. Throughout the course of the project, the document flow may include change orders authorized by the construction manager at risk. In addition to the formal legal arrangements, the project owner may require bid, performance, and payment bonds from all entities in the supply chain. The proofs of comprehensive general liability insurance, worker's compensation, and other insurance coverages are typically submitted by all supply chain members to the construction manager at risk. There is a trend to have downstream supply chain entities name the project owner and the construction manager at risk contractor as an additional insured on their policies. In the event of payment disputes, lien filings can become a part of the document flow with unpaid downstream supply chain entities filing against the project property.

Supply Chain Coordination and Information Flows

For high-profile projects, such as sports arenas and convention centers, there are frequently dedicated websites with information on how and when to bid. Bid packages may be advertised in the newspaper, and also advertised, produced, and sold by independent local reprographics firms. The contractor subscription services and reprographics firms may publish plan holders' lists so that the construction community has information on who is bidding what projects. In the vertical sector, pre-bid meetings may be held to disseminate information and answer questions about the project. The bids in this sector can be submitted electronically for more sophisticated project owners, or manually with immediate dissemination of the identity of the low responsive bidder. During the course of construction on some projects, partnering meetings are held with all supply chain members represented. There are often work site postings, including billboard size announcements that credit major supply chain entities for their performance. However, there are so many different trades represented on a large vertical project, that the coordination of information can be a challenge absent the implementation of supply chain philosophies.

Supply Chain Money Flows

The vertical construction market is the most vulnerable to bankruptcy because of the many private owners. The project owner obtains financing from commercial banks, insurance company investment divisions, and other financial institutions, and then makes periodic draws to pay the project invoices. Some high-profile private projects, hotels, and the like are subsidized with government dollars which can mean a more reliable cash flow. Inspection is performed by the construction manager. Payment can be slow especially for downstream entities when there are disputes upstream.

Implementation of Construction Supply Chain Management

Before firms align based on capabilities and interest in a supply chain configuration, they must first excel as individual firms in their internal and external operations. Each perspective supply chain member should perform a focus analysis. A focus analysis consists of thought provoking questions that challenge the construction supply chain member to consider all aspects of their businesses. The purpose of performing a focus analysis is to investigate the following questions: Is the "how to make money" in my business and industry changing? Who is winning profitable projects in my work category; who is not winning profitable projects and why? An example focus analysis checklist is given in Table 8.1.

Profit and Growth
1. How are profitable projects defined?
• The top 20% of the profit generation
2. How is profitability for your company measured?
• Quality of revenue streams
3. What proportion of the business development expenditures and incentives are directed toward bidding on profitable projects?
• Bidding on profitable projects is important
4. What percentage of profitable projects does your company win?
• What percentage of the profitable projects does your primary competitor win?
Customer (project owner) Satisfaction
5. Are customer satisfaction data collected?
6. How is information concerning/customer satisfaction used to solve customer problems?
Employee Productivity
7. How do you measure employee/subcontractor productivity?

TABLE 8.1 Construction Company Focus Analysis Example

Employee Loyalty
8. How do you create employee/subcontractor loyalty?
9. Has your company made an effort to determine the right level of worker retention?
Employee Satisfaction
10. Is employee satisfaction measured in ways that can be linked to similar measures of customer satisfaction with sufficient frequency and consistency to establish trends?
11. How are new employees hired? How are current employees dismissed?
12. To what extent are measures of customer satisfaction, customer loyalty, or the quality used in recognizing and rewarding employees/subcontractors.
Internal Service Quality
13. Do employees know who their customers are?
14. Are employees satisfied with the technological, training, and personal support they receive on the job?
Leadership
15. To what extent is your company's leadership?
• Energetic, creative versus conservative
• Participatory versus removed
• Listening and teaching versus supervising and managing
• Motivating by mission versus. motivating by fear
• Leading by personality versus company policies

TABLE 8.1 Construction Company Focus Analysis Example (*Continued*)

Conclusion

Horizontal and vertical infrastructure construction projects are increasing at an impressive rate. Two construction supply chain models encompass the variety of specific project types discussed in Chap. 1. Horizontal projects are usually publicly funded and characterized by government agencies in the role of the project owner. In addition to the project owner's own in-house technical capabilities, the supply chain members have substantial engineering expertise. Vertical projects may have public or private funding. Construction managers are a key supply chain entity in the vertical model. Because of private ownership issues there can be vulnerability to bankruptcy in some variations of the vertical model.

Reference

1. American Recovery and Reinvestment Act, H.R. 1—92-94.

APPENDIX A
Joint Venture Agreement

<u>JOINT VENTURE AGREEMENT</u>

This Joint Venture Agreement entered into this ___ day of _____, 200_, by and between (name), whose principal place of business is located (address), (hereinafter _____) and (name), whose principal place of business is located (address), (hereinafter _____)

WITNESSETH:

WHEREAS, the parties hereto desire to jointly prepare and submit certain joint bids for certain construction projects as set forth in paragraph 2 (hereinafter referred to as the "Work"), and if such Joint Venture is the successful bidder for the Work to jointly complete the Work, and

WHEREAS, the parties further represent to each other and to the project owner that each is qualified to perform highway construction in the State of _____ each has the ability to provide its share of finances, personnel, equipment, and supervision to complete the Work in the event the Joint Venture is the successful bidder and to sustain and pay for any losses which may be incurred.

NOW THEREFORE, in consideration of the representations and promises of the parties to each other herein contained, the parties do hereby mutually agree to form a Joint Venture in accordance with the following terms and conditions:

1. <u>Name</u>. The name of the Joint Venture shall be:_____

   If required by (state) Law, an assumed name certificate in such name shall be filed in each County wherein the Joint Venture maintains an office.

2. <u>Business</u>. The Joint Venture is formed for the sole purpose of bidding on, and if the Joint Venture is the successful bidder, pursuing to completion certain construction projects. The

construction projects that fall under this agreement will be jointly agreed to by signing a Pre-bid Joint Venture Agreement for each project (see attached Exhibit "A"). Only projects with jointly signed Pre-Bid Joint Venture Agreement will be covered by this Agreement.

The parties agree to use their best efforts to jointly prepare and submit timely bids for the work, and if contracts are awarded pursuant to such bids, such contracts shall be executed in the name of the Joint Venture. If no agreement is reached by the parties as to the amount of the bid to be submitted or if such agreement is reached by the parties as to the amount of bid to be submitted and a bid is submitted but no contract is awarded to the Joint Venture for the Work, then this Agreement shall automatically terminate as it pertains to that specific project. If no Work is acquired prior to_____the parties hereto shall not be partners for any purpose other than to liquidate, wind up, and account for the affairs of the Joint Venture.

3. <u>Principal Office</u>. The principal office of the Joint Venture shall be at_____

4. <u>Interests of Joint Venturers</u>. The name and ownership interest of each of the joint venturers is as follows:_____

5. <u>Capital Contribution</u>. The initial capital contributions of the joint venturers shall be as follows:

In addition to the initial capital contributions, each joint venturer agrees to make further capital contributions in proportion to the ownership percentages set forth above, as may be necessary to carry out or complete the Work in a timely and satisfactory manner, but no joint venturer shall be required hereunder to contribute additional capital in excess of $5,000.00 without its consent.

No interest shall be paid on capital contributions except to the extent either joint venturer's capital contribution is proportionately greater than the ownership percentage set out above.

6. <u>Depositary</u>. All funds of this Joint Venture shall be deposited in the name of the Joint Venture in an account to be established with_____, and to be used solely for the purposes of this Joint Venture, with all financial records and accounting relating thereto to be maintained separate and apart from other_____records and accounting not related to this Joint Venture.

7. <u>Fiscal Year</u>. The fiscal year of the Joint Venture shall be the same as the calendar year, ending on December 31 of each year.

8. <u>Books and Records</u>. Complete and accurate accounts of all transactions of the Joint Venture shall be kept in proper books of account, and each party shall enter or cause to be entered a full accurate account of all of its transactions on behalf of the partnership.

   (a) The books of account and other records of the partnership shall, at all times, be kept in the office of the Joint Venture partnership, which will be_____

   (b) The partnership books shall be kept on a percentage of completion basis for the calendar year and shall be closed and balanced at the end of each year. An audit shall be made as of the closing date.

   (c) Each partner shall, at all times, have access to the books and records of the Joint Venture and may inspect and copy any of such records.

9. <u>Division of Profits and Losses</u>. Net profits and losses of the Joint Venture shall be determined upon the completion of the Work and upon payment being received from the owner and also immediately following the end of any Joint Venture fiscal year, if the same shall end prior to completion of the Work. Such profits or losses shall be determined in accordance with generally accepted accounting principles consistently applied under methods used for Federal income tax purposes. Such profits or losses shall be allocated between the joint venturers and credited or charged to their capital on the following basis:

10. <u>Property Used By Joint Venture</u>. Each of the joint venturers agrees to make available on lease basis certain machinery, equipment, and personnel to be used in the performance of the Work. Prior to beginning the Work, if the Joint Venture is the successful bidder, the parties shall supplement this Agreement by preparing a list of the machinery, equipment, and personnel to be used to complete the Work. Such supplement shall be filed with and made a part of this Agreement and shall also set forth the agreed lease rental price of all machinery and equipment and compensation to be paid to personnel made available to the Joint Venture by the parties. Any further requirements for equipment rentals, tools, and materials purchased or the hiring of labor shall be done by the Joint Venture in its own name on the basis set out herein.

11. <u>Management of the Joint Venture</u>. _____ shall be designated the Managing Partner of the Joint Venture and shall control the day-to-day operations involved in completing the Work in a timely and satisfactory manner. The Joint Venture partners shall be responsible for and accept financial liability

for that portion of the Work, and all expenses related thereto, which corresponds to the ownership interest and profits and losses interest of each Joint Venture partner set out in Paragraphs 4 and 9 above.

The Managing Partner shall maintain the Joint Venture's books and records, subject to the rights of inspection set forth in Paragraph 8 above, and shall diligently record all transactions affecting the Joint Venture therein. Managing Partner shall supply_____with reports on at least a monthly basis, of all activities and transactions of the Joint Venture, financial and otherwise. The activities of the Joint Venture shall be conducted in accordance with the following:

(a) Managing Partner shall execute and deliver in the name of the Joint Venture such purchase orders, rental agreements, and other agreements for the acquisition of materials, labor, and equipment required by the Joint Venture for completion of the work. However, any expenditure for such purposes in excess of $1,000.00 shall require the approval of both Joint Venture partners;

(b) Neither Joint Venture partner shall receive any salary or fees for services rendered to the Joint Venture, except as set forth on the Supplement to be attached hereto pursuant to paragraph 10;

(c) The Joint Venture partners shall each execute any and all indemnity agreements required by the surety or sureties on any bonds furnished in connection with the award or performance of the Work, and each shall assume and bear its proportionate share (as designated in Paragraph 4 above) of any loss which may result therefrom;

(d) The Joint Venture shall obtain and maintain in force during the term of the Joint Venture the following insurance coverage (with the limits indicated), which coverage shall be paid for by the Joint Venture:

1. Comprehensive General Liability—Combined single limit bodily injury and property damage of one million dollars each occurrence and one million dollars in aggregate;

2. Automobile Liability—Combined single limit bodily injury and property damage of one million dollars per accident;

3. Workmen's Compensation and Employer's Liability ($500,000 limit);

4. Commercial Umbrella Policy—Nine million dollars per occurrence and nine million dollars in the aggregate.

12. Division of Work. _____ and its employees will assist in training personnel to perform the kind of projects awarded. _____will purchase or lease the equipment necessary to perform these projects, buy the materials necessary to perform these projects, and hire the employees necessary to perform these projects, except such employees will be provided by_____to train_____to perform these projects (with_____to reimburse_____for such employees).

13. Acts Requiring Unanimous Consent. Neither of the joint venturers shall do any of the following without the unanimous consent of both Joint Venture partners:

    (a) Use the Joint Venture name or assets in any way, except for the transaction of the legitimate Joint Venture business, nor to do any act in contravention of the Joint Venture Agreement;

    (b) Have any power or authority to do any act prohibited by law to be done by a single joint venturer, unless authorized specifically herein;

    (c) Release or discharge any indebtedness owed the Joint Venture in excess of $1,000.00 for less than the full amount thereof without the express consent of the other Joint Venturer;

    (d) Impart to any other person, any information concerning the financial statements or operations of Joint Venture, except as may be necessary to carry on the business of the Joint Venture, or to disclose the financial condition of a partner;

    (e) Assign, transfer, encumber, pledge, or dispose of all or any part of its Joint Venture interest or withdraw or retire from the Joint Venture, except as specifically authorized herein;

    (f) Make, execute and deliver any assignment for the benefit of creditors, or any bond, confession of judgment, chattel, mortgage, guarantee, indemnity bond, surety bond, or contract of sale of, any of its personal property;

    (g) Hire, lease, purchase, sell, or mortgage any real estate or any interest or enter into any contract for any such purpose;

    (h) Borrow or loan money or make, execute, deliver, accept, or endorse, except for deposit and collection, any commercial paper, or except for the ordinary purposes of the Joint Venture, use or employ the credit, money, or other property of the Joint Venture;

Any partner who shall violate any of the terms, provisions, and conditions of this agreement shall, in addition to being subjected to other remedies, liabilities, and obligations that may be imposed upon, and save harmless the other partner from any and all claims, demands, and actions that may arise out of, or by reason of, such a violation of any of these terms, provisions and conditions.

14. Dissolution of Joint Venture. The Joint Venture shall be dissolved upon the occurrence of any one of the following events:

    (a) Completion of the Work and the complete acceptance and payment;

    (b) In the event of the bankruptcy, insolvency, or the appointment of a receiver for the assets of any joint venturer not dissolved within sixty (60) days;

    (c) Failure of either joint venturer to perform its designated portion of the Work in a manner satisfactory to the owner and in keeping with good construction practices in a timely manner;

    (d) In the case of any dissolution pursuant to subsections (b) and (c), the joint venturer not causing the dissolution shall have the right to substitute another contractor for the joint venturer causing the dissolution in order to complete the Work;

    (e) The failure of the joint venturers to agree upon and submit a bid for the Work or the failure of the Joint Venture to be awarded a contract or contracts for the Work.

15. Distribution of Purchase Equipment. Upon completion of the Work, the Managing Partner will secure a bona fide bid for each item or group of items of equipment purchased by or for the Joint Venture, from one or more reputable dealers, and each of the partners shall have the right to purchase any item or group of items, at the highest prices bid therefor by such dealers, but no partner without the prior written consent of the other partner shall be entitled to purchase a greater percent of such equipment than the percentage of its interest in the Joint Venture. All equipment not so disposed of shall be sold by the Managing Partner for the best price obtainable to outsiders.

16. Liquidation of the Joint Venture. Upon completion, acceptance of the Work, and payment therefor, (in addition to the monthly reports prepared by the Managing Partner) a

full, true, and accurate account shall be made in writing of all of the assets and liabilities of the Joint Venture and of all of its receipts and disbursements, and the interest of each partner in the capital and other assets of the partnership and in the net profits or losses, shall be ascertained and the amount of net profits earned, or the amount of net loss sustained, shall be respectively credited or debited on the books of account of the partnership to the respective partners.

Thereupon, liquidation shall proceed as follows:

(a) To the payment of liabilities of creditors including joint venturers and to the expenses of liquidation.

(b) To the setting up of any reserves which the joint venturers determine reasonably necessary for the contingent liabilities of the Joint Venture or any joint venturer arising out of or in connection with a Joint Venture liability;

(c) To the joint venturers in an amount equal to their respective capital accounts, excluding any account with a negative balance, or if the amount available for such payment be insufficient, then pro-rata on account thereof; and

(d) The balance of the payment in full satisfaction of the Joint Venture interests of all joint venturers in proportion to their respective percentage shares, adjusted as provided in the succeeding provisions of this paragraph. To such balance shall be added the aggregate amount of the negative capital accounts of the joint venturers. This balance shall be distributed in accordance with the joint venturers' respective percentage shares reduced for each by the amount, if any, of this negative capital amount.

17. Miscellaneous.

    (a) Notice. All notices under the Agreement shall be in writing and shall be effectively given to any joint venturer if delivered to any joint venturer, or if mailed by United States Certified Mail, return receipt requested, to such joint venturer at the address furnished by her to the Joint Venture, and to the Joint Venture if mailed in such manner to its principal office.

    (b) Construction. This Agreement shall be construed in accordance with the laws of the State of (name of state).

18. Effective Date. This Joint Venture Agreement shall become effective upon execution by the named joint venturers.

19. <u>Prior Agreements</u>. This Agreement constitutes the entire agreement of the parties relating to the Work and shall supersede and render void all prior agreements, letters or memoranda, including but not limited to the Pre-Bid Joint Venture Agreements dated between_____ and _____

ATTEST: COMPANY A _____

_____   _____

STATE OF _____)
)SS:
COUNTY OF _____)

Before me, a Notary Public in and said County and State, personally appeared   , and who, being first duly sworn did execute the foregoing Joint Venture Agreement on behalf of said corporation.

_____
                                              Notary Public
            Printed _____

My Commission Expires: County of Residence:

_____   _____

ATTEST: COMPANY B _____

_____ _____

STATE OF _____)
) SS:
COUNTY OF _____)

Before me, a Notary Public in and said County and State, personally appeared   , and who, being first duly sworn did execute the foregoing Joint Venture Agreement on behalf of said corporation.

_____
                          Notary Public
Printed _____

My Commission Expires: County of Residence:

_____   _____

Exhibit A

Pre-Bid Joint Venture Agreement

Pursuant to paragraph 1 of the master Joint Venture Agreement dated (   ), the parties, (name) and (name) hereby enter into this pre-bid Joint Venture on this date (   ) for the purpose of preparing and submitting a competitive bid in the name of the Joint Venture to perform work as the prime contractor on DOT project RC -2801. The bid date for the project is (date). RC-2801 is an accelerated project on I-98 in (city) to add travel lanes and modify interchanges near the airport expressway south of I-79. This project involves substantial bridge replacement, concrete base-pavement, and heavy grading and requires prequalification types A, C, and D. If the Joint Venture submits a bid for the referenced project, but no contract is awarded, then this pre-bid Joint Venture Agreement is terminated and another pre-bid agreement must be made to bid upon a different project.

ATTEST: COMPANY A _____

_____   _____

STATE OF _____)
) SS:
COUNTY OF _____)

Before me, a Notary Public in and said County and State, personally appeared, and who, being first duly sworn did execute the foregoing Joint Venture Agreement on behalf of said corporation.

_____
            Notary Public

Printed _____

My Commission Expires: County of Residence:

_____   _____

ATTEST: COMPANY B _____

_____   _____

STATE OF _____)
) SS:
COUNTY OF _____)

Before me, a Notary Public in and said County and State, personally appeared_____, and who, being first duly sworn did execute the foregoing Joint Venture Agreement on behalf of said corporation.

_____
            Notary Public

Printed _____

My Commission Expires: County of Residence:

_____   _____

APPENDIX B

Subcontractor's Bid Package and Pre-Bid Invitation

Lane Avenue Parking Garage &
Student Academic Services
Building
OSU Project Numbers
#315-2005-992-1 & #315-2005-992-2
EDGE Compliance

PRE-BID INVITATION

Pre-Bid Date:	February 7, 2010	
Pre-Bid Time:	Parking Garage, Phase 2a	10:00 a.m. – 11:00 a.m. (approx.)
	Student Academic Svcs. Bldg.	01:00 p.m. – 02:00 p.m. (approx.)
	Parking Garage, Phase 2b	03:00 p.m. – 04:00 p.m. (approx.)
Architect:	Acock Associates Architects	
Pre-Bid Address:	Fawcett Center – Clinton Room	
	2400 Olentangy River Road	
	Columbus, OH 43210	
	Phone: 614/292-1342	Fax: 614/292-3072
Prevailing Wage:	Yes	
Tax Exempt:	TBD	

A complete description of all pertinent information for each phase is attached (15 pages to follow); information including each trade's Estimated Contract Value, where Contract Documents can be obtained, actual Bid dates, and the EDGE Program.

The intent of the EDGE program is to reach or surpass the overall goals and community outreach objectives for these projects and is an integral

Appendix B

part of the Miles-McClellan Equal Employment Opportunity and Business Utilization Policies.

The inclusion of Minority, Female and Disadvantage Business "fair share" participation of the construction projects under the management of Miles-McClellan is an ongoing corporate policy. It is based on our concern for their development to enable them to competitively participate in the construction industry mainstream.

Prime contractors bidding on work are expected to make a results-oriented effort to utilize EDGE compliant/eligible subcontractors in accordance with the established goals assigned to the program. Larger contractors are encouraged to subcontract out portions of work to an EDGE participant (that may be smaller in size). Smaller contractors are encouraged to seek out larger firms to inform them of services you offer to determine how budgets can be met without compromising time, costs, and quality. In efforts to increase EDGE Compliance and to assist in this effort do not hesitate to call.

Project Notes:

Contact Ernie Lewis @ 614/487-7744 ext. 2327 or Matthew Recchiuti @ ext. 2313 for questions.

Please fax back to 614/487-7747 with your company information and intent.

Contractor: _____.
Contact: _____.
Email: _____.
Will you be attending the Pre-Bid?
Yes _____ No _____ Maybe _____

Document 00 10 00—Solicitation   **OhioDAS**
Ohio Department of Administrative   www.ohio.gov/sao
   Services   e: StateArchOff@das.state.oh.us
General Services Division   v: 614.466.4761 • f: 614.644.7982
State Architect's Office • 4200 Surface Road
   • Columbus, Ohio 43228-1395

Sealed bids will be received on behalf of the Board of Trustees of Ohio State University, Business and Finance, at:

   Facilities Operations and Development
   4th Floor Central Classroom Building
   2009 Millikin Road
   Columbus, Ohio 43210

Subcontractor's Bid Package and Pre-Bid Invitation   175

for the following Project:

Project No. 315-2005-992-1
Lane Ave. Parking Garage – Phase 2b
The Ohio State University, Facilities Operations and Development
Columbus, Franklin

in accordance with the Contract Documents prepared by:

Acock Associates Architects
383 North Front Street
Columbus, Ohio 43215
Phone: 614-228-1586
Fax: 614-228-2780
Pete Confar, AIA LEED AP
pconfar@acock.com

The Construction Manager is:

Ruscilli/Miles-McClellan
2041 Arlingate Lane
Columbus, Ohio 43228
Phone: 614-876-9484
Fax: 614-921-1183
Adam Drexel
adrexel@ruscilli.com

Bidders may submit requests for consideration of a proposed Substitution for a specified product, equipment, or service to the Associate no later than 10 days prior to the bid opening. Additional products, equipment, and services may be accepted as approved Substitutions only by written Addendum.

From time to time, the State Architect's Office issues new editions of the "State of Ohio Standard Requirements for Public Facility Construction" and may issue interim changes. Bidders must submit Bids that comply with the version of the Standard Requirements included in the Contract Documents.

Prevailing Wage rates and Equal Employment Opportunity requirements are applicable to this Project.

This Project is subject to the State of Ohio's Encouraging Diversity, Growth, and Equity ("EDGE") Business Development Program. A Bidder is required to submit with its Bid and with its Bidder's Qualifications form, certain information about the certified EDGE Business Enterprise(s) participating on the Project with the Bidder. Refer to subparagraph 6.1.12 of the Instructions to Bidders.

The EDGE Participation Goal for the Project is 5.0 percent.

Appendix B

The percentage is determined by the contracted value of goods, services, materials, and labor that are provided by EDGE-certified business(es). The participation is calculated on the total amount of each awarded contract. For more information about EDGE, contact the State of Ohio EDGE Certification Office at www.EDGE.ohio.gov, or at its physical location: 30 E. Broad St., 18th Floor, Columbus, Ohio 43215-3414; or by telephone at (614) 466-8380.

DOMESTIC STEEL USE REQUIREMENTS AS SPECIFIED IN OHIO REVISED CODE SECTION 153.011 APPLY TO THIS PROJECT. COPIES OF OHIO REVISED CODE SECTION 153.011 CAN BE OBTAINED FROM ANY OF THE OFFICES OF THE OHIO DEPARTMENT OF ADMINISTRATIVE SERVICES.

Bidders are required to be enrolled in and to be in good standing in a Drug-Free Workplace Program ("DFWP") approved by the Ohio Bureau of Workers' Compensation ("OBWC") prior to submitting a Bid and are required to provide, on the Bid Form with its Bid, certain information relative to their enrollment in such a program; and, if awarded a Contract, shall comply with other DFWP criteria described in General Conditions Paragraph 1.10—Drug Free Workplace Program Participation.

Bidders entering into a contract greater than $2,000,000 are required to submit their bid information into escrow. Refer to subparagraph 6.1.10 of the Instructions to Bidders.

Separate bids will be received for:

Trade	**Estimate**
Sitework—Bid Package 102	**$2,950,836**
Alternate #5	($100,100)
Alternate #8	$135,000
Landscaping—Bid Package 103	**$519,961**
Alternate #5	($75,100)
Structural Concrete—Bid Package 104	**$14,685,625**
Alternate #1	$84,000
Alternate #3	$18,000
Alternate #7	$2,250,000
General Trades—Bid Package 105	**$1,207,889**
Alternate #1	$210,000
Alternate #2	$15,000
Alternate #4	$15,000
Alternate #6	$6,000

Subcontractor's Bid Package and Pre-Bid Invitation

Trade	Estimate
Misc. Metals—Bid Package 106	**$2,656,548**
Alternate #1	$2,500
Alternate #3	$490,000
Fire Protection—Bid Package 107	**$145,070**
Plumbing—Bid Package 8	**$187,724**
Alternate #1	$2,500
HVAC—Bid Package 109	**$265,649**
Alternate #1	$25,000
Electrical—Bid Package 110	**$1,112,144**
Alternate #1	$15,000

until **February 26, 2010 at 1:00 p.m.**, when all Bids will be opened and read aloud.

All Bidders are strongly encouraged to attend the Pre-Bid Meeting on **February 7, 2010, at 10:00 a.m.** until approximately 11:00 a.m., at the following location:

> Fawcett Center—Clinton Room
> 2400 Olentangy River Rd.
> Columbus, Ohio 43210
> Phone: 614-292-1342 | Fax: 614-292-3072

The Contract Documents are available for purchase from Atlas Blueprint & Supply Co., Inc., at 372 West Spring Street Columbus, Ohio 43215, Phone: 614-224-5149, Fax: 614-224-2583, www.atlasblueprint.com at the non-refundable cost of approximately $200 per set, plus shipping, if requested.

The Contract Documents may be reviewed for bidding purposes without charge during business hours at the office of the Associate, Ruscilli Construction Co., Inc., and the following locations:

Allied Construction Industries
3 Kovach Drive
Cincinnati, Ohio 45215
Phone: (513) 221-8020
Fax: (513) 221-8023
Contact: Dan Wright [PDF]
E-mail: dwright@aci-construction.org
Web site: www.aci-construction.org

BB-Bid Plan Room
Contractor's Register
800 East Main Street
Jefferson Valley, NY 10535
Phone: (800) 431-2584 ext: 3618
Fax: (866) 790-8024
Contact: Gabriel Rivera [PDF]
E-mail: plans@thebluebook.com
Web site: www.thebluebook.com

Appendix B

Builder's Exchange of East Central Ohio
2521 34th Street, N.E.
Canton, Ohio 44705
Phone: (330) 452-8039 Ext 203
Fax: (330) 452-4323
Contact: Chris Zimmerman [PDF]
E-mail: czimmerman@bxofeco.com
Web site: www.bxofeco.com

Cincinnati Builders Exchange
4350 Glendale-Milford, Suite 120
Blue Ash, Ohio 45252
Phone: (513) 3769-4800
Fax: (513) 769-7888
Contact: Ashley Mazurek [None]
E-mail: amazurek@bxohio.com
Web site: www.bxohio.com

Dayton Builder's Exchange
2077 Embury Park Road
Dayton, Ohio 45414
Phone: (937) 278-5723
Fax: (937) 278-3843
Contact: John Grandetti [None]
E-mail: jgrandetti@bxcleve.com
Web site: www.bxohio.com

Reed Construction Data
30 Technology Parkway South – Suite 500
Norcross, Georgia 30092
Phone: (877) 891-0601
Fax: (800) 508-5370
Contact: Jen Gallam [PDF]
E-mail: rcdcentralnews@reedbusiness.com
Web site: www.reedconstructiondata.com

The Builder's Exchange
9555 Rockside Rd., Suite 300
Valley View, Ohio 44125
Phone: (216) 393-6300 /
(866) 907-6300
Fax: (216) 393-6304 / (866) 907-6304
Contact: Lori Romaro [PDF]
E-mail: lromano@bxohio.com
Web site: www.bxcleve.com

Builder's Exchange of East Central Ohio
495 Wolf Ledges Parkway
Akron, Ohio 44311
Phone: (330) 434-5165 Ext 12
Fax: (330) 434-6088
Contact: Bridget Foreman [PDF]
E-mail: bforeman@bxofeco.com
Web site: www.bxofeco.com

Construction News Corporation
7261 Engle Road – Suite 304
Middleburg Heights, Ohio 44130
Phone: (800) 969-4700 / (440) 826-4700
Fax: (800) 229-4626
Contact: Ted Blaicher [PDF]
E-mail: aab3@cncnewsonline.com
Web site: www.cncnewsonline.com

McGraw-Hill Construction/Dodge at the Builder's Exchange of Central Ohio
1175 Dublin Road
Columbus, Ohio 43215
Phone: (614) 486-6575
Fax: (614) 486-0544
Contact: Reid DeCoursey [PDF]
E-mail: Dodge_ReocMW@mcgraw-hill.com
Web site: www.dodge.construction.com

Subcontractors Association of Northeast Ohio
76 East North St.
Akron, Ohio 44304
Phone: (330) 762-9951
Fax: (330) 762-9960
Contact: Matt Smith [PDF]
E-mail: matt@saneo.Com
Web site: www.saneo.com

Toledo Builder's Exchange
5555 Airport Highway
Suite 140
Toledo, Ohio 43615
Phone: (419) 865-3833
Fax: (419) 865-8014
Contact: Sarah Skiver [None]
E-mail: sskiver@bxohio.com
Web site: www.bxohio.com

Ohio PTAC at Athens
Ohio University's Voinovich Center for Leadership and Public Affairs
143 Technology & Enterprise Bldg
Athens, Ohio 45701
Phone: (740) 597-1868
Fax: (740) 593-1795
Contact: Sharon Hopkins [Paper]
E-mail: hopkins1@ohio.edu
Web site: ohio.edu/ptac

University of Toledo Capacity Building and Construction
2225 Nebraska Avenue
Toledo, Ohio 43606
Phone: (419) 530-3120
Fax: (419) 530-6228
Contact: Brenda Jackson-Cross [PDF]
E-Mail: brendajacksoncross@utoledo.edu
Web site: www.utoledo.edu

Cincinnati MCBAP
Cincinnati B.D.S., Inc.
3 Kovach Drive
Cincinnati, Ohio 45215
Phone: (513) 631-7666
Fax: (513) 631-7613
Contact: Onnie Martin [PDF]
E-mail: omartin@mcbap.biz
Web site: www.mcbap.biz

Columbus MCBAP
Central Ohio Minority Business Association
1393 E. Broad Street, Floor 2
Columbus, Ohio 43205
Phone: (614) 252-8005 Ext 101
Fax: (614) 258-9667
Contact: Rhonda Barber [Paper & PDF]
E-mail: rbarber@comba.com
Web site: www.comba.com

Ohio PTAC at Cleveland
Lake Erie College Campus
391 West Washington Street
Painesville, Ohio 44077
Phone: (440) 357-2294
Fax: (440) 357-2296
Contact: Jane Stewart [PDF]
E-mail: jstewart@Lcedc.org
Web site: www.Lcedc.org/ptac/ptac.htm

Akron Community Service Center and Urban League
Minority Business Development Center
440 Vernon Odom Boulevard
Akron, Ohio 44307
Phone: (330) 434-3101
Fax: (330) 434-7339
Contact: Triva Manley [PDF]
E-mail: aultmanley@aol.com
Web site: www.Akronul.org

Cleveland MCBAP
Myers University
3921 Chester Avenue
Cleveland, Ohio 44114
Phone: (216) 432-9025
Fax: (216) 432-9027
Contact: Michelle Spain [PDF]
E-mail: csbaemcap@ao1.com
Web site: www.clevelandmcbap.biz

Dayton MCBAP
City of Dayton MCBAP
201 Riverside Drive, Suite 1E
Dayton, Ohio 45405-4956
Phone: (937) 223-2164
Fax: (937) 223-8495
Contact: Goodie Gillespie [PDF]
E-mail: mcbaphrc@dayton.net
Web site: www.daytonmcbap.com

Appendix B

Portsmouth MCBAP
Portsmouth Inner City Development Corp.
1206 Waller Street, Box 847
Portsmouth, Ohio 45662
Phone: (740) 354-6626
Fax: (740) 353-2695
Contact: Maxine Malone [PDF]
E-mail: pidc@zoomnet.com
Web site: www.pidcovmba.org

Youngstown MCBAP
Youngstown Area Development Corp.
2133 Belmont Avenue
Youngstown, Ohio 44504
Phone: (330) 746-5681
Fax: (330) 746-4332
Contact: William Carter [Paper]
E-mail: YADC@sbcglobal.net
Web site: www.Youngstown-mcbap.org

The Ohio State University
Facilities Operations and Development
4th Floor Central Classroom Building
2009 Millikin Road
Columbus, Ohio 43210

Document 00 10 00—Solicitation **OhioDAS**
Ohio Department of Administrative Services www.ohio.gov/sao
General Services Division e: StateArchOff@das.state.oh.us
State Architect's Office • 4200 Surface Road v: 614.466.4761 • f: 614.644.7982
• Columbus, Ohio 43228-1395

Sealed bids will be received by:

> Facilities Operations and Development
> 4th Floor Central Classroom Building
> 2009 Millikin Road
> Columbus, Ohio 43210

for the following Project:

> Project No. 315-2005-992-2
> Lane Ave. Parking Garage – Phase 2a
> The Ohio State University, Facilities Operations and Development
> Columbus, Franklin

in accordance with the Contract Documents prepared by:

> Acock Associates Architects
> 383 North Front Street
> Columbus, Ohio 43215
> Phone: 614-228-1586
> Fax: 614-228-2780
> Pete Confar, AIA LEED AP
> pconfar@acock.com

Subcontractor's Bid Package and Pre-Bid Invitation

The Construction Manager is:

Ruscilli/Miles-McClellan
2041 Arlingate Lane
Columbus, Ohio 43228
Phone: 614-876-9484
Fax: 614-921-1183
Adam Drexel
adrexel@ruscilli.com

Bidders may submit requests for consideration of a proposed Substitution for a specified product, equipment, or service to the Architect/Engineer ("A/E") no later than 10 days prior to the bid opening. Additional products, equipment, and services may be accepted as approved Substitutions only by written Addendum.

From time to time, the State Architect's Office issues new editions of the "State of Ohio Standard Requirements for Public Facility Construction" and may issue interim changes. Bidders must submit Bids that comply with the version of the Standard Requirements included in the Contract Documents.

Prevailing Wage rates and Equal Employment Opportunity requirements are applicable to this Project.

This Project is subject to the State of Ohio's Encouraging Diversity, Growth, and Equity ("EDGE") Business Development Program. A Bidder is required to submit with its Bid and with its Bidder's Qualifications form, certain information about the certified EDGE Business Enterprise(s) participating on the Project with the Bidder. Refer to subparagraph 6.1.1.12 of the Instructions to Bidders.

The EDGE Participation Goal for the Project is 5.0 percent.

The percentage is determined by the contracted value of goods, services, materials, and labor that are provided by certified EDGE business(es). The participation is calculated on the total amount of each awarded contract. For more information about EDGE, contact the State of Ohio EDGE Certification Office at www.EDGE.ohio.gov, or at its physical location: 30 E. Broad St., 18th Floor, Columbus, Ohio 43215-3414; or by telephone at (614) 466-8380.

DOMESTIC STEEL USE REQUIREMENTS AS SPECIFIED IN OHIO REVISED CODE SECTION 153.011 APPLY TO THIS PROJECT. COPIES OF OHIO REVISED CODE SECTION 153.011 CAN BE OBTAINED FROM ANY OF THE OFFICES OF THE OHIO DEPARTMENT OF ADMINISTRATIVE SERVICES.

Bidders are required to be enrolled in and to be in good standing in a Drug-Free Workplace Program ("DFWP") approved by the Ohio Bureau of Workers' Compensation ("OBWC") prior to submitting a Bid and are required to provide, on the Bid Form with their bid, certain information relative to their enrollment in such a program; and, if awarded a Contract, shall comply with other DFWP criteria described in General Conditions Paragraph 1.10–Drug-Free Workplace Program Participation.

Bidders entering into a contract greater than $2,000,000 are required to submit their bid information into escrow. Refer to subparagraph 6.1.10 of the Instructions to Bidders.

Separate bids will be received for:

<u>Trade</u>	<u>Estimate</u>
General Conditions—Bid Package 101	**$547,000**

until **February 26, 2010, at 3:00 p.m.**, when all Bids will be opened and read aloud.

All Bidders are strongly encouraged to attend the Pre-Bid Meeting on **February 7, 2010, at 3:00 p.m.** until approximately 4:00 p.m., at the following location:

Fawcett Center—Clinton Room
2400 Olentangy River Rd.
Columbus, Ohio 43210
Phone: 614-292-1342
Fax: 614-292-3072

The Contract Documents are available for purchase from Atlas Blueprint & Supply Co., Inc., at 372 West Spring Street Columbus, Ohio 43215, Phone: 614-224-5149, Fax: 614-224-2583, www.atlasblueprint.com at the non-refundable cost of approximately $450 per set, plus shipping, if requested.

The contract Documents may be reviewed for bidding purposes without charge during business hours at the office of the Associate, Ruscilli Construction Co., Inc., and the following locations:

Allied Construction Industries
3 Kovach Drive
Cincinnati, Ohio 45215
Phone: (513) 221–8020
Fax: (513) 221-8023
Contact: Dan Wright [PDF]
E-mail: dwright@aci-construction.org
Web site: www.aci-construction.org

BB-Bid Plan Room
Contractor's Register
800 East Main Street
Jefferson Valley, NY 10535
Phone: (800) 431-2584 ext: 3618
Fax: (866) 790-8024
Contact: Gabriel Rivera [PDF]
E-mail: plans@thebluebook.com
Web site: www.thebluebook.com

Subcontractor's Bid Package and Pre-Bid Invitation

Builder's Exchange of East Central Ohio
2521 34th Street, N.E.
Canton, Ohio 44705
Phone: (330) 452-8039 Ext 203
Fax: (330) 452-4323
Contact: Chris Zimmerman [Paper]
E-mail: czimmerman@bxofeco.com
Web site: www.bxofeco.com

Cininnati Builders Exchange
4350 Glendal-Milford, Suite 120
Blue Ash, Ohio 45252.
Phone: (513) 3769-4800
Fax: (513) 769-7888
Contact: Ashley Mazurek [None]
E-mail: amazurek@bxohio.com
Web site: www.bxohio.com

Dayton Builder's Exchange
2077 Embury Park Road
Dayton, Ohio 45414
Phone: (937) 278-5723
Fax: (937) 278-3843
Contact: John Grandetti [None]
E-mail: jgrandetti@bxcleve.com
Web site: www.bxohio.com

Reed Construction Data
30 Technology Parkway South – Suite 500
Norcross, Georgia 30092
Phone: (877) 891-0601
Fax: (800) 508-5370
Contact: Jen Gallam [PDF]
E-mail: redcentralnews@reedbusiness.com
Web site: www.reedconstructiondata.com

The Builder's Exchange
9555 Rockside Rd., Suite 300
Valley View, Ohio 44125
Phone: (216) 393-6300/(866) 907-6300
Fax: (216) 393-6304/(866) 907-6304
Contact: Lori Romano [PDF]
E-mail: lromano@bxohio.com
Web site: www.bxcleve.com

Builder's Exchange of East Central Ohio
495 Wolf Ledges Parkway
Akron, Ohio 44311
Phone: (330) 434-5165 Ext 12
Fax: (330) 434-6088
Contact: Bridget Foreman [Paper]
E-mail: bforeman@bxofeco.com
Web site: www.bxofeco.com

Construction News Corporation
7261 Engle Road – Suite 304
Middleburg Heights, Ohio 44130
Phone: (800) 969-4700 / (440) 826-4700
Fax: (800) 229-4626
Contact: Ted Blaicher [PDF]
E-mail: aab3@cncnewsonline.com
Web site: www.cncnewsonlin.com

McGraw-Hill Construction/Dodge at the Builder's Exchange of Central Ohio
1175 Dublin Road
Columbus, Ohio 43215
Phone: (614) 486-6575
Fax: (614) 486-0544
Contact: Reid DeCoursey [PDF]
E-mail: Dodge_ReocMW@mcgraw-hill.com
Web site: www.dodge.construction.com

Subcontractors Association of Northeast Ohio
76 East North St.
Akron, Ohio 44304
Phone: (330) 762-9951
Fax: (330) 762-9960
Contact: Matt Smith [PDF]
E-mail: matt@saneo.Com
Web site: www.saneo.com

Toledo Builder's Exchange
5555 Airport Highway
Suite 140
Toledo, Ohio 43615
Phone: (419) 865-3833
Fax: (419) 865-8014
Contact: Sarah Skiver [None]
E-mail: sskiver@bxohio.com
Web site: www.bxohio.com

Appendix B

Ohio PTAC at Athens
Ohio University's Voinovich Center for Leadership and Public Affairs
143 Technology & Enterprise Bldg
Athens, Ohio 45701
Phone: (740) 597-1868
Fax: (740) 593-1795
Contact: Sharon Hopkins [Paper]
E-mail: Hopkins1@ohio.edu
Web site: ohio.edu/ptac

University of Toledo Capacity Building and Construction
2225 Nebraska Avenue
Toledo, Ohio 43606
Phone: (419) 530-3120
Fax: (419) 530-6228
Contact: Brenda Jackson-Cross [PDF]
E-Mail: brendajacksoncross@utoledo.edu
Web site: www.utoledo.edu

Cincinnati MCBAP
Cincinnati B.D.S., Inc
7162 Reading Road, Suite 630
Cincinnati, Ohio 45237
Phone: (513) 631-7666
Fax: (513) 631-7613
Contact: Marcus Maddox [PDF]
E-mail: mmaddox@ohiostatewidembdc.org
Web site: www.ohiostatewidembdc.org

Columbus MCBAP
Central Ohio Minority Business Association
1393 E. Broad Street, Floor 2
Columbus, Ohio 43205
Phone: (614) 252-8005
Fax: (614) 258-9667
Contact: Rhonda Barber [Paper & PDF]
E-mail: rbarber@comba.com
Web site: www.comba.com

Northeast Ohio PTAC (NEO – PTAC)
391 West Washington Street
Painesville, Ohio 44077
Phone: (440) 357-2294
Fax: (440) 357-2296
Contact: Grace Laurio [PDF]
E-mail: Glaurio@Lcedc.org
Web site: www.Lcedc.org/ptac.htm

Akron Community Service Center and Urban League
Minority Business Development Center
250 East Market Street
Akron, Ohio 44308
Phone: (330) 434-5052
Fax: (330) 434-7339
Contact: crystal Bell [PDF]
E-mail: aulcbell@aol.com
Web site: www.Akronul.org

Cleveland MCBAP
Myers University
3921 Chester Avenue
Cleveland, Ohio 44114
Phone: (216) 432-9025
Fax: (216) 432-9027
Contact: Michelle Spain [PDF]
E-mail: csbaemcap@aol.com
Web site: www.clevelandmcbap.biz

Dayton MCBAP
City of Dayton MCBAP
201 Riverside Drive, Suite 1E
Dayton, Ohio 45405-4956
Phone: (937) 223-2164
Fax: (937) 223-8495
Contact: Goodie Gillespie [PDF]
E-mail: mcbaphrc@dayton.net
Web site: www.daytonmcbap.com

Subcontractor's Bid Package and Pre-Bid Invitation

Portsmouth MCBAP
Portsmouth Inner City Development Corp.
1206 Waller Street, Box 847
Portsmouth, Ohio 45662
Phone: (740) 354-6626
Fax: (740) 353-2695
Contact: Maxine Malone [PDF]
E-mail: pidc@zoomnet.com
Web site: www.pidcovmba.org

Youngstown MCBAP
Youngstown Area Development Corp.
2133 Belmont Avenue
Youngstown, Ohio 44504
Phone: (330) 746-5681
Fax: (330) 746-4332
Contact: William Carter [Paper]
E-mail: YADC@sbcglobal.net
Web site: www.Youngstown-mcbap.org

The Ohio State University
Facilities Operations and Development
4th Floor Central Classroom Building
2009 Millikin Road
Columbus, Ohio 43210
Phone: (614) 292-4458
Fax: (614) 292-2539
Web site: www.fod.osu.edu

Document 00 10 00—Solicitation
Ohio Department of Administrative
   Services
General Services Division
State Architect's Office • 4200 Surface Road
   • Columbus, Ohio 43228-1395

OhioDAS
www.ohio.gov/sao
e: StateArchOff@das.state.oh.us
v: 614.466.4761 • f: 614.644.7982

Sealed bids will be received by:

   Facilities Operations and Development
   4th Floor Central Classroom Building
   2009 Millikin Road
   Columbus, Ohio 43210

for the following Project:

   Project No. 315-2005-992-2
   Student Academic Services Building (SASB)
   The Ohio State University, Facilities Operations and Development

Columbus, Franklin in accordance with the Contract Documents prepared by:

   Acock Associates Architects
   383 North Front Street
   Columbus, Ohio 43215
   phone: 614-228-1586
   fax: 614-228-2780
   Pete Confar, AIA LEED AP
   pconfar@acock.com

Appendix B

The Construction Manager is:

Ruscilli/Miles-McClellan
2041 Arlingate Lane
Columbus, Ohio 43228
phone: 614-876-9484
fax: 614-921-1183
Adam Drexel
adrexel@ruscilli.com

Bidders may submit requests for consideration of a proposed Substitution for a specified product, equipment, or service to the Architect/Engineer ("A/E") no later than 10 days prior to the bid opening. Additional products, equipment, and services may be accepted as approved Substitutions only by written Addendum.

From time to time, the State Architect's Office issues new editions of the "State of Ohio Standard Requirements for Public Facility Construction" and may issue interim changes. Bidders must submit Bids that comply with the version of the Standard Requirements included in the Contract Documents.

Prevailing Wage rates and Equal Employment Opportunity requirements are applicable to this Project.

This Project is subject to the State of Ohio's Encouraging Diversity, Growth, and Equity ("EDGE") Business Development Program. A Bidder is required to submit with its Bid and with its Bidder's Qualifications form, certain information about the certified EDGE Business Enterprise(s) participating on the Project with the Bidder. Refer to subparagraph 6.1.12 of the Instructions to Bidders.

The EDGE Participation Goal for the Project is 5.0 percent.

The percentage is determined by the contracted value of goods, services, materials, and labor that are provided by EDGE-certified business(es). The participation is calculated on the total amount of each awarded contract. For more information about EDGE, contact the State of Ohio EDGE Certification Office at www.EDGE.ohio.gov, or at its physical location: 30 E. Broad St., 18th Floor, Columbus, Ohio 43215-3414; or by telephone at (614) 466-8380.

DOMESTIC STEEL USE REQUIREMENTS AS SPECIFIED IN OHIO REVISED CODE SECTION 153.011 APPLY TO THIS PROJECT. COPIES OF OHIO REVISED CODE SECTION 153.011 CAN BE OBTAINED FROM ANY OF THE OFFICES OF THE OHIO DEPARTMENT OF ADMINISTRATIVE SERVICES.

Bidders are required to be enrolled in and to be in good standing in a Drug-Free Workplace Program ("DFWP") approved by the Ohio Bureau of Workers' Compensation ("OBWC") prior to submitting a Bid and are required to

Subcontractor's Bid Package and Pre-Bid Invitation

provide, on the Bid Form with its Bid, certain information relative to their enrollment in such a program; and, if awarded a Contract, shall comply with other DFWP criteria described in General Conditions Paragraph 1.10 – Drug Free Workplace Program Participation.

Bidders entering into a contract greater than $2,000,000 are required to submit their bid information into escrow. Refer to subparagraph 6.1.10 of the Instructions to Bidders.

Separate bids will be received for:

Trade	Estimate
Steel – Bid Package 201	**$3,009,825**
Concrete – Bid Package 202	**$501,572**
Masonry – Bid Package 203	**$1,386,875**
Alternate #2	($65,561)
General Trades/Elevators – Bid Package 204	**$2,922,525**
Alternate #7	($160,732)
Alternate #9	($82,114)
Alternate #11	$33,936
Curtainwall – Bid Package 205	**$1,100,455**
Alternate #1	$26,800
Roofing – Bid Package 206	**$398,101**
Drywall/Painting/Ceilings – Bid Package 207	**$1,813,171**
Alternate #2	$21,524
Alternate #3	($2,474)
Alternate #6	($102,897)
Alternate #8	$2,400
Alternate #9	$2,822
Alternate #10	($1,000)
Flooring/Tile – Bid Package 208	**$1,158,170**
Alternate #5	($94,070)
Alternate #8	($105,297)
Alternate #10	$19,828
Fire Protection – Bid Package 209	**$386,253**
Plumbing – Bid Package 210	**$722,109**
HVAC – Bid Package 211	**$3,515,624**
Alternate #4	$25,750
Electrical – Bid Package 212	**$2,606,045**
Technology – Bid Package 213	**$837,400**

until **February 29, 2010, at 1:00 p.m.,** when all Bids will be opened and read aloud.

Appendix B

All Bidders are strongly encouraged to attend the Pre-Bid Meeting on **February 7, 2010, at 1:00 p.m.** until approximately 2:00 p.m., at the following location:

Fawcett Center – Clinton Room
2400 Olentangy River Rd.
Columbus, Ohio 43210
Phone: 614-292-1342 | Fax: 614-292-3072

The Contract Documents are available for purchase from Atlas Blueprint & Supply Co., Inc. at 372 West Spring Street Columbus, Ohio 43215, phone: 614-224-5149 fax: 614-224-2583, www.atlasblueprint.com at the non-refundable cost of approximately $250 per set, plus shipping, if requested.

The contract Documents may be reviewed for bidding purposes without charge during business hours at the office of the Associate, Ruscilli Construction Co., Inc., and the following locations:

Allied Construction Industries
3 Kovach Drive
Cincinnati, Ohio 45215
Phone: (513) 221–3020
Fax: (513) 221-8023
Contact: Dan Wright [PDF]
E-mail: dwright@aci-construction.org
Web site: www.aci-construction.org

BB-Bid Plan Room
Contractor's Register
800 East Main Street
Jefferson Valley, NY 10535
Phone: (800) 431-2584 ext: 3618
Fax: (866) 790-8024
Contact: Gabriel Rivera [PDF]
E-mail: plans@thebluebook.com
Web site: www.thebluebook.com

Builder's Exchange of East Central Ohio
2521 34th Street, N.E.
Canton, Ohio 44705
Phone: (330) 452-8039 Ext 203
Fax: (330) 452-4323
Contact: Chris Zimmerman [PDF]
E-mail: czimmerman@bxofeco.com
Web site: www.bxofeco.com

Builder's Exchange of East Central Ohio
495 Wolf Ledges Parkway
Akron, Ohio 44311
Phone: (330) 434-5165 Ext 12
Fax: (330) 434-6088
Contact: Bridget Foreman [PDF]
E-mail: bforeman@bxofeco.com
Web site: www.bxofeco.com

Cincinnati Builders Exchange
4350 Glendale-Milford, Suite 120
Blue Ash, Ohio 45252.
Phone: (513) 3769-4800
Fax: (513) 769-7888
Contact: Ashley Mazurek [None]
E-mail: amazurek@bxohio.com
Web site: www.bxohio.com

Construction News Corporation
7261 Engle Road – Suite 304
Middleburg Heights, Ohio 44130
Phone: (800) 969-4700/(440) 826-4700
Fax: (800) 229-4626
Contact: Ted Blaicher [PDF]
E-mail: aab3@cncnewsonline.com
Web site: www.cncnewsonline.com

Subcontractor's Bid Package and Pre-Bid Invitation   189

Dayton Builder's Exchange
2077 Embury Park Road
Dayton, Ohio 45414
Phone: (937) 278-5723
Fax: (937) 278-3843
Contact: John Grandetti [None]
E-mail: jgrandetti@bxcleve.com
Web site: www.bxohio.com

Reed Construction Data
30 Technology Parkway South – Suite 500
Norcross, Georgia 30092
Phone: (877) 891-0601
Fax: (800) 508-5370
Contact: Jen Gallam [PDF]
E-mail: redcentralnews@reedbusiness.com
Web site: www.reedconstructiondata.com

The Builder's Exchange
9555 Rockside Rd., Suite 300
Valley View, Ohio 44125
Phone: (216) 393-6300 / (866) 907-6300
Fax: (216) 393-6304 / (866) 907-6304
Contact: Lori Romano [PDF]
E-mail: lromano@bxohio.com
Web site: www.bxcleve.com

Ohio PTAC at Athens
Ohio University's Voinovich Center for
Leadership and Public Affairs
143 Technology & Enterprise Bldg
Athens, Ohio 45701
Phone: (740) 597-1868
Fax: (740) 593-1795
Contact: Sharon Hopkins [Paper]
E-mail: hopkins@ohio.edu
Web site: ohio.edu/ptac

McGraw-Hill Construction / Dodge at the Builder's Exchange of Central Ohio
1175 Dublin Road
Columbus, Ohio 43215
Phone: (614) 486-6575
Fax: (614) 486-0544
Contact: Reid DeCoursey [PDF]
E-mail: Dodge_ReocMW@mcgraw-hill.com
Web site: www.dodge.construction.com

Subcontractors Association of Northeast Ohio
76 East North St.
Akron, Ohio 44304
Phone: (330) 762-9951
Fax: (330) 762-9960
Contact: Matt Smith [PDF]
E-mail: matt@saneo.Com
Website: www.saneo.com

Toledo Builder's Exchange
5555 Airport Highway
Suite 140
Toledo, Ohio 43615
Phone: (419) 865-3833
Fax: (419) 865-8014
Contact: Sarah Skiver [None]
E-mail: sskiver@bxohio.com
Web site: www.bxohio.com

Northeast Ohio PTAC (NEO-PTAC)
391 West Washington Street
Painesville, Ohio 44077
Phone: (440) 357-2294
Fax: (440) 357-2296
Contact: Grace Laurio [PDF]
E-mail: glaurio@Lcedc.dog
Web site: www.Lcedc.org/ptac.htm

Appendix B

University of Toledo Capacity Building and Construction
2225 Nebraska Avenue
Toledo, Ohio 43606
Phone: (419) 530-3120
Fax: (419) 530-6228
Contact: Brenda Jackson-Cross [PDF]
E-Mail: brendajacksoncross@utoledo.edu
Web site: www.utoledo.edu

Cincinnati MCBAP
Cincinnati B.D.S., Inc.
3 Kovach Drive
Cincinnati, Ohio 45215
Phone: (513) 631-7666
Fax: (513) 631-7613
Contact: Onnie Martin [PDF]
E-mail: omartin@mcbap.biz
Web site: www.mcbap.biz

Columbus MCBAP
Central Ohio Minority Business Association
1393 E. Broad Street, Floor 2
Columbus, Ohio 43205
Phone: (614) 252-8005 Ext 101
Fax: (614) 258-9667
Contact: Rhonda Barber [Paper & PDF]
E-mail: rbarber@comba.com
Web site: www.comba.com

Portsmouth MCBAP
Portsmouth Inner City Development Corp.
1206 Waller Street, Box 847
Portsmouth, Ohio 45662
Phone: (740) 354-6626
Fax: (740) 353-2695
Contact: Maxine Malone [PDF]
E-mail: pidc@zoomnet.com
Web site: www.pidcovmba.org

Facilities Operations and Development
4th Floor Central Classroom Building
2009 Millikin Road
Columbus, Ohio 43210
Phone: (614) 292-4458
Fax: (614) 292-2539
Web site: www.fod.osu.edu

Akron Community Service Center and Urban League
Minority Business Development Center
440 Vernon Odom Boulevard
Akron, Ohio 44307
Phone: (330) 434-3101
Fax: (330) 434-7339
Contact: Triva Manley [PDF]
E-mail: aultmanley@aol.com
Web site: www.Akronul.org

Cleveland MCBAP
Myers University
3921 Chester Avenue
Cleveland, Ohio 44114
Phone: (216) 432-9025
Fax: (216) 432-9027
Contact: Michelle Spain [PDF]
E-mail: csbaemcap@aol.com
Web site: www.clevelandmcbap.biz

Dayton MCBAP
City of Dayton MCBAP
201 Riverside Drive, Suite 1E
Dayton, Ohio 45405-4956
Phone: (937) 223-2164
Fax: (937) 223-8495
Contact: Goodie Gillespie [PDF]
E-mail: mcbaphrc@dayton.net
Web site: www.daytonmcbap.com

Youngstown MCBAP
Youngstown Area Development Corp.
2133 Belmont Avenue
Youngstown, Ohio 44504
Phone: (330) 746-5681
Fax: (330) 746-4332
Contact: William Carter [Paper]
E-mail: YADC@sbcglobal.net
Web site: www.Youngstown-mcbap.org

APPENDIX C
CD 300, Standard Form of Tri-Party Agreement for Collaborative Project Delivery*

---

*Materials are reproduced with the express written permission of Consensus DOCS under license No. 0122. These documents are available in electronic form at www.ConsensusDocs.org.

Appendix C

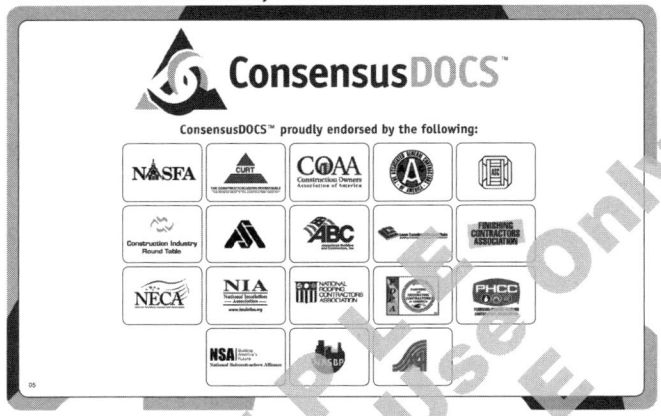

NOT FOR REPRODUCTION
TO ORDER DOCUMENT, VISIT WWW.CONSENSUSDOCS.ORG

CONSENSUSDOCS 300
STANDARD FORM OF TRI-PARTY AGREEMENT FOR COLLABORATIVE PROJECT DELIVERY

This document was developed through a collaborative effort of entities representing a wide cross-section of the construction industry. The organizations endorsing this document believe it represents a fair and reasonable consensus among the collaborating parties of allocation of risk and responsibilities in an effort to appropriately balance the critical interests and concerns of all project participants.

These endorsing organizations recognize and understand that users of this document must review and adapt this document to meet their particular needs, the specific requirements of the project, and applicable laws. Users are encouraged to consult legal, insurance and surety advisors before modifying or completing this document. Further information on this document and the perspectives of endorsing organizations is available in the ConsensusDOCS Guidebook.

TABLE OF ARTICLES

1. AGREEMENT
2. DEFINITIONS
3. COLLABORATIVE PRINCIPLES
4. MANAGEMENT BY THE MANAGEMENT GROUP

IMPORTANT: A vertical line in the margin indicates a change has been made to the original text. Prior to signing, recipients may wish to request from the party producing the document a "redlined" version indicating changes to the original text. Consultation with legal and insurance counsel and careful review of the entire document are strongly encouraged.

ConsensusDOCS 300 • STANDARD FORM OF TRI-PARTY AGREEMENT FOR COLLABORATIVE PROJECT DELIVERY Copyright © 2007, ConsensusDOCS LLC. YOU ARE ALLOWED TO USE THIS DOCUMENT FOR ONE CONTRACT ONLY. YOU MAY MAKE 9 COPIES OF THE COMPLETED DOCUMENT FOR DISTRIBUTION TO THE CONTRACT'S PARTIES. ANY OTHER USES, INCLUDING COPYING THE FORM DOCUMENT, ARE STRICTLY PROHIBITED.

Standard Form of Tri-Party Agreement for Collaborative Project Delivery

NOT FOR REPRODUCTION
TO ORDER DOCUMENT, VISIT WWW.CONSENSUSDOCS.ORG

5. OWNER PROVIDED INFORMATION
6. DEVELOPMENT OF DESIGN AND COLLABORATIVE PRECONSTRUCTION SERVICES
7. PROJECT PLANNING AND SCHEDULE
8. PROJECT BUDGET, COST MODELING AND PROJECT TARGET COST ESTIMATE
9. DESIGNER'S COMPENSATION
10. CONSTRUCTOR'S COMPENSATION
11. INCENTIVES AND RISK SHARING
12. TRADE CONTRACTORS AND SUBCONTRACTORS
13. CONSTRUCTION OPERATIONS
14. DESIGNER'S CONSTRUCTION PHASE SERVICES
15. TIME
16. DESIGNER'S COMPENSATION AND PAYMENT
17. COST OF WORK
18. PAYMENT
19. RIGHT TO AUDIT
20. CHANGES
21. INDEMNITY, INSURANCE AND BONDS
22. SUSPENSION, NOTICE TO CURE AND TERMINATION OF THE AGREEMENT
23. DISPUTE RESOLUTION
24. MISCELLANEOUS
25. CONTRACT DOCUMENTS

This Agreement has important legal and insurance consequences. Consultation(s) with an attorney and with insurance and surety consultants are encouraged with respect to its completion or modification.

ARTICLE 1
AGREEMENT

This Agreement is made this _____ day of _____ in the year _____ by and between the

OWNER (Name and Address)

and the DESIGNER (Name and Address)

Appendix C

and the CONSTRUCTOR (Name and Address)

for the following PROJECT (Address and Brief Project Description)

Notice to the parties shall be given at the above addresses.

ARTICLE 2
DEFINITIONS

2.1 Agreement means this ConsensusDOCS 300 Standard Form of Agreement For Collaborative Project Delivery, as modified by the Parties, and Exhibits and Attachments made part of this Agreement upon its execution.

2.2 A Change Order is a written order approved by the Management Group after execution of this Agreement, indicating changes in the scope of the Work, the PTCE or Contract Time, including substitutions proposed to and accepted by the Management Group.

2.3 Collaborative Project Delivery Team (CPD) shall have the meaning ascribed in Paragraph 3.3.

2.4 The Construction Budget is the Owner's total cost of Project components and construction services. The Construction Budget does not include the Design Budget and other costs that make up the overall Project Target Cost Estimate.

2.5 The Construction Schedule is the document that specifies the dates on which the Constructor plans to begin and complete various parts of the Work, including dates on which information and approvals are required from the Management Group.

2.6 The Contract Documents consist of:

a. Change Orders and written amendments to this Agreement including exhibits and appendices and amendments;

b. this Agreement;

c. the most current documents approved by the Management Group;

d. the information provided by the Owner pursuant to Article 5;

e. the Contract Documents in existence at the time of execution of this Agreement which are set forth in Article 25;

f. the Owner's Program.

Except as specifically provided in this Agreement, in case of any inconsistency, conflict or ambiguity among the Contract Documents, the documents shall govern in the order in which they are listed above. Among all the Contract Documents, the term or provision that is most specific or includes the latest date shall control. Information identified in one Contract Document and not identified in another shall not be considered to be a conflict or inconsistency.

2.7 The Contract Time is the period between the Date of Commencement and Substantial Completion.

2.8 The Constructor is the person or entity identified in Article 1.

2.9 The term Day shall mean calendar day unless otherwise specifically defined.

2.10 The Design Budget is the Owner's total cost for design services required for the completion of the Project.

2.11 Designer means the Architect, Designer or Engineer identified in Article 1 and its consultants and includes the Designer's representative, licensed in the state where the Project is located. The use of the term Designer in this Agreement is for convenience and is not intended to imply or infer that the individual or entity named in Article 1 will provide design professional services in a discipline in which it is not licensed.

2.12 Final Completion occurs on the date when the Constructor's obligations under this Agreement are complete and accepted by the Owner and final payment becomes due and payable. This date shall be confirmed by a Certificate of Final Completion signed by the Owner and the Constructor.

2.13 A Material Supplier is a person or entity retained by the Constructor to provide material or equipment for the Work.

2.14 Others means other contractors, material suppliers and persons at the Worksite who are not employed by the Constructor or Subcontractors.

2.15 Owner is the person or entity identified in Article 1, and includes the Owner's Representative.

2.16 Owner's consultants means those consultants retained by Owner identified by attachment to this Agreement who will assist Owner in carrying out the Project.

2.17 The Owner's Program is an initial description of the Owner's objectives, that may include budget and time criteria, space requirements and relationships, flexibility and expandability requirements, special equipment and systems, and site requirements.

2.18 The Project, as identified in Article 1, is the building, facility or other improvements for which the Owner, Designer and Constructor have agreed to work collaboratively to achieve the design and construction under this Agreement.

2.19 Project Plan means the resource-loaded plan prepared by Designer and Designer's consultants (or any other party as requested by the Management Group) depicting the activities to be accomplished in each phase of the Project and the anticipated labor (and resulting personnel costs), together with anticipated Reimbursable Expenses.

2.20 The Project Schedule is the document that shows the timing and sequencing of the design and construction required to meet the time criteria set forth in the Owner's Program.

2.21 The Project Target Cost Estimate (PTCE) shall have the meaning ascribed in Paragraph 8.3.

2.22 Responsible Designer shall mean the person or entity that has responsibility for preparing the design, including drawings or specifications, for a particular portion of the Work.

2.23 Services means the services provided by the Designer or by consultants retained by the Designer for the Project.

2.24 A Subcontractor is a person or entity retained by the Constructor as an independent contractor to provide the labor, materials, equipment or services necessary to complete a specific portion of the Work. The term Subcontractor shall include Trade Contractors as defined in Paragraph 2.27. The term Subcontractor does not include the Designer or Others.

Appendix C

NOT FOR REPRODUCTION
TO ORDER DOCUMENT, VISIT WWW.CONSENSUSDOCS.ORG

2.25 Substantial Completion of the Work, or of a designated portion, occurs on the date when the Work is sufficiently complete in accordance with the Contract Documents so that the Owner may occupy or utilize the Project, or a designated portion, for the use for which it is intended. The issuance of a certificate of occupancy is not a prerequisite for Substantial Completion if the certificate of occupancy cannot be obtained due to factors beyond the Constructor's control. This date shall be confirmed by a Certificate of Substantial Completion signed by the Owner and Constructor.

2.26 A Sub-subcontractor is a person or entity who has an agreement with a Subcontractor to perform any portion of the Subcontractor's Work.

2.27 A Trade Contractor is a person or entity retained by the Constructor to provide collaboration and services during the Preconstruction Phase of the Project. It is anticipated that a Trade Contractor will continue to serve as a Subcontractor during the Construction Phase provided that the Management Group determines that its performance merits continued participation and accepts its price proposal.

2.28 Work means the construction and services necessary or incidental to fulfill the Constructor's obligations for the Project in conformance with this Agreement and the other Contract Documents. The Work may refer to the whole Project or only a part of the Project if work is also being performed by the Owner or Others.

    2.28.1 Changed Work means work that is different from the original scope of Work; or work that changes the PTCE or Contract Time.

    2.28.2 Defective Work is any portion of the Work that is not in conformance with the Contract Documents.

2.29 Worksite means the geographical area at the location of the Project as identified in Article 1 where the Work is to be performed.

ARTICLE 3
COLLABORATIVE PRINCIPLES

3.1 OBJECTIVES The Project consists of the design, construction and commissioning of the Project as more fully described in Exhibit A to this Agreement. The Project objectives are to design and construct the facilities called for in the Owner's Program, within the Project Target Cost Estimate and the Schedule developed under the Agreement.

3.2 COLLABORATIVE PROJECT DELIVERY The Parties agree that the Project objectives can be best achieved through a relational contract that promotes and facilitates strategic planning, design, construction and commissioning of the project, through the principles of collaboration and lean project delivery. This approach recognizes that each Party's success is tied directly to the success of all other members of the Collaborative Project Team and encourages and requires the Parties to organize and integrate their respective roles, responsibilities and expertise, to identify and align their respective expectations and objectives, to commit to open communications, transparent decision-making, proactive and non-adversarial interaction, problem-solving, the sharing of ideas, to continuously seek to improve the Project planning, design, and construction processes, and to share both the risks and rewards associated with achieving the Project objectives.

3.3 COLLABORATIVE PROJECT DELIVERY TEAM The Parties shall perform as a Collaborative Project Delivery (CPD) Team to facilitate the design, construction and commissioning of the Project. CPD Team members shall share information and collaborate for the benefit of the Project. CPD Team members shall initially include the Owner, the Designer and the Constructor. In forming a Collaborative Project

---

IMPORTANT: A vertical line in the margin indicates a change has been made to the original text. Prior to signing, recipients may wish to request from the party producing the document a "redlined" version indicating changes to the original text. Consultation with legal and insurance counsel and careful review of the entire document are strongly encouraged.

ConsensusDOCS 300 • STANDARD FORM OF TRI-PARTY AGREEMENT FOR COLLABORATIVE PROJECT DELIVERY Copyright © 2007, ConsensusDOCS LLC. YOU ARE ALLOWED TO USE THIS DOCUMENT FOR ONE CONTRACT ONLY. YOU MAY MAKE 9 COPIES OF THE COMPLETED DOCUMENT FOR DISTRIBUTION TO THE CONTRACT'S PARTIES. ANY OTHER USES, INCLUDING COPYING THE FORM DOCUMENT, ARE STRICTLY PROHIBITED.

APPENDIX D

Standard Form of Agreement between Owner and Contractor for Integrated Project Delivery*

AIA® Document A295™–2008 Instructions

General Conditions of the Contract for Integrated Project Delivery

GENERAL INFORMATION

Purpose. Integrated Project Delivery is a project delivery approach that integrates people, systems, business structures, and practices into a process that collaboratively harnesses the talents and insights of all participants to reduce waste and optimize efficiency through all phases of design, fabrication, and construction. AIA Document A295–2008, a general conditions form, provides the terms and conditions under which the Owner, Contractor, and Architect will work together on a Project that utilizes Integrated Project Delivery and is the cornerstone of this delivery model.

A295–2008 integrates the duties and services of the Owner, Architect, and Contractor through each phase of Integrated Project Delivery. A295–2008 describes the services and duties of the Owner, Contractor,

---

*Reproduced with permission of The American Institute of Architects, 1735 New York Avenue, NW, Washington, D.C., 2006.

and Architect in six phases: Conceptualization; Criteria Design; Detailed Design; Implementation Documents; Construction; and Closeout. Throughout the Conceptualization, Criteria Design, and Detailed Design phases, the Architect performs its design services in close collaboration with the Owner and Contractor. The Contractor, during the design phases, provides estimating and other advisory services, such as constructability reviews, to inform the Architect's design. At the conclusion of the Detailed Design Phase, the Owner and Contractor negotiate a Guaranteed Maximum Price and the GMP Documents are identified. The Contractor is thereafter required to construct the Project in accordance with the GMP Documents. Upon establishment of the Guaranteed Maximum Price, A295–2008 provides essential terms for the construction contract, clearly delineating the duties of the Owner, Contractor, and Architect through the Implementation Documents, Construction, and Closeout Phases.

In addition to the unique manner in which A295–2008 describes the Owner, Architect, and Contractor's duties, it also requires the utilization of a building information model to the greatest extent practicable. A building information model is a digital representation of the physical and functional characteristics of the Project. The building information model may consist of a single model or multiple models used in the aggregate. In order to utilize the building information model and any other digital information used on the Project in the most efficient manner, A295–2008 requires the Owner, Architect, and Contractor to meet and delineate the types of software to be used, standards and tolerances required, and the permitted uses for all such digital information. Such determinations are to be set forth in AIA Form E201™–2007, or a similar protocol document, that is incorporated by reference into all agreements for services or construction for the Project.

In order to achieve this highly collaborative process, the terms of A295–2008 are incorporated by reference into the Owner-Architect and Owner-Contractor Agreements. A295–2008 should also be incorporated by reference into any consultant and subcontractor agreements the Architect and Contractor may enter into. The result is that the parties establish a common basis for the primary and secondary relationships of Integrated Project Delivery.

Related Documents. A295–2008 is incorporated by reference into B195™–2008, Standard Form of Agreement between Owner and Architect for Integrated Project Delivery and A195™–2008, Standard Form of Agreement between Owner and Contractor for Integrated Project Delivery. A295–2008 may also be adopted by indirect reference into the Architect-Consultant agreement when the prime Agreement between Owner and Architect adopts A295–2008 and it is in turn adopted into the Architect-Consultant agreement AIA Document C401™–2007. Such incorporation by reference is a valid legal drafting method, and documents so incorporated are generally interpreted as part of the respective contract. Pursuant to Section 9. 19. 3 of A295–2008, the Contractor must require each Subcontractor to be bound to the Contractor by the terms of A295–2008, and to assume toward the Contractor all obligations and responsibilities which the Contractor, under the A295–2008, assumes toward the Owner and Architect.

The GMP Documents, including A295–2008, record the Contract for Construction between the Owner and the Contractor. The other GMP Documents are the A195–2008, Supplementary Conditions, Drawings, Specifications, and Modifications. Although the AIA does not produce standard documents for Supplementary Conditions, Drawings, or Specifications, a variety of model and guide documents are available, including AIA's MASTERSPEC and AIA Document A503™–2007, Guide for Supplementary Conditions.

As mentioned above and diagrammed below, A295–2008 is a vital document used to allocate the proper legal responsibilities of the parties.

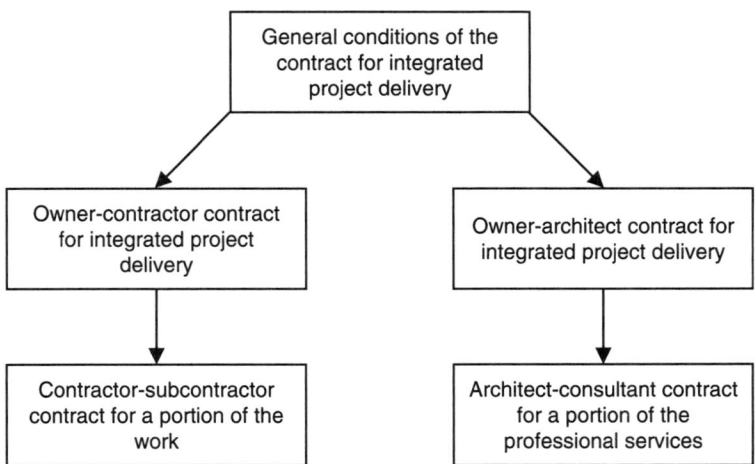

Dispute Resolution—Mediation and Arbitration. This document contains provisions for mediation and arbitration of claims and disputes. Mediation is a non-binding process, but is mandatory under the terms of this agreement. Arbitration is also mandatory under the terms of this agreement. Arbitration is binding in most states and under the Federal Arbitration Act. In a minority of states, arbitration provisions relating to future disputes are not enforceable but the parties may agree to arbitrate after the dispute arises. Even in those states, under certain circumstances (for example, in a transaction involving interstate commerce), arbitration provisions may be enforceable under the Federal Arbitration Act.

The AIA does not administer dispute resolution processes. To submit disputes to mediation or arbitration or to obtain copies of the applicable mediation or arbitration rules, call the American Arbitration Association at (800) 778–7879, or visit their Web site at www.adr.org.

Why Use AIA Contract Documents. AIA contract documents are the product of a consensus-building process aimed at balancing the interests of all parties on the construction project. The documents reflect actual industry practices, not theory. They are state-of-the-art legal documents, regularly revised to keep up with changes in law and the industry—yet they are written, as far as possible, in everyday language. Finally, AIA contract documents are flexible: they are intended to be modified to fit individual projects, but in such a way that modifications are easily distinguished from the original, printed language.

Use of Non-AIA Forms. If a combination of AIA documents and non-AIA documents is to be used, particular care must be taken to achieve consistency of language and intent among documents.

Standard Forms. Most AIA documents published since 1906 have contained in their titles the words "Standard Form." The term "standard" is not meant to imply that a uniform set of contractual requirements is mandatory for AIA members or others in the construction industry. Rather, the AIA standard documents are intended to be used as fair and balanced baselines from which the parties can negotiate their bargains. As such, the documents have won general acceptance within the construction industry and have been uniformly interpreted by the courts. Within an industry spanning 50 states—each of them free to adopt different, and perhaps contradictory, laws affecting that industry—AIA documents form the basis for a generally consistent body of construction law.

Use of Current Documents. Prior to using any AIA Contract Document, users should consult www.aia.org or a local AIA component to verify the most recent edition.

Reproductions. This document is a copyrighted work and may not be reproduced or excerpted from without the express written permission of the AIA. There is no implied permission to reproduce this document, nor does membership in The American Institute of Architects confer any further rights to reproduce this document.

This document is intended for use as a consumable—that is, the original document purchased is to be consumed in the course of its use.

This document may not be reproduced for project manuals. If a user wishes to include a sample or samples of this document in a project manual, the normal practice is to purchase a quantity of the pre-printed forms, binding one in each of the manuals.

Unlike many other AIA Contract Documents, AIA Document A295–2008 does not include the AIA's express written permission to reproduce copies of the document. The AIA will not permit reproduction outside of the limited license for reproduction granted above, except upon written request and receipt of written permission from the AIA.

Rights to reproduce the document may vary for users of AIA software. Licensed AIA software users should consult the End User License Agreement (EULA).

To report copyright violations of AIA Contract Documents, e-mail The American Institute of Architects' legal counsel, copyright@aia.org.

USING A295–2008

Modifications

Particularly with respect to professional or contractor licensing laws, building codes, taxes, monetary and interest charges, arbitration, indemnification, format, and font size, AIA Contract Documents may require modification to comply with state or local laws. Users are encouraged to consult an attorney before completing or modifying a document.

In a purchased paper AIA Contract Document, necessary modifications may be accomplished by writing or typing the appropriate terms in the blank spaces provided on the document, or by attaching Supplementary Conditions, special conditions, or referenced amendments. Modifications directly to purchased paper AIA Contract Documents may also be achieved by striking out language. However, care must be taken in making these kinds of deletions.

Under NO circumstances should standard language be struck out to render it illegible. For example, users should not apply blocking tape, correction fluid, or Xs that would completely obscure text. Such practices may raise suspicion of fraudulent concealment, or suggest that the completed and signed document has been tampered with. Both parties should initial handwritten changes.

Using AIA software, modifications to insert information and revise the standard AIA text may be made as the software permits.

By reviewing properly made modifications to a standard AIA Contract Document, parties familiar with that document can quickly understand the essence of the proposed relationship. Commercial exchanges are greatly simplified and expedited, good faith dealing is encouraged, and otherwise latent clauses are exposed for scrutiny.

AIA Contract Documents may not be retyped or electronically scanned. Retyping can introduce typographic errors and cloud legal interpretation given to a standard clause. Furthermore, retyping and electronic scanning are not permitted under the user's limited license for use of the document, constitute the creation of a derivative work and violate the AIA's copyright.

Cover Page
Project: The Project should be identified with the same name and location or address as set forth in the Owner-Architect and Owner-Contractor agreements.

Owner: The Owner should be identified using the same legal name and the address as set forth in the Owner-Architect and Owner-Contractor agreements.

Architect: Similarly, the Architect should be identified using the same legal name and the address as set forth in the Owner-Architect and Owner-Contractor agreements.

Contractor: Similarly, the Contractor should be identified using the same legal name and the address as set forth in the Owner-Architect and Owner-Contractor agreements.

Article 1 General Provisions
§ 1.2 Initial Information
Initial Information is provided in Section 1.2. The parties should take care to be as explicit and detailed as possible with respect to the relevant Initial Information.

Article 5 Conceptualization Phase
The Architect and the Contractor meet with the Owner and provide a preliminary evaluation of the Owner's program and budget requirements during the Conceptualization Phase. The Architect provides a schedule for its services and the Contractor prepares a Project Schedule that it will periodically update throughout the Project.

Article 6 Criteria Design Phase
During the Criteria Design Phase, the Architect, in consultation with the Contactor, prepares Criteria Design Documents for the Owner's

review and approval. The Contractor, based on the Architect's Criteria Design Documents, prepares an estimate of the total cost to the Owner to construct all elements of the Project.

Article 7 Detailed Design Phase

The Architect develops the Detailed Design Documents from the approved Criteria Design Documents. Prior to conclusion of the Detailed Design Phase, the Contractor provides an update to its previous estimates. At the completion of the Detailed Design Phase, the Architect submits Detailed Design Documents that are consistent with the Owner's Budget for the Work. Thereafter, the Contractor and Owner negotiate a Guaranteed Maximum Price. The negotiated Guaranteed Maximum Price is set forth in an amendment to the Owner-Contractor Agreement. Upon acceptance of the Guaranteed Maximum Price, the Detailed Design Documents become part of the GMP Documents. The Contractor is required to construct the Project in accordance with the GMP Documents.

Article 8 Implementation Documents Phase

During the Implementation Documents Phase, the Architect and Contractor further develop the GMP documents in order to provide the detail and quality levels of materials, systems, and other requirements for construction of the Project. The Implementation Documents incorporate the traditional shop drawing process and are not part of the GMP Documents.

Article 9 Construction Phase

During the Construction Phase, the Contractor constructs the Project in accordance with the GMP documents and the Architect provides construction administration services.

Article 10 Closeout Phase

During the Closeout Phase, the Architect, Contractor, and Owner perform activities associated with Substantial Completion, Final Completion, Final Payment, and other post-construction requirements.

APPENDIX E

Construction Manager At Risk Contract

State Construction File #

This Agreement, entered into this_____day of (Month), (Year) for (Title of Project) between:_____ and _____

(Hereinafter: The Construction Manager at Risk), and the State of North Carolina, by the Constituent Institution of the University of North Carolina listed below:

(Hereinafter: the Owner)

WITNESSETH

Whereas the Owner has published a Request for Proposals seeking the submission of competitive proposals to act as a construction manager at risk to furnish professional construction management services during the design and construction of the Project identified and described in that Request for Proposals; and,

Whereas, the undersigned Construction Manager submitted a competitive proposal that was evaluated by the Owner; and,

Whereas, the Owner, through its awarding authority, has made an award of the work to the undersigned Construction Manager, and pursuant to the terms of the Request for Proposals this form is to be executed to form and memorialize the contractual relationship between the parties;

Now therefore, the Construction Manager and the Owner agree as follows:

Appendix E

1. This form of contract hereby shall be incorporated and accompanied by: Owner's recommendation for award letter (Date), Owner's request for proposal (Date), Contractor's (CM @ Risk) response to proposal (Date), Contractor's HUB plan approved by Owner (Date), Designer's drawing and specification lists (Date), Contractor's payment and performance bond (Date), Power of Attorney, Insurance Certificate (Date), Statement of GMP including schedule of values for cost of the work and General Conditions (Date), and incorporate herein by reference the contract for preconstruction services dated (Date of contract).
2. For the sums set forth in the Construction Manager's fee proposal (or any subsequently amended fee agreement), the Construction Manager undertakes to act as the Owner's fiduciary (GS143–128.1) and to furnish professional construction management services during the design and construction of the Project.
3. The providing of the Construction Manager's services shall be in compliance with the requirements of the RFP (including all its appendices and attachments) and the Construction Manager's proposal (hereinafter, together: the Contract Documents). To the extent that any term, requirement, or specification in the Construction Manager's proposal shall be in conflict with the RFP, the terms, requirements, and specifications of the RFP shall control and the conflicting contents of the Construction Manager's proposal shall be deemed surplussage except where provided otherwise.
4. That the Construction Manager shall commence provision of construction phase services under this agreement on a date to be specified in a written order of the Owner and shall fully complete all services hereunder and accomplish the final completion of the project within____consecutive calendar days from the date of Notice to Proceed. The Construction Manager shall furnish to the Owner various schedules as provided in the Contract Documents setting forth planned progress of the project broken down by the various divisions or part of the work and by calendar days. If the Construction Manager fails to begin the work under the contract within the time specified, or the progress of the work is not maintained on schedule, or the work is not completed within the time above specified, or shall allow the work to be performed unsuitably, or shall discontinue the prosecution of the work, or if the Construction Manager shall become insolvent, or be declared bankrupt, or commit any act of bankruptcy or insolvency, or allow any final judgment to stand against him unsatisfied for a period of forty-eight (48) hours, or shall make an assignment for the benefit of creditors, or for any other cause

whatsoever shall not carry on the work in an acceptable manner, the Owner may give notice in writing, sent by certified mail, return receipt requested, to the Construction Manager and his surety of such delay, neglect or default, specifying the same, and if the Construction Manager within a period of fifteen (15) days after such notice shall not proceed in accordance therewith, then the Owner shall, declare this contract in default, and, thereupon, the surety shall promptly take over the work and complete the performance of this contract in the manner and within the time frame specified. In the event the surety shall fail to take over the work to be done under this contract within fifteen (15) days after being so notified and notify the Owner in writing, sent by certified mail, return receipt requested, that he is taking the same over and stating that he will diligently pursue and complete the same, the Owner shall have full power and authority, without violating the contract, to take the prosecution of the work out of the hands of said Construction Manager, to appropriate or use any or all contract materials and equipment on the grounds as may be suitable and acceptable and may enter into an agreement, either by public letting or negotiation, for the completion of said contract according to the terms and provisions thereof or use such other methods as in his opinion shall be required for the completion of said contract in an acceptable manner. All costs and charges incurred by the Owner, together with the costs of completing the work under contract, shall be deducted from any monies due or which may become due said Construction Manager and surety. In case the expense so incurred by the Owner shall be less than the sum which would have been payable under the contract, if it had been completed by said Construction Manager, then the said Construction Manager and surety shall be entitled to receive the difference, but in case such expense shall exceed the sum which would have been payable under the contract, then the Construction Manager and the surety shall be liable and shall pay to the Owner the amount of said excess.

5. It is further mutually agreed between the parties hereto that if at any time after the execution of this agreement and the surety bonds hereto attached for its faithful performance, the Second Party shall deem the surety or sureties upon such bonds to be unsatisfactory, or if, for any reason, such bonds cease to be adequate to cover the performance of the work, the First Party shall, at its expense, within five (5) days after the receipt of notice from the Second Party so to do, furnish an additional bond or bonds in such form and amount, and with such surety or sureties as shall be satisfactory to the Second Party. In such event no further payment to the First Party

shall be deemed to be due under this agreement until such new or additional security (surety) for the faithful performance of the work shall be furnished in manner and form satisfactory to the Second Party.

6. Guaranteed Maximum Price

Cost of the Work	$
Construction Manager's construction contingency	$
Construction Manager's construction fee	$
General Conditions Allowance	$_____
Total Guaranteed Maximum Price	$

IN WITNESS WHEREOF, the Parties hereto have executed this agreement on the day and date first above written in four (4) counterparts, each of which shall without proof or accounting for other counterparts, be deemed an original contract.

Witness: Contractor:(Trade or Corporate Name)

_____ By: _____

_____
(Proprietorship or Partnership)

Attest: (Corporation)   Title:_____
                                     (Owner, Partner, or Corp.
                                     Pres. or Vice Pres. only)

By:_____

Title:_____

     (Corp. Sec. or Asst.
     Sec. only)

(CORPORATE SEAL)   The State of North Carolina through

Witness: _____

                               (Agency, Department or Institution)

_____ By:_____

                               Title:_____

Glossary

Acceptance A draft on which the debtor indicates by the word "accepted" his or her intention to pay or honor.

Acknowledgment A standard form used by a vendor or supplier to advise that the purchase order has been received.

Act of God Danger beyond human control; any accident produced by an irresistible physical cause, such as hurricane, flood, earthquake, or lightning. In no way connected with negligence.

Actual weight Gross shipping or transport weight

Addendum A document used to modify bid documents prior to receipt of bids. An addendum is incorporated into the formal contract.

Ad valorem The total value of goods or materials against which tariff rates are imposed.

Advertisement for bids A published notice of an owner's intention to award a contract for construction work to a contractor who submits an acceptable proposal in accordance with the owner's instructions to bidders. In its usual form, the advertisement is published in a convenient form of news media (e.g., newspaper, magazine) in order to attract contractors who are willing to prepare and submit proposals for the completion of the project.

Advice of shipment A notice sent to the purchaser from the seller advising that the shipment has gone forward; usually contains details of packing, routing, delivery date, and so on.

Agency Implies a relationship between two parties in which one is empowered to perform certain functions or business transactions for the other.

Agent An agent is authorized by the principal to act in the principal's behalf and interest. An agent's actions generally bind the principal as if the principal had acted directly.

Aggregated shipments An indefinite number of shipments from different supply sources to a single buying organization, consolidated and considered as a single consignment.

Agreement A consensus by two or more parties. As it relates to construction, the term is synonymous with contract. An example of this is the agreement between owner and contractor.

Airbill A shipping or manifest document used by airlines for air freight; contains shipping instructions to the airline.

Air freight To transport or ship goods by air.

Airway bill Document used for shipment and transport of air freight by air carriers; lists the materials shipped along with instructions, costs, and other specific details.

Allowance A stated requirement of contract documents whereby a specified sum of money is incorporated, or allowed, into the contract sum in order to sustain the cost of a stipulated material, assembly, piece of equipment, or other element of a construction contract. This device is convenient in cases where the particular item cannot be fully described in the contract documents. The allowance can be stated as a lump sum or as a provisional sum.

All risk insurance An insurance policy that covers specific risks of damage or loss from any number of potential events during and after the construction process.

Amortization The distribution of the initial cost of an asset by periodic charges to ongoing operations, as in the case of depreciation.

Application for payment A financial statement prepared by the contractor or subcontractor stating the amount of work completed and materials purchased and stored to date. The statement includes the sum of previous payments and current payments due in accordance with payment terms of the contract.

Approve To accept and endorse as satisfactory; implies that the object approved has the endorsement of the approving agency or body. However, the approval may still require confirmation by another party.

Arbitration The process by which parties agree to submit their disputes and claims to the determination and resolution of a third, impartial, and unbiased party (referred to as the arbitrator), rather than pursuing their claims in a court of law.

Architect A design professional who, by education, experience, and examination, is licensed by state government to practice the art of building design and technology.

Arrival date The date purchased materials and equipment are scheduled to arrive at the construction site.

Arrival notice Notice that a freight carrier sends to the purchaser when a shipment has arrived.

Glossary

Artisan's lien   The lien of a mechanic or other skilled worker in connection with something on which he or she has applied labor or materials, giving him or her the right to keep possession of it until final payment is made.

As-built drawings   Record drawings made during construction. As-built drawings record the locations, sizes, and nature of concealed items such as structural elements, accessories, fixtures, devices, values, and mechanical equipment. These record drawings form a permanent record of the as-built condition of the building or facility.

As is   Indicates that the materials and equipment offered for sale are without warranty or guarantee. The purchaser has no recourse on the vendor or supplier for the quality of the materials and equipment.

Assignment   The transfer of rights or title to another party, frequently involving rights originating from a contract.

Back order   The part of an order that cannot be delivered at the scheduled date, but will be delivered at a later date.

Banker's acceptance draft   A document or draft used in financing a foreign transaction, making possible the payment of cash to an exporter, covering all or part payment for a shipment made by the exporter.

Bargain   Agreement on the terms and conditions of a purchase. Purchase of articles at a price favorable to the buyer.

Barter   The process of exchanging one kind of article for another, as opposed to trading by use of money.

Bid   A complete and properly executed proposal to perform work or supply goods or services that have been described verbally or in the bidding documents and submitted in accordance with instructions to bidders. A bid is an offer.

Bid bond   A form of bid security purchased by a bidder; provided, subject to forfeit, to guarantee that the bidder will enter into a contract with the owner for construction of the facility within a specified time period.

Bidding documents   Documents that typically include the advertisement or invitation to bidders, instructions to bidders, bid form, form of contract, forms of bonds, conditions of contract, specifications, drawings, and any other information necessary to completely describe the work for which bidders can prepare bids for the owner's consideration.

Bid opening   A formal meeting held at a specified place and time at which sealed bids are opened, tabulated, read aloud, and made available for public inspection.

Bill   An invoice the freight carrier uses to show consignee, consignor, shipment description, weight, freight charges, and other relevant information.

Glossary

Bill of exchange A formal written document used to settle and pay for an existing obligation.

Bill of lading A transport company's contract and receipt for materials and equipment; agrees to transport from one location to another and to deliver to a designated individual or party.

Bill of materials A list of all permanent materials required on the construction project. The bill of materials list consists of all items described on a drawing and specification.

Binder A temporary but binding commitment by an insurance company to provide insurance coverage.

Blanket order Provides for the vendor or supplier to furnish certain materials for a certain period of time and at a predetermined price; acts as a master purchase order, reducing the number of smaller purchase orders.

Boiler plate A term used to describe the terms and conditions on the back of a purchase order or the specific clauses described in a contract.

Bonded warehouse A warehouse under the surveillance of the U.S. Treasury Department for observance of revenue and excise laws.

Bond performance A bond obtained in connection with a contract; ensures the performance and completion of all the scope, terms, conditions, and agreements contained within the contract.

Bonds Formal documents, given by an insurance company, in the name of a principal to an obligee to guarantee a specific obligation. In the construction industry the main types of bonds are the bid bond, performance bond, and payment bond.

Breach of contract The failure to perform any of the obligations that are stated within the terms and conditions of the contract.

Bulk materials Materials bought in lots; purchased from a generic description or standard catalog description and bought in medium to large quantity for issue as required. Examples are pipe fittings, conduit, cable, timber, and stone.

Bulletin A document used to request pricing for a modification to the design after a contract is issued. If pricing is acceptable, a change order to the contract incorporates the requirements of the bulletin into a project.

Burden In construction, the cost of operating a home branch or site office with staff other than operating site personnel. Also means federal, state, and local taxes, fringe benefits, and other union contract obligations. In manufacturing operations, burden typically means operating overhead costs.

Cancellation of order Annulment or cessation of order.

Glossary

Certificate of material compliance A written statement signed and approved by an authorized person stating that the materials comply with the material specification.

Certificate of origin A document, issued by the appropriate authority in an exporting country, that certifies the origin of the equipment, materials, or labor used in the manufacture of the equipment or materials being exported to another country.

Certified test report A written document, approved by an appropriate body, that contains sufficient information to verify the actual properties of the materials and equipment and the actual results of the tests.

Change in scope A change in requirements, objectives, work content, or schedule that results in a difference from the terms and conditions of the contract.

Change order A written order, issued after execution of the construction contract, that authorizes a change in the construction work and contract time and/or value.

CIF (Cost, Insurance, Freight) When seller quotes CIF, the quote includes the cost of the materials or equipment, marine insurance, and all transportation charges to the stated destination point.

C.L. Carload.

Claim A request for additional payment.

COD Cash on delivery.

Commercial terms The terms and conditions of a purchase order or contract that relate to the business and commercial aspects of the purchase order or contract. The price, quantity, and delivery date are the main elements covered under the commercial terms.

Compensatory damages Damages awarded to compensate the injured party by granting a monetary value equal to the loss or injury encountered.

Competitive bidding The offer of proposals by individuals or organizations competing for a purchase order or contract to supply specific materials, equipment, or services.

Conditional sale A sale made with the knowledge that title will not pass to the buyer until some stated condition has been achieved.

Conditions of the contract A document describing the rights, responsibilities, and relationships of the parties to a contract.

Consequential damages Payment for loss or damage that is not directly attributable to a wrongful action on the part of another party, but is the result of one or more of the consequences of the action.

Consideration A term used to describe the value that shall be reimbursed to one party to a contract by another party in return for services or articles rendered.

Containerization The use of road and marine transportation containers are normally 20 or 40 feet in length. Shipment of large sealed freight containers via rail, air, truck, or water to optimized transit time, security, packaging, and turnaround time.

Contract A written or oral agreement between two or more competent parties to perform a specific act or acts enforceable by law.

Contract administration Administering contracts and purchase orders to protect the interest of a specific organization and to satisfy the conditions and requirements of the contract and/or purchase order.

Contract documents A term applied to a collection of related documents (contract, specifications, drawings, and any additional data) that define the extent of an agreement between two or more parties.

Cost plus A contract or pricing method in which the purchaser agrees to pay the supplier an amount determined by the actual cost incurred by the supplier to provide the materials, equipment, or services purchased, plus a fixed percentage of that cost or a fixed sum as profit.

Counteroffer To decline an offer by submitting a new offer with different conditions or terms than the original offer.

Damage claim A formal claim document filed for damages to materials and equipment.

Damages Compensation or payment for damage to materials and equipment, individuals, or property that is the fault or cause of another party.

Davis-Bacon Act An act passed into law by the U.S. Congress in the 1930s. The act provides that wages and fringe benefits paid to workers employed by contractors and subcontractors under contract with the federal government be paid not less than the local prevailing wage rate for each trade.

Debit notice An invoice used to offset a previous overpayment, showing the difference between the previous invoice and the correct value.

Deliverable A product or report that must be delivered to satisfy a contractual obligation.

Delivering carrier The carrier that transports and delivers the materials and equipment to the purchaser.

Delivery The act of transferring possession; applied to shipping, occurs when lading is surrendered and title, materials, and equipment pass to the receiving party.

Demurrage A charge made on freight cars, vehicles, or ships held by or for consignor or consignee for subsequent loading or unloading.

Detail specification A description of the requirements for a specific item or material or equipment.

Discount   An allowance or deduction given by the seller to the buyer that reduces the cost of the item purchased when certain conditions are met by the buyer (e.g., prompt payment within a stipulated period).

Distribution   The broad range of activities targeted at the efficient movement of finished materials and equipment from the end of the production line to the eventual end user or consumer.

Dock   The loading or unloading ramp or platform at an industrial facility or factory.

Draft   A legal document instructing one individual to pay another.

Due date   The date when purchased materials and equipment will be available for installation at the project location.

Dunnage   Protective matter used around materials or equipment to prevent movement, damage, or breakage while in transit.

Durable goods   Consumer products that are used repeatedly over a period of years (e.g., household appliances, vehicles).

Duty   The charge assessed by a government on materials and equipment imported or exported. An obligation established by law or contract is not formalized.

Earnest money   Money that one party gives to another at the time of entering into a contract to "seal the deal." Earnest money can be forfeited if a contract is not formalized.

Error and omission excepted   Printed on invoices or other statement(s) to safeguard the originator's right to amend or modify the value if found to be incorrect.

Escalation   The value of adjustment permitted by an escalation clause (see below). An allowance for an anticipated increase in the cost of equipment, materials, and labor as a result of continuing price inflation experienced over time.

Escalation clause   A contract clause that provides for a price adjustment based on specific changes.

Ex   (Ex mill, Ex factory, Ex warehouse, Ex dock) Prefix used to denote point of origin. When a seller quotes a price Ex, the seller proposes only to make the materials and equipment available at the Ex point of origin and includes no transportation costs in the quoted prices.

Excess freight   Freight in excess of that indicated on the original freight carrier billing.

Exchange bill of lading   A bill of lading compiled and exchanged for another bill of lading.

Excise tax   A tax on the manufacture, sale, or use of certain articles made, sold, or used within a country.

Export Shipment of materials or equipment to a foreign country.

Export permit A permit given by the government of an exporting country allowing a party within that country to export the materials and equipment to another country.

Fabrication Manufacturing operations for materials or equipment as opposed to the final installation operation.

Facilitation A system to decrease the time of international cargo transportation through the use of the latest customs methods, duty and tariff collection, and other related functions of international traffic activities.

Factor An agent selling goods or materials on a commission basis for his or her principal.

Fair market value The value of an article as determined by negotiation between buyer and seller; considered acceptable as a basis of a purchase and sale of the particular article.

FAS (Free Along Side) When a seller quotes a price FAS, the price includes the cost of transportation and delivery alongside the oceangoing vessel and within reach of the vessel's loading equipment. The price does not include costs for any export permits or the payment of any export duties or tariffs.

Field inspection A thorough examination of the equipment and materials shortly after delivery to determine if they meet the requirements of the specifications and to find any hidden defects or damage.

Field purchase order A purchase order used in field construction situations where authority to make the type of purchase involved is usually restricted or has a predetermined not-to-exceed value.

Field required date The date required for an item of material or equipment to be delivered to a construction site for the maintenance of the project schedule.

FIFO An accounting procedure based on a "first-in, first-out" treatment of stock or inventory; the articles that are received earliest are used first. The opposite of this procedure is LIFO (last-in, first-out).

Firm offer A definite proposal or offer to buy or sell some article on stated terms and conditions. Such an offer binds the proposal to a stipulated time period.

FOB (Free On Board) Indicates that the seller pays the transportation costs up to the delivery location indicated. For example, a contractor's purchase order frequently specifies delivery as "F.O.B. construction site" or "F.O.B. storage yard." If the purchase order stipulates that the seller is to pay the delivery costs to a designated location, the title to the article does not pass until the article has been delivered to that location. Under

F.O.B. agreement, title goes to the purchaser when the carrier delivers the article to the location stipulated.

F.O.B. destination, freight prepaid   A term used in reference to the title passing to the buyer and to the freight cost being paid by the seller.

F.O.B. factory, freight allowed   Free on board factory, freight prepaid from point of origin.

F.O.B. origin, freight collect   A term used in reference to the title passing to the buyer. The buyer pays the freight costs, owns the goods in transit, and files all claims for any loss or damage while in transit.

F.O.B. origin, freight prepaid and charged   A term used in reference to the title passing to the buyer. Freight costs are paid by the seller and then collected from the buyer by adding the value of freight costs to the invoice.

F.O.B. shipping point   The location at which title to the articles passes from the seller to the buyer. The seller is liable for transportation costs and the risks of loss or damage to the goods up to the point where title passes to the buyer. The buyer is liable for such costs and risks after the passing of the title.

Follow-up record   Information used in the expediting and delivery from vendors and suppliers.

F.O.R.   Free on rail.

Force majeure   Circumstances beyond an individual's control; pleadable as an excuse for the nonfulfillment of a contract or purchase order.

Forward purchasing   The purchase of quantities exceeding the immediate requirement, that is, in anticipation of any significant price increase or market shortage.

F.O.T.   Free on truck.

Freight forwarder   Some freight forwarder organizations act as agents on behalf of shippers in organizing the transportation of articles without handling any of the articles. Others act as freight carriers in consolidating small- and mid-sized shipments and delivering them to the purchaser.

General conditions   Guidelines that define many of the rights, responsibilities, obligations, and limitations of authority of the owner and contractor, and include a general procedure governing the performance of the work. When organized under the Construction Specification Institute Master Format, they are described under 16 divisions.

General contractor   A construction organization who has a direct relationship with project owners and is also referred to as a prime contractor.

General liability insurance A broad form of liability insurance covering claims for bodily injury and property damage.

Generic A term used to generally describe a group, type, or class of materials and equipment, rather than name a specific trade name or source of manufacture.

Goods received note A document detailing all equipment and materials after they have been audited and checked for quantity at the receiving point.

Gross ton 2240 lb of weight.

Gross weight The total weight of a shipment, including containers, packaging, and miscellaneous materials.

Guarantee A promise, pledge, or formal assurance given as a pledge that another's obligation or debt will be fulfilled.

Guaranteed maximum cost contract A contract for construction in which the contractor's or subcontractor's compensation is stated as a combination of actual cost incurred, plus a fee, with a guarantee by the contractor or subcontractor that the total compensation will be limited to a specific stated amount.

Heavy-lift charge A fee imposed by a transportation organization for lifting materials and equipment of excessive weight.

Hedging A method of selling for future delivery whereby the parties protect themselves against potential loss.

Hold The below-deck cargo storage space aboard ship; the cargo compartment of an aircraft.

Hold order A purchaser's order to hold a particular delivery at a designated location for a specific period of time.

Hold points Inventory or warehouse areas set aside for storing semicomplete articles.

Hundredweight The transport of 100 lb "cwt."

Implied contract A contract formed when parties express, through their conduct, their agreement to be bound to its conditions and terms. An agreement is inferred and understood without express statements.

Indemnification An obligation contractually taken on or legally imposed on one party to protect another party against any loss or damage from specific liability.

Indemnity A responsibility of one person to make good a loss or damage incurred by another. A payment for damage, loss, or expense incurred.

Indirect materials A group of materials used in making a product that are not incorporated or part of the finished product.

Glossary 219

Injunction A formal order issued by a court of law ordering a person or a group to do or refrain from doing some activity.

Inland bill of lading A bill of lading used in transporting materials and equipment overland to the exporter's international transporter. A through-bill of lading can be used in some circumstances; however, it is usually necessary to prepare both an inland bill of lading and an ocean bill of lading for foreign export of materials and equipment.

Inland carrier A transportation organization that moves export or import materials and equipment between seaports and inland locations.

Inquiry A request for information related to the schedule, location, availability, interest, cost, or quantity of construction-related items.

Inspection The examination, audit, measuring, and testing of materials and equipment including, when necessary, raw materials, fabrication elements, components, intermediate assemblies, subassemblies, and end products to determine if the materials, equipment, and services meet the contract specification requirements. This activity can be completed either by visual inspection or with the use of special equipment.

Inspection plan A procedure that defines the material or equipment requiring inspection and describes the method and order of performing the tests or inspections.

Inspection report A report to inform the purchaser of the quality and workmanship of the items of materials and equipment delivered.

Inspector A qualified inspector employed by an organization to examine and review the fabrication, manufacture, and installation of construction-related equipment and materials.

Instructions to bidders A document that is part of the bidding requirements, usually prepared by a design professional, architect, or engineer. Instructions to bidders describe specific instructions to the potential contractors on procedures, requirements of the owner, and other necessary information for the preparation and submission of bids for consideration and review by the owner.

Insurance A contract, typically called an insurance policy, in which the insurer, in return for the payment of a premium, agrees to pay the insured for any losses or damages incurred by the insured during the execution of a specified undertaking (e.g., construction of a building or facility).

Insurance certificate A document supplied by a contractor, subcontractor, or vendor stating the coverage of insurance related to a particular contract.

Inventory Items of materials and equipment that are in the storeroom or warehouse, or work-in-progress consisting of raw materials, fabrication elements, components, parts of intermediate materials and equipment, and finished materials and equipment ready for distribution and sale.

Physical inventory is ascertained and established by actual count. It includes materials and equipment that are physically available for allocation and distribution, and stored and controlled in a warehouse or outside laydown area.

Invitation to bid Written notice of an owner's desire to receive competitive bids for a particular construction project where a select number of contractors are invited to submit bids for the construction of the project.

Invoice Seller's itemized bill of quantities and prices of materials, equipment, and/or services that have been delivered to the purchaser.

ITC Investment tax credit

JIT (just-in-time) A system for planning and scheduling fabrication through the manufacturing sequence, optimizing the purchase and storage of materials and equipment, and eliminating any inventory or stock on hand.

Job lot A small number of specific materials or items of equipment that are produced at one specific time.

Job-lot ordering The buying of necessary materials, equipment, and components to fabricate in accordance with a customer's specifications.

Joint agent An official designated to act for two or more principals.

Joint venture An organization in which two or more parties join together to form a business operation with the legal characteristics of a partnership to achieve a specific goal.

Journeyman A qualified workman who has completed an apprenticeship.

Judgment A decision rendered as a result of a course of action in a court of law.

KD Knocked down or disassembled to reduce bulk.

Key activity An activity that is considered of major importance, sometimes referred to as a milestone event.

Kitting The process of sending components of a total assembly to another location in a kit form for assembly.

Labor and material payment bond A contract between a contractor and a surety, in which the surety, for a premium payment by the contractor, agrees to reimburse subcontractors, vendors, and material suppliers any amounts due for their materials and services, should the contractor default in payment to them.

Lading The act of loading, or the contents of a specific shipment.

Laydown area A space of ground, usually without a roof, that is used for the delivery and storage of materials and equipment.

L&D Loss and damage.

Lead time The period of time required to perform a specific activity of work.

Lease A contract whereby an individual or organization lets another use property or equipment for a definite term and for an agreed rental cost. The lessor retains title to such property or equipment.

Legal tender Money issued by the government to satisfy a debt or obligation.

Letter of credit A letter addressed by a bank to a correspondent bank certifying that an individual or organization named therein is entitled to draw upon an account.

Liability A state of being under obligation; exposure to potential claim by which an individual or organization may be subject to pay for compensation for loss, damage, or other acts to another individual or organization.

Lien A legal claim on the assets or property of another.

LIFO (last-in, first-out) An accounting practice of determining the cost of stock inventory used in a manufactured product or process (opposite of FIFO).

Liquidated damages A sum of money agreed to by the contracting parties as to damages to be given in case of a failure to meet the obligations of the contract.

Litigation To engage in a lawsuit; the process by which parties submit their disputes to the jurisdiction of federal or state law courts for resolution.

Load factor A ratio that applies to the utilization of a physical plant or piece of equipment; the ratio or percentage of average load utilized to maximum load available for use.

Logistics The science of transportation and supply; the art of obtaining and distributing finished products in the marketplace.

Long ton 2240 lb, same as gross ton.

Lot size The amount of specific materials and equipment items ordered from a vendor.

LTL Less than truckload.

Lump sum An amount or value used in a proposal, bid, or contract representing the total cost that an organization is prepared to contract to perform an item of work.

Manifest A list of the cargo loaded in ships, trucks, containers, and the like; an oceangoing transportation, referred to as a ship's manifest.

Marketable title A title about which no uncertainty exists concerning its legal soundness or validity.

Marketing research The systematic gathering, recording, and analyzing of data and intelligence about tasks and activities related to the marketing of materials and services.

Markup A percentage that can be added to the total of all direct costs to determine a final price or contract sum. Allows the contractor or subcontractor to recover the costs associated with overhead.

Material The raw elements, parts, or semiprocessed components from which a finished product is created.

Material cost The cost of all items that are essential to the construction process or operation of a facility, including the direct and indirect related costs.

Material man A term used to describe an individual from whom the contractor may obtain the materials of construction. The material man may be a manufacturer's sales representative or agent or distributor; a salesman of materials and equipment could also be considered a material man.

Materials management A concept whereby all materials and equipment procurement functions are combined under one management function, including contracting, purchasing, quality assurance, quality control, inspection and expediting, trafficking, and receiving.

Material status A report detailing the current availability of materials.

Materials test report A report usually referred to as a Certified Materials Test Report or Mill Test Report. The actual test results are usually described, detailing chemical analyses, material composition tests, and procedures used in testing.

MC Minimum charge.

Mechanic's lien A type of lien filed by an individual or organization who has performed work for which payment is either in dispute or remains unpaid.

Minimum carload weight A minimum weight for which a carload of materials and equipment can be charged.

Mixed truckload rate A rate applied to a truckload shipment made up of two or more different materials.

Modifications A term used to signify changes that may be made to contract documents and a construction contract. Modifications made before the award of a contract are called addenda; modifications made after the contract is in place are called change orders.

Multiple-consignee A container car, truck, or ship loaded with materials and equipment for two or more consignees.

Multiple source buying A container car, truck, or ship loaded with materials and equipment for two or more consignees.

Need date The date when a particular article is required at the construction site.

Negligence Under the law, failure to exercise the care and consideration a prudent person would exercise; lack of care and attention.

Negotiation The process by which a buyer and seller reach an agreement on the terms and conditions regarding the purchase of materials, equipment, goods, or services.

Net price The price reached after all allowable discounts, rebates, and the like are deducted from the original selling price.

Net ton 2000 lb

Net weight The weight of the materials and equipment without the shipping container and dunnage.

Notary A public officer empowered to administer oaths, take depositions, and certify deeds and contracts.

OBL Ocean bill of lading.

Obligation A duty that is the result of a promise or contract; an agreement which an individual or organization is responsible to fulfill.

Obsolete Outmoded, worn out, discarded, or no longer in use.

Offer A proposal or bid made by an individual or organization to another individual to perform a service or action; the acceptance of such an offer results in contract. The individual or organization who makes the offer is called an offeror, and the individual or organization who receives the offer is called an offeree. A bid or proposal is an example of an offer.

Open competitive bidding selection A process of contractor selection wherein an advertisement to bidders is published in newspapers and trade magazines notifying contractors of the owner's intention to receive and consider sealed competitive bids for a construction contract. Typically the lowest conforming and responsible bid will be successful.

Open-end order Purchases made against the buyer's purchase order or contract. The purchase order or contract contains price, conditions, and terms. The purchase order or contract may not specify the final quantity to be purchased.

Order lead time Period of time required to obtain an item from a vendor or supplier once the purchase order requirements are known.

OS&D (over, short, and damage report) A report or log showing discrepancies in materials received, together with a damage evaluation.

Overhead   A cost inherent in the operating of a business. A cost that cannot be charged to a specific part of the work, materials, or equipment.

Owner   The individual, group, or organization that has title to a building or facility.

Packing list   A document or log prepared by the shipper to indicate in detail the particular package contents.

Partial payment   A stage payment made upon delivery of one or more completed units.

Patent   A government grant to an inventor by which he or she is the only person allowed to make or sell the new invention for a certain number of years.

Payment bond   A form of security purchased by a contractor from a surety; guarantees that the contractor will pay all costs of labor, materials, and other services associated with a construction.

Penalty clause   A clause in a contract that stipulates the sum of money to be forfeited in the case of nonperformance of the terms and conditions of the contract.

Performance bond   A form of security purchased by a contractor from a surety; guarantees that the contractor will satisfactorily perform all of the work associated with a construction project.

Physical distribution   The activities associated with the transportation and movement of materials and equipment from the manufacturer to the end user.

Piggyback   The carrying of anything that usually moves alone by a large vehicle. The transportation of highway trailers or containers on specially equipped railroad flat cars.

Pledge   To bind by a promise.

Point of origin   The actual location of origin of a shipment.

Port of entry   A port designated by a government as the entry point for materials, equipment, and services from an overseas country.

Prime contractor   The prime contractor works directly for the project owner to build and coordinate the project. In some sectors, for example, heavy highway, the prime self performs a significant portion of construction items. In other sectors, the prime's role is consistent with that of a general contractor.

Prefabrication   A manufacturing or fabrication technique, generally taking place at a location other than the construction site, in which various materials and equipment are combined to form a larger component element for final installation at the construction location.

Procurement   The activity related to the acquisition of articles, land, property, or services by the means of purchasing.

Glossary

Procurement lead time The time required by a buyer to select and negotiate with a vendor or supplier and place a purchase order.

Promissory note A written pledge or promise by one individual or organization to pay another unconditionally a certain sum of money (principal and interest) at a specified time.

Purchase Obtaining an article for money; something acquired for a specific amount of money or its equivalent.

Purchase order A written contract made between a buyer and a seller that describes the articles being purchased, the price of the articles and the method of delivery.

Purchase requisition A written request issued to a purchasing department from an individual or group that requires a specific article.

Purchasing The act of buying materials, equipment, and services that conform to the correct quality, in the correct quantity, at the market price, and are delivered in accordance with the promised delivery date.

Purchasing cycle The activities in the acquisition of materials, equipment, and services.

Purchasing manual An operating guide that explains the policies and procedures for purchasing personnel to follow in the performance of their work activities.

Quality The essential attributes that permit materials and equipment to function in the desired manner.

Quality assurance A formal procedure that ensures that the materials and equipment will perform satisfactorily when installed.

Quality control The procedure and activities that ensure adequate quality is maintained in the materials and equipment utilized in the construction process.

Quantification A list of actual quantities of materials and equipment from a set of drawings and specifications.

Quantity The amount of equipment or material units required.

Quantity discount The reduction in unit price cost established by a predetermined minimum number.

Quasi-contract An obligation under which an individual or organization that received a benefit must pay the individual or organization who gave the benefit, despite the absence of a contract.

Quotation A summary of price, terms of sale, and general description of materials, equipment, or services offered for sale by a contractor or vendor to a potential buyer. When issued in response to a purchase inquiry, it is considered an offer to sell.

Quotation expiration date The date after which a quotation is no longer valid.

Quotation request A purchaser's invitation to potential vendors or suppliers to bid on a list of articles.

Rate of exchange The rate at which the currency of one country is exchanged for the currency of another country.

Reactive expediting A form of expediting conducted primarily by telephone contact; reacts to situations and problems as they occur.

Rebate The amount refunded to a purchaser for the purchase of an agreed quantity or value within a stipulated period of time.

Receipt inspection An audit and examination of materials and equipment prior to acceptance; to review the completeness of the delivery and to note any obvious damage.

Receipt of bids The action of an owner in receiving sealed bids that have been invited or advertised in accordance with the owner's intention to award a construction contract.

Receiving The receipt and delivery of articles at a designated location.

Receiving and storage The action of processing materials and equipment from vendors and suppliers, including maintaining and controlling all elements in storage, and the eventual distribution of the materials and equipment.

Receiving report A form or log used by an organization's receiving department for recording the materials and equipment received and the differences, if any, from the quantities indicated on the purchase order.

Recourse The procedure a buyer or seller may use to have a seller or buyer satisfactorily comply with the terms of the contract.

Repair To mend or put in good condition. The process of restoring a nonconforming material or equipment item so that it can perform its intended function.

Request for bid A request by a purchaser for the submission of an offer or proposal from the supplier to be considered, accepted, or rejected by the purchaser.

Requirements The total scope of work to be performed together with specifications, drawings, and cost of the work.

Requisition An internal form that an individual or department sends to the purchasing department requesting materials, equipment, or other services.

Retention The percentage or value withheld from a contractor that is paid when the contract has been satisfactorily completed.

Glossary

Review The examination of any form of data, documentation, or drawings, for the purpose of establishing acceptability and conformance to the requirements of the contract.

Rework The procedure by which a nonconforming element is made to conform to the established need by repairs or modifications.

RFQ (Request For Quotation) The process of soliciting bids or proposals for a stated scope of work.

Routing The determination of each road to be used in the transportation of materials and equipment to a construction job site.

Sales price The value received for items sold. Gross sales price is the total value paid. Net sales is the gross value less discounts, rebates, and freight costs.

Sales representative An individual acting for a supplier or vendor who is familiar with the products that the buyer may be considering for purchase.

Sales revenue Funds received as the result of a sales transaction.

Sales tax A tax levied on the sale of materials, equipment, or services; calculated as a percentage of the purchase price. Different states use different percentages.

Salvage The material or equipment that is saved after damage or demolition has been completed.

Salvage value The value recovered or realized when an article or facility is demolished, scrapped, or sold.

Samples Examples of completed materials, products, equipment, or workmanship that establish standards by which the installed work will be evaluated.

Scope Defines the work to be performed and completed; usually documented and described in the contract.

Scope change A deviation from the original project scope of work agreed to in the contract. A scope change can be an activity either added to or deleted from the original scope of work.

Seller's lien The seller's right to withhold or to lay claim on materials or equipment sold, giving up these rights upon receipt of payment.

Shop drawings The various drawings created by contractors, subcontractors, vendors, or manufacturers that illustrate construction, materials, dimensions, and installation data for the incorporation of a specific element into the construction project.

Shop fabrication The manufacturing assembly of components or elements in a vendor's or manufacturer's shop.

Shop inspection A detailed inspection and audit at the vendor's or fabricator's shop of the conformance of materials and equipment to the project specifications.

Short ton 2000 lb.

Small tools In construction, a saw, shovel, hammer, trowel, and the like, that is operated by hand.

Sourcing The process of researching and determining qualified sources of materials and equipment.

Specifications A precise, detailed description and presentation of some article.

Standard The requirements of a specific standardization method approved by a recognized and appropriate authority.

Start-up The systematic audit and check-out of all plant equipment and systems in accordance with prescribed procedures and tests, commencing prior to completion of construction and extending through mechanical completion.

Status report A type of log or schedule report, chart, or graph that monitors planned and actual physical progress.

Stop order A document used to direct a work stoppage. Contractor, subcontractor, or vendor is required to acknowledge receipt of a stop order.

Storage The function of placing materials and equipment in a designated area for safekeeping and distribution.

Subcontract An agreement between a general contractor and a contractor who specializes in a specific trade for the performance of a portion or element of work for which the general contractor is responsible to the owner.

Submittal A sample manufacturer's cut sheet or data, shop or fabricate drawing, or other item that is submitted to the owner, architect, or engineer by a contractor for approval or other action.

Subsystem A group or set of assemblies, components, or elements that, when combined, perform a single function.

Supplier Vendor, seller, manufacturer, contractor, or subcontractor.

Supplier evaluation The procedure of evaluating a supplier's ability to perform the required quantity, quality, and schedule requirements.

Surety An individual or company that issues a bond to guarantee that another person or company will perform in accordance with the terms and conditions of an agreement or contract.

Glossary

Surplus The usable materials, equipment, components, or parts that are in excess of the construction requirements.

Surveillance The monitoring and witnessing of construction work.

Surveillance inspection The observation and inspection of the manufacturing of materials and equipment used in construction.

Tagged item A separate, identifiable item, generally tracked and controlled separately from the bulk materials of commodities; an example of this is the instrumentation items.

Takeoff (or quantity takeoff) The process of compiling the required material quantities from the contract drawings.

Tariff, freight A listing of duties or taxes on imports or exports.

Tax exemption certificate A document given by the purchaser to the seller with the purchase order to indicate that the transportation is not subject to sales tax.

Technical bid evaluation The ranking of vendor or supplier bids based on the quality, cost, compliance with specifications, and delivery requirements.

Terms of payment The method of payment for materials, equipment, and services stipulated in a contract.

Testing Confirming an article's ability to meet preestablished requirements by subjecting the article to a set of physical, chemical, or operating evaluations.

Title The legal right to the possession of property.

Tracing Locating the current position of a shipment after it has entered the delivery and transportation phase.

Trademark A mark, picture, name, or letters owned and used by a manufacturer or merchant to distinguish his or her goods from the goods of another.

Traffic The action of transporting materials and equipment by a freight carrier.

Transit Action of being conveyed from one location to another.

Transit charges Costs of services rendered while a shipment is being transported.

Transit rate A rate applying to traffic stopped en route for milling, painting, packing, treating, storage, and so on.

Transload Shipment stopped while being transported in order to be partially unloaded.

Transmittal A form or letter indicating the action to be taken on an article being transmitted from one party to another.

Trial The term commonly applied to an action in a court of law; the examining and deciding of a case in court.

Turn key A form of contract that provides all of the necessary services to complete a building, facility, or other construction project.

Unit cost contract A construction contract in which reimbursement is based on a preestablished cost per unit of measure for the quantities produced or installed.

Unit load Several articles that are loaded on one pallet, or placed in a crate, enabling transportation of the items at one time, as one unit.

Unit of measure Used to specify the number of units or items to be purchased.

Unit train Freight trains that move large quantities of bulk materials between two or more locations.

Usage The number of units or articles of an inventory item consumed over a period of time.

Use tax A tax imposed on the user of materials and equipment.

Valuation The appraisal of the value of exported or imported materials and equipment.

Value The real worth of an article; marketable price. Intrinsic worth of an item. The value of an article is determined by the lowest cost at which a satisfactory supply of materials and equipment or services can be obtained.

Value analysis The application of techniques that establish a value for a necessary action at the lowest evaluated cost.

Value engineering A discipline that reviews the real value of various life cycle costs, materials, equipment, and construction techniques. Value engineering reviews the initial cost of design construction, coupled with the costs associated with maintenance, energy use, and life cycle.

Variable costs The costs associated with raw materials and all manufacturing operating costs, which vary with manufacturing output (e.g., water, electricity, gas, and catalysts).

Variance The permission granted to an owner of land or property to depart from the requirements of a specific zoning ordinance. A variance allows the owner of land or property to use his or her land in a different manner than is specified in the original ordinance.

VAT Value added tax.

Vendor An individual or organization that sells something to a purchaser.

Glossary 231

Vendor performance evaluation   A ranking and evaluation of vendors' and suppliers' performance based on quality of work, compliance with specifications, delivery, and cost.

Vendor's lien   A seller's right to retain possession of materials or equipment until he or she has received payment.

Verification   Witnessing of certain steps in the fabrication and manufacturing process, such as metallurgical analysis, hydrostatic and performance, or operational tests. Review and audit of nondestructive testing, x-rays, and bench tests.

Vessel-ton   One hundred cubic feet of volume.

Vicarious liability   An individual or organization that is liable for the results of another individual's or organization's failure to act.

Visual inspection   Manual inspection of materials and equipment.

VNX   Value not exceeding.

Volume discount   A reduction in unit cost predicted on the size of a particular purchase.

Waive   To give up a right or claim; to refrain from claiming or pressing.

Warehouse   A facility for the receiving, storage, and eventual distribution of materials and equipment.

Warehouse receipt   A document given by the warehouseman as a receipt for materials and equipment placed in the warehouse.

Warranty   A promise or pledge that something is what it is claimed to be. The seller makes a specific assurance concerning the nature, quality, and character of the goods.

Waste   The refuse from the fabrication and manufacturing process that cannot be reclaimed or reused.

Waybill   A document compiled at the point of origin of a shipment indicating the point of origin, final destination, route, purchaser, seller, description of shipment, and the cost of the transportation.

Weight, gross   The actual combined weight of the item, container, or any dunnage materials.

Weight, net   The actual weight of the item; does not include container, or any dunnage materials.

Weight, tare   The difference between the gross weight and the net weight of an item being shipped; weight of empty container, including dunnage packing material used in transport.

Wholesaler   An individual or organization that acquires products, materials, and equipment for resale to retailers or other users.

Workers' compensation insurance The insurance required of employers that provides compensation for injury and loss of wages for a work-related accident.

Work in progress Materials or equipment in various states of fabrication or completion.

Work Order A written form that describes an activity to be completed.

Index

A

Acceptance, 209
Acknowledgment, 209
Acquisition process (for capital equipment), 104
Act of God, 209
Actual weight, 209
Ad valorem, 209
Addendum, 209
Adhesives, 48
Advertisements, 45, 209
Advice of shipment, 209
Affirmative Action Certification, 151
Affirmative action programs, 79
AGC (*see* Associated General Contractors of America)
Agency, 209
Agent, 209
Aggregated shipments, 209
Agreements:
 contractual, 132–138
 defined, 210
 standard, 42
AIA (*see* American Institute of Architects)
AIA Document A 195TM–2008, 197–203
AIA Document A 295–2008, 138
AIA Document A 401–2007 (Instructions, General Conditions of the Contract for Integrated Project Delivery), 42
Air freight, 210
Airbill, 210
Airway bill, 210
All risk insurance, 210
Alliances, strategic, 16
Allowance, 210
American Institute of Architects (AIA), 9, 133–134, 136–138
American Recovery and Reinvestment Act, 155–156
Amortization, 210
Analytical knowledge, 1
Annual review periods, 56
Antitrust violations, 53
Application for payment, 210
Approve, 210
Arbitration, 210
Architects, 5–6, 9, 12, 133–134, 156–158, 210
ARR (*see* Average rate of return)
Arrival date, 210
Arrival notice, 210
Artisan's lien, 211
As is, 211
As-built drawings, 211
Asphalt, 63
Assignment, 211
Associated General Contractors of America (AGC), 9, 66, 133
At risk contract, construction manager, 205–208
Attitude adjustment, 11
Attitudinal barriers, 21
Audits, 119
Average rate of return (ARR), 109–110

B

Back order, 211
Backhoes, 124
Banker's acceptance draft, 211
Bankruptcy:
 risk of, 8
 of U. S. auto manufacturers, 14
Bargaining, 93–95, 135, 211
Barter, 211
Benchmarking, 67

234 Index

Bid, defined, 211
Bid bond, 211
Bid opening, 211
Bid packages:
  components of, 83–85
  development of, 159–160
  evaluation of, 86
  preparation of, 80–83
  sample form, 173–190
Bidding, 45, 47, 131–132, 148, 151, 160, 213
Bidding documents, 211
Bilateral monopoly systems, 94
Bill, 211
Bill of exchange, 212
Bill of lading, 212
Bill of materials, 212
Billing systems, 128
Binder, 212
Blanket order, 212
Boiler plate, 212
Boilerplate provisions, 39
Bond performance, 212
Bonded warehouse, 212
Bonds, 212
Breach of contract, 212
Broad form indemnity, 137
Brown-Root, 146
Building codes, 46, 100
Bulk materials:
  availability of, 71
  defined, 212
  multiple sourcing for, 72
  prices of, 64
Bulletin, 212
Burden, 212
Buying, multiple source, 223

C

California, 86–87
Cancellation of order, 211
Capacity analysis, 80
Capital equipment, 103–125
  acquisition process for, 104
  cash-flow analysis for investment in, 108–109
  disposal of, 119, 124
  and financial plan analysis, 112–118, 120–121
  implementation stage with, 118, 122–123
  leasing vs. purchasing, 112–118
  and long-term objectives, 105
  and market niches, 105, 108
  methods for evaluating investment in, 109–112

Capital equipment, (*Cont*):
  new vs. used, 124–125
  requisition process for, 105–107
  sources for, 103
Capital leases, 115
Capitalism, 72
Cash-flow analysis, 108–109
Categorical method (for supplier evaluation), 54, 67–68
CD 200 (Standard Agreement and General Conditions between Owner and Contractor), 136
CD 240 (Standard Form Agreement between Owner and Architect/Engineer), 134
CD 300 (Standard Form of Tri-Party Agreement for Collaborative Project Delivery), 138, 191–196
CD 750 (Agreement between Contractor and Subcontractor), 137
Cellular telephones, 141
Certificate of material compliance, 213
Certificate of origin, 213
Certification programs (for suppliers), 75–76
Certified test report, 213
Chambers of commerce, 66
Change in scope, 213
Change orders:
  and contract types, 93
  defined, 213
  and INDOT, 154
  and subcontracting, 99–101
Chrysler, 14
Claim, 213
CM At Risk (*see* Construction manager at risk)
Collaboration, 6
Collaborative project delivery, standard form of tri-party agreement for, 192–196
Collaborative relationships, 52–53
Commercial terms, 213
Commodity materials, 52
Communication:
  between buyer and supplier, 66
  at field level, 97
  gaps in, 15
  for integration, 29
  lack of, 6
  with single sources, 72–73
  strategies for, 54
Compensatory damages, 213
Competitive bidding, 213

Index

Competitive pressures, 32
Competitive relationships, 52
Competitive strategy, 34–37
Completion date, 84
Computerized supplier performance reports, 74–75
Conceptual knowledge, 1
Concrete, 63
Conditional sale, 213
Conditions of the contract, 213
ConsensusDOCS, 9, 133–138, 192–196
Consequential damages, 213
Consideration, 213
Construction manager agents, 49
Construction manager at risk (CM At Risk), 49–50
Construction manager at risk contract, 205–208
Construction managers, 27–28, 49–50, 158–159
Construction plans, 80–81, 84
Construction projects, types of, 7–10
Construction Resource Managers (CRMs), 50
Construction risks, 2–7
Construction supply chain management (CSCM), 8–10, 16, 130–131
Containerization, 214
Content, of information, 129
Continuous improvement, 11, 50
Contract(s):
 defined, 214
 design-build, 93
 guaranteed maximum cost, 218
 implied, 218
 long-term, 73
 negotiation of, 93–95
 outsourced supply, 73
 prime, 43
 purchase orders as, 39
 subcontracts, 41–42, 44
 types of, for subcontracting, 88, 90–93
 unit cost, 230
Contract administration, 214
Contract documents, 214
Contractor selection, 9
Contractual agreements, 132–138
Coolants, 47
Cooperation, 9, 21
 in prime-subcontractor relationships, 77
 with single sources, 72–73
Cooperative relationships, 52–53
Coordination, 6, 130
Cost plus, 214

Cost plus pricing, 6, 91, 93
Cost responsibility, 33
Cost-ratio method (for supplier evaluation), 54, 68–70
Costs:
 competitive advantages from, 34, 36
 direct and indirect, 139
 fixed, 73, 90
 indirect, 139
 and profit, 33–34
 reduction of, 11–13, 76
Counteroffer, 214
Counterproductive relationships, 52
CPM (*see* Critical path method)
Critical path method (CPM), 31, 131
CRMs (Construction Resource Managers), 50
Cross-sourcing, 74
CSCM (*see* Construction supply chain management)
Cumberland Gap Tunnel, 90
Cumulative learning, 4
Customer service, 57, 66
Customers, 4–5, 10

D

Damage claim, 214
Damages, 214
Data file, 80
Davis-Bacon Act, 154, 214
DBEs (*see* Disadvantaged business enterprises)
Deadlines, 65
Debit notice, 214
Decentralization, 6
Delays, 6, 128, 131
Delivering carrier, 214
Delivery, 214
Delivery dependability, 64–65
Demurrage, 214
Departments of transportation (DOTs), 79, 85, 87, 146
Design engineers, 49–50
Design errors, 99
Design-build contracts, 93
Design-build projects, 77–78
Detail specification, 214
Differentiation, by construction organizations, 34, 36
Direct costs, 139
Disadvantaged business enterprises (DBEs), 53, 79, 85, 148–149, 151, 158
Discount, 114, 215, 225
Disposal, of capital equipment, 119, 124
Distribution, 39, 215

Dock, 215
Document flows, 154–155, 160
Documents, for supply sourcing, 43–44
DOTs (see Departments of transportation)
Downstream information technology, 50
Draft, 215
Due date, 215
Dunnage, 215
Durable goods, 215
Duty, 215

E

Early payment, 39
Earnest money, 215
EATCF (estimated after-tax cash flows), 109
Economic trends, 80
Efficiency, operational, 11–12
EIS (Federal Environmental Impact Statement), 148
EJCDC (see Engineers Joint Contract Documents Committee)
Electronic bidding, 148, 151, 160
Elimination of waste, 11–12
E-mails, 141
Employees, 10, 11
Empowerment, of employees, 11
Engineering, 146
Engineering drawings, 39, 47
Engineering specifications, 46
Engineers, 5, 6, 12
Engineers Joint Contract Documents Committee (EJCDC), 9, 133, 137
Equipment suppliers, 153–154
Error and omission excepted, 215
Escalation, 215
Escalation clause, 215
Estimated after-tax cash flows (EATCF), 109
Estimates, 131–132, 142, 153
Evaluation:
 of investment in capital equipment, 109–112
 supplier (see Supplier evaluation)
Ex (prefix), 215
Excavation, 91
Excess freight, 215
Exchange bill of lading, 215
Excise tax, 215
Execution, of projects, 140–142
Explicit bargaining, 94
Export, 216
Export permit, 216

F

Fabrication, 216
Facilitation, 216
Factor, 216
Fair market value, 216
Federal Aid Highway Act, 146
Federal Environmental Impact Statement (EIS), 148
Federal Highway Administration (FHWA), 79, 146, 148, 155
Ferrous metal products, 63
FHWA (see Federal Highway Administration)
Field inspection, 216
Field intelligence, 80
Field measurements, 141
Field purchase order, 216
Field required date, 216
FIFO, 216
Financial plan analysis, 112–118, 120–121
Financial Standards Accounting Board, 115
Firm offer, 216
Fixed costs, 73, 90
Flexibility, 36
Flow-down terms, 136
FOB, 216–217
FOB destination, freight prepaid, 217
FOB factory, freight allowed, 217
FOB origin, freight collect, 217
FOB shipping point, 217
Follow-up record, 217
Force majeure, 217
Ford Motor Company, 14
Forward purchasing, 217
Freight forwarder, 217

G

General conditions, 217
"General Conditions of the Contract for Construction," 134
General contractor, 217
General liability insurance, 160, 218
General Motors, 14
Generic, 218
Global markets, 145–146
Goods received note, 218
Goodwill, 21
Government agencies, 45
Governmental regulations, 157
Grade methods (for supplier evaluation), 74–75
Gross ton, 218
Gross weight, 218
Guarantee, 218
Guaranteed maximum cost contract, 218

Index **237**

H

Halliburton, 146
Harvard Business School study on competitiveness, 17
Heavy/horizontal construction supply chain model(s), 8, 145–156
  components of, 147–148
  equipment suppliers in, 153–154
  flows in, 154–156
  and international demand, 146
  material suppliers in, 153
  prime contractor in, 149, 151–152
  project owner in, 148, 150
  public vs. private projects in, 154
  subcontractors in, 152–153
Heavy-lift charge, 218
Hedging, 218
Highway projects, 53, 90, 97, 131, 146
Historical maintenance records, 124
Hold, 218
Hold order, 218
Hold points, 218
Hundredweight, 218
Hurdle methods (for supplier evaluation), 75

I

IDM (initial decision maker), 137
Implementation stage (with capital equipment), 118, 122–123
Implied contract, 218
Improvement, continuous, 11, 50
Improvement curve techniques, 4
Income statements, 33
Income tax effect, 115–117
Indemnification, 218
Indemnity, 137, 218
Indiana Department of Transportation (INDOT), 148–156
Indirect costs, 139
Indirect materials, 48, 218
INDOT (*see* Indiana Department of Transportation)
Inflation, 32
Information:
  flow of, 155
  management of, 10
  on suppliers, 66
Information sharing, 29, 129–131
Information technology (IT), 8
Initial decision maker (IDM), 137
Injunction, 219
Inland bill of lading, 219
Inland carrier, 219
Inquiry, 219

Inspection:
  defined, 219
  of materials, 65
  of used equipment, 125
Inspection plan, 219
Inspection report, 219
Inspector, 219
Instructions to bidders, 219
Insurance, 79, 137, 149, 155, 160, 210, 219
Insurance certificate, 219
Integrated project delivery, standard form of agreement between owner and contractor for, 197–203
Integrated Project Delivery system, 138
Intermediate form indemnity, 137
Internal rate of return (IRR), 111–112
International demand, 146
Internet, 29, 66, 142
Inventory, 219–220
Inventory investment, 29
Invitation to bid, 220
Invoice, 220
Iraq, 32, 146
IRR (internal rate of return), 111–112
IT (information technology), 8

J

Japanese manufacturers, 13
Job lot, 220
Job-lot ordering, 220
Joint agent, 220
Joint venture(s), 21–23, 163–171, 220
Journeyman, 220
Judgment, 220
Just-in-time purchasing concepts, 29, 46

K

KD, 220
Keiretsu, 13
Key activity, 220
Kim Construction, 60–62
Kitting, 220
Knight, F., 2

L

Labor and material payment bond, 220
Lading, 220
Laydown area, 220
Lead time, 221
Leadership, 11
"Lean" construction, 12, 17
Lean purchasing concepts, 29
Leases, 44, 112–118, 221

Legal tender, 221
Letter of credit, 221
Letters of intent, 95–98
Liability, 221
Libraries, 66
Lien laws, 78
Liens, 211, 221, 222, 227, 231
Life cycle, for projects, 26–28
Life cycle costing, 109
Limited form indemnity, 137
Linear averaging method (for supplier evaluation), 54, 70
Liquidated damages, 221
Litigation, 221
Load factor, 221
Loans, 113
Location, of suppliers, 66
Logistics, 221
Long ton, 221
Long-term contracts, 73
Long-term equipment investments, 104
Long-term relationships, 53, 73–75
Lot size, 221
Lubricants, 47
Lump sum, 221
Lump sum pricing, 6, 90

M

MacNeil, Ian R., 17
Maintenance, 114
Maintenance, repair, and operating supplies, 47–48
Mandatory pre-bid meetings, 85
Manifest, 221
Manufacturing risks, 2–7
Market niches, 105, 108
Marketable title, 222
Marketing research, 222
Markup, 222
Masonry, 63
Material, 222
Material cost, 222
Material man, 222
Material status, 222
Material suppliers, 5, 8, 12, 153, 159
Materials management, 222
Materials purchasing, 46–47
Materials specifications, 46–47
Materials test report, 222
MBEs (minority business enterprises), 158
MC, 222
Mechanic's lien, 222
Mendel, Kevin, 60
Metal products, ferrous, 63

Minimum carload weight, 222
Minority business enterprises (MBEs), 158
Minutes (from meetings), 57–58
Mixed truckload rate, 222
Modifications, 222
Monopoly systems, bilateral, 94
Multiple source buying, 223
Multiple-consignee, 222
Mutual indemnity, 137

N

Natural resources, 32
Need date, 223
Negligence, 223
Negotiated pricing, 6, 65, 93
Negotiation, 93–95, 223
Net adjusted cost, 69
Net cash flows, 108–109
Net present value (NPV), 109–111
Net price, 223
Net ton, 223
Net weight, 223
New capital equipment, 124–125
Niche marketing, 127–128
Notary, 223
Notice of Award, 45
Notice to Contractors, 149
Notices of furnishing, 78
NPV (see Net present value)

O

Objectives, of organizations, 105
Obligation, 223
Obsolete, 223
Offer, 223
Open bid subcontractor selection, 80, 81
Open Competitive Bidding Selection, 223
Open-end order, 223
Operating leases, 113–115
Operating supplies, 47–48
Operational efficiency, 11–12
Operations, 3
Order lead time, 223
Outsourced supply contracts, 73
Overhead, 224
Owners, 78, 224

P

Packing list, 224
Partial payment, 224
Patent, 224
Payback, 109–110
Payment bond, 224

Payments, flow of, 155–156
Penalty clause, 224
Performance bond, 224
Performance data, 80
Performance measurement, 34, 140
Performance reports, 40
Performance reviews, 56–57
Performance-based evaluations, 67
Personnel:
    for equipment acquisition, 108
    for supply chain relationship
        management, 49–50
Phones, cellular, 141
Physical distribution, 224
PI (profitability index), 112
Piggyback, 224
Plan holder lists, 151
Planning:
    for subcontracting, 80
    for supply sourcing, 37–41
Pledge, 224
Point of origin, 224
Port of entry, 224
Powerpoint presentations, 142
Pre-bid conferences:
    and prime contractors, 151
    and subcontracting, 85–86
Pre-bid invitation (form), 173–190
Preconstruction design, 9
Prefabrication, 222
Preferred/Tier 2 suppliers, 53–55
Pre-liens, 78
Prequalification, 79, 146–147, 149, 152
Price, as factor in supplier selection,
    64–65
Pricing, 6, 9
Prime contractor(s), 5, 6, 12–14
    architects' relationships with, 133–134
    defined, 224
    in heavy/horizontal construction
        supply chain model, 149, 151–152
    selection of, 9
    subcontractors' relationships with,
        77–79
    and supplier partnerships, 18–19
    and supply chain relationship
        management, 50
    and supply sourcing, 27–28
Prime contracts, 43
Private projects, 154
Private sector commercial projects, 7
Private sector heavy (horizontal)
    market, 8
Private sector housing market, 7
Process flowcharts, 67
Process-based evaluations, 67

Processed steel, 46
Procurement, 224
Procurement lead time, 225
Productivity, 124, 128, 139–140
Profit, 33–34
Profitability, 127–143
Profitability index (PI), 112
Progress information, 141–142
Project management, 138–140
Project owners:
    in heavy/horizontal construction
        supply chain model, 148, 150
    in vertical construction supply chain
        model, 157–158
Promissory note, 225
Public projects, 154
Public sector building (vertical) market, 8
Public sector heavy (horizontal) market, 8
Public works, 53, 80, 131, 154–155
Purchase, 225
Purchase order, 225
Purchase orders, 37, 39–41, 44, 119
Purchase requisition, 225
Purchasing, 112–118, 225
Purchasing cycle, 225
Purchasing departments, 71, 103
Purchasing manual, 225
Purchasing/supply management, 86

Q

Quality:
    defined, 225
    of information, 129
    of materials, 64–65
    in performance review, 57
Quality assurance/control, 95–100, 225
Quantification, 225
Quantity, 225
Quantity discount, 225
Quasi-contract, 225
Questionnaire, for subcontractors, 82–84
Quotation, 225
Quotation expiration date, 226
Quotations, 41–42, 45, 64, 151–153
    (*See also* Requests for quotations)

R

Rate of exchange, 226
Reactive expediting, 226
Rebate, 226
Receipt inspection, 226
Receipt of bids, 226
Receiving, 226
Receiving and storage, 226
Receiving report, 226

Index

Recertification, 75
Record of Decision (ROD), 148
Recourse, 226
Regulations, governmental, 157
Reimbursable costs, 91
Renting, of equipment, 27
Repair, 226
Repair supplies, 47–48
Replacement, of equipment, 108
Request for bid, 226
Request for proposal (RFP), 9
Requests for quotations (RFQs), 64, 227
Requirements, 226
Requisition, 226
Requisition process (for capital equipment), 105–107
Residential housing market, 70
Responsibility, cost, 33
Retention, 226
Review, 227
Review process (for supply chain relationship management), 56–59
Reward, 2
Reward criteria, 34
Rework, 227
RFQ (request for quotation), 227
Risk management, 10
Risks:
    allocation of, 133, 138
    assessment of, 88, 90
    manufacturing vs. construction, 2–7
    reasonable, 1
Routing, 227

S

Safety, 128
Sale and leasebacks, 114–115
Sales price, 227
Sales representative, 227
Sales revenue, 227
Sales tax, 227
Salvage, 227
Salvage value, 114, 227
Samples, 227
SCDOT (South Carolina Department of Transportation), 50
Schedules, for projects, 82
Scheduling start times, 54
SCM (*see* Supply chain management)
Scope, 227
Scope change, 227
Scoring system, for strategic supplier relationships, 57, 59
Second Gulf War, 32
Segmentation (within supply chain relationship management), 53–56
Selection, supplier (*see* Supplier selection)
Seller's lien, 227
Sharing, information (*see* Information sharing)
Shop drawings, 43, 99, 159, 227
Shop fabrication, 227
Shop inspection, 228
Short ton, 228
Shortages, 32
Short-term equipment investments, 104
Small tools, 228
SMS Construction, 53–54, 56–57
Source selection, 80
Sourcing (*see* Supply sourcing)
South Carolina Department of Transportation (SCDOT), 50
Specialty subcontractors, 5
Specifications, 46–47, 80–81, 84, 228
Standard, 228
Standard agreements, 42
"Standard Form of Agreement Between Contractor and Subcontractor," 42
Start-up, 228
Status report, 228
Steel, 43, 46, 65
Stop order, 228
Storage, 228
Strategic alliances, 16
Strategic supplier relationship management, 54, 56
Strategic supplier selection, 66
Strategic/Tier 1 suppliers, 53–56
Strengths, weaknesses, opportunities, threats (SWOT) analysis, 56, 80
Subcontract, 228
Subcontracting, 8–10, 12, 77–102
    bid package for, 80–86, 173–190
    and change orders, 99–101
    major subcontractors, 95–98
    and negotiation, 93–95
    planning for, 80
    and pre-bid conferences, 85–86
    and prime-subcontractor relationship, 77–79, 135–136
    and purchasing/supply management, 86
    and quality assurance/control, 95–100
    source selection for, 80
    submission of bids for, 86–89
    and supplier partnerships, 18–19, 51–52
    and supply chain relationship management, 50–51
    and supply sourcing, 41–42, 44–45
    types of contracts, 88, 90–93

Index

Subcontractors:
  in heavy/horizontal construction supply chain model, 152–153
  reduction of, 51–52
  in vertical construction supply chain model, 159
Subcontracts, 41–42, 44
Submission, of bids, 86–89
Submittal, 228
Subsystem, 228
Supplier(s):
  defined, 228
  reduction of, 51–52, 74
Supplier certification programs, 75–76
Supplier evaluation, 54, 63–64, 228
  categorical method for, 54, 67–68
  and certification programs, 75–76
  cost-ratio method for, 54, 68–70
  criteria for, 67
  example of, 70–72
  linear averaging method for, 54, 70
  and long-term relationship issues, 73–75
Supplier selection, 63–66
  factors for successful, 64–66
  mistakes made in, 64
  and single vs. multiple sources, 72–73
  and sources of supplier information, 66
  strategic, 66
Supplies, operating, 47–48
Supply chain control, 13
Supply chain management (SCM), 3–4, 8, 128–142
  barriers to, 14–16
  and bid preparation, 131–132
  and competitive construction operations, 13–14
  and contractual agreements, 132–138
  implementation of, 161–162
  and information sharing, 129–131
  and project execution, 140–142
  and project management, 138–140
  and supplier partnerships, 16–23
Supply chain management business models, 145–162
  for heavy/horizontal construction segment, 145–156
  for vertical construction segment, 156–161
Supply chain relationship management, 49–62
  behavioral dimensions of, 52–53
  example of supplier profile, 60–62
  fundamental principles of, 50–51

Supply chain relationship management, (*Cont.*):
  personnel for, 49–50
  preferred supplier relationship management, 54
  and reduction of subcontractors/suppliers, 51–52
  review process for, 56–59
  segmentation within, 53–56
  strategic supplier relationship management, 54, 56
Supply management process, 30–32
Supply sourcing, 25–48
  and competitive strategy, 34–37
  and cost responsibility, 33
  cycle of, 42–43
  documents needed for, 43–44
  fragmentation of, 25
  maintenance, repair, and operating supplies, 47–48
  materials purchasing, 46–47
  objectives of, 28–30
  planning for, 37–41
  profit from, 33–34
  and project life cycle, 26–28
  and subcontracting, 41–42, 44–45
  and supply management process, 30–32
Supply sourcing managers, 27–29
Surety, 228
Surplus, 229
Surveillance, 229
Surveillance inspection, 229
SWOT analysis (*see* Strengths, weaknesses, opportunities, threats analysis)

T

Tagged item, 229
Takeoff (or quantity takeoff), 229
Tariff, freight, 229
Tax exemption certificate, 229
Tax planning process, 103
Taxes:
  and leasing vs. purchasing equipment, 113–114
  on motor fuels, 146
TCO (total cost of ownership), 109
Technical bid evaluation, 229
Technical risk, 88, 90
Technology:
  and change orders, 99
  and competition, 64
  and information sharing, 129